#MeToo and Feminism

Karen Boyle

#MeToo and Feminism

Weinstein and Beyond

Second Edition

Karen Boyle
Department of Humanities
University of Strathclyde
Glasgow, UK

ISBN 978-3-031-67313-9   ISBN 978-3-031-67314-6 (eBook)
https://doi.org/10.1007/978-3-031-67314-6

© The Editor(s) (if applicable) and The Author(s), under exclusive license to Springer Nature Switzerland AG 2019, 2024

This work is subject to copyright. All rights are solely and exclusively licensed by the Publisher, whether the whole or part of the material is concerned, specifically the rights of translation, reprinting, reuse of illustrations, recitation, broadcasting, reproduction on microfilms or in any other physical way, and transmission or information storage and retrieval, electronic adaptation, computer software, or by similar or dissimilar methodology now known or hereafter developed.
The use of general descriptive names, registered names, trademarks, service marks, etc. in this publication does not imply, even in the absence of a specific statement, that such names are exempt from the relevant protective laws and regulations and therefore free for general use.
The publisher, the authors and the editors are safe to assume that the advice and information in this book are believed to be true and accurate at the date of publication. Neither the publisher nor the authors or the editors give a warranty, expressed or implied, with respect to the material contained herein or for any errors or omissions that may have been made. The publisher remains neutral with regard to jurisdictional claims in published maps and institutional affiliations.

This Palgrave Macmillan imprint is published by the registered company Springer Nature Switzerland AG
The registered company address is: Gewerbestrasse 11, 6330 Cham, Switzerland

If disposing of this product, please recycle the paper.

Acknowledgements for the Second Edition

This second edition arose from a conversation with Lina Aboujieb at Palgrave who commissioned and championed the first edition and has been a supporter of the second: thank you. During the writing of this second edition, I have been fortunate to have worked with fantastic Ph.D. students whose work on gender, violence and representation has inspired and informed my own. My thanks to Charlotte James Robertson, Camila Cavalcante Pereira, Emma Flynn, Melody House, Marie McDermott, Elisa Sajed and Abeera Baig. I am particularly grateful to Emma, Melody and Marie for their comments on Chapters 4 and 6. I have been privileged to co-supervise PhDs with colleagues from a range of disciplinary contexts and our supervisory conversations have sparked new ideas and connections so many thanks to: Lynn Abrams, Catherine Spencer, Caroline Verdier, Michael Higgins, Laura Piacentini, Melanie McCarry and Fiona McKay. Over the past 4 years, collaborating with Susan Berridge has provided much-needed motivation, connection and inspiration in times of lockdown and beyond. I have also benefitted enormously from collaborating with Chamil Rathnayake on related projects. As I was finalising this second edition, I took on a new role as Head of the Department. Continuing to function in this context, never mind finding time for research, would have been impossible without the support and general brilliance of David Murphy, Churnjeet Mahn, Tanja Bueltmann, Katie McGlynn and Christina Crawley.

To my family and friends: thank you all for your encouragement from near and far. Special thanks to my mum and dad, Eliz and Sandy, who have been my biggest supporters, and Gavin, who has organised us all. Thanks to Alec, Carys and Niko: without you I might have finished this earlier, but there would have been less fun along the way. Special mention to Carys for introducing me to the restorative properties of a Taylor Swift singalong. Finally, to Ian Garwood a huge thanks for, well, everything. You are the very best of humans.

Contents

1 **#MeToo and Feminism: Weinstein and Beyond** 1
   Introduction 1
   Feminism(s) in the Long #MeToo Moment 3
   Weinstein and Beyond 13
   Victims, Survivors, Naming and Anonymity 19
   Outline of the Chapters 22
   References 25

2 **Silence Breaking** 33
   Introduction 33
   Speaking Out 36
   Speaking Out Online 42
   What's Feminism Got To Do With It? 46
   Conclusion 58
   References 59

3 **Theorising the Relationships of Gender and Violence Through #MeToo: Continuum Thinking** 69
   Introduction 69
   From "the" Continuum to Continuum Thinking 71
   Damonsplaining 82
   Violence or Sex, Violence and Sex 87
   Conclusion 92
   References 93

4	**The Long #MeToo Moment**	97
	Introduction	97
	Origins, Invisible Work and Permanence	98
	The Long #MeToo Moment	102
	The Entwining of Popular Feminism and Popular Misogyny	112
	Endings: Part 1	115
	Endings: Part 2	121
	References	126
5	**Men in the #MeToo Era**	133
	Introduction	133
	Men in #MeToo as Victim/Survivors	134
	#HimToo and Himpathy	141
	Credible Perpetrators	150
	Conclusion	156
	References	157
6	**The Cultural Value of Abuse**	165
	Introduction	165
	Hiding in Plain Sight	168
	Weinstein and the Cultural Value of Abuse	173
	"You Loved It": Complicity, Cancellation and Comebacks	179
	Cancellations?	185
	Conclusion	194
	References	195
7	**Reconsidering Survivor Speech in the Media: Against Testimony**	201
	Introduction	201
	Breaking the Silence (Again)	202
	Breaking the Story	211
	Experience and Expertise	215
	Surviving Speech	222
	Conclusion	229
	References	230
8	**Conclusion: #MeToo, Now What?**	237
	References	241
Index		243

CHAPTER 1

#MeToo and Feminism: Weinstein and Beyond

INTRODUCTION

This book takes as its starting point reports from a number of women that self-styled movie mogul Harvey Weinstein sexually assaulted them. Jodi Kantor and Megan Twohey broke the Weinstein story in the *New York Times* on 5 October 2017 and the findings of Ronan Farrow's simultaneous investigation for the *New Yorker* swiftly followed (Farrow 2017a). These stories prompted an outpouring of victim/survivor testimony, most prominently under the hashtag #MeToo, connecting the experiences of women in the US film industry to those of women in vastly different geographic and socio-economic locations.

The first edition of this book was published as *#MeToo, Weinstein and Feminism* in 2019. In the years since, there has been an explosion of #MeToo discourse, cultural production and academic analysis, with which this second edition is in conversation. This introductory chapter thus begins by offering an expanded discussion of the relationship of feminism(s) to #MeToo. Central to this discussion is an evaluation of the critiques of #MeToo. In asking who—or what—is being critiqued, I seek to ensure that the intersectional failures of mainstream media and some feminist scholarship do not become self-perpetuating, marginalising the speech of the very victim/survivors such critiques are intended to centre. In this section, I also reconsider the distinction I proposed in 2019 between the #MeToo moment (initiated by Alyssa Milano's #MeToo

© The Author(s), under exclusive license to Springer Nature Switzerland AG 2024
K. Boyle, *#MeToo and Feminism*,
https://doi.org/10.1007/978-3-031-67314-6_1

tweet in October 2017) and the Me Too movement, linked to the work of Tarana Burke. Work since 2019 has complicated the "origin" stories of both moment and movement, however, I argue that this distinction remains helpful in keeping in view the timebound nature of the hashtag's virality whilst not losing sight of wider feminist movements to end sexual and other forms of gender-based violence with which it is connected. This second edition offers an expanded account of #MeToo's temporalities and offers the *long* #MeToo moment as a way of thinking about the explosion of discourse and activism around sexual and gender-based violence over the past decade or so. The long #MeToo moment not only allows for a discussion of the diverse contexts in which #MeToo has been taken up, but additionally provides the possibility of placing the moment and movement in *ongoing* conversation.

At the heart of #MeToo and Me Too are the experiences of victim/survivors of sexual harassment and assault predominately, but not exclusively, women. A recurring concern throughout this book is how sexual harassment and assault, those who perpetrate it and those who experience it, are represented. In introducing these themes in this chapter, I consider first the position of Harvey Weinstein—and other men accused of sexual harassment and abuse in the #MeToo moment—in this book. The first edition (which was published before Weinstein's criminal trials) used Weinstein as an exemplar of the moment of cultural "reckoning" around sexual harassment and assault whilst acknowledging the limitations of a monster-of-the-moment approach. The second edition is similarly concerned with this tension, but in moving *beyond* Weinstein I partly want to argue for the importance of keeping him in view lest complacency creep in that his imprisonment brings sexual harassment and assault in the film industry to an end. This raises a number of questions about naming, authority and accountability, questions which I then explore in relation to the position of those who report sexual harassment and abuse. In both of these sections, I am concerned not only with *media* representations, but with the ethical implications for feminist research and writing. The final section of this introduction provides an overview of the remaining chapters and, for readers already familiar with the first edition, identifies where the new and updated materials can be found.

Feminism(s) in the Long #MeToo Moment

One of the aims of this book is to interrogate the stories *about* feminism(s) which are told through, and in response to, #MeToo. The definition of feminism which guides this discussion is that provided by bell hooks:

> Simply put, feminism is a movement to end sexism, sexist exploitation, and oppression.
>
> (hooks 2000: 1)

hooks' definition serves as a reminder that feminism seeks to have a practical application in changing the world around it. As such, it should never be static but continue to evolve. In this book, I am concerned with interdisciplinary bodies of scholarship focusing on feminism itself, on violence as a feminist issue, and from within feminist media studies. I draw primarily on work developed in Britain and the US from the early second wave onwards, though Chapter 4 takes a broader approach in order to understand claims made about #MeToo's "global" reach and significance. I am interested in how ideas have developed within and across the periods and—in assessing how #MeToo has evolved—across place and sectors. This is an understanding of feminism *in* movement: a feminism which is itself continually being refined and contested, not least in response to internal and external critique. As I will argue, this is a feminism which has been largely missing from mainstream media accounts of #MeToo which have been strangely untethered from history and in which feminism—if it appears at all—figures as a curiously static and almost exclusively white identity.

In this, I am informed by the work of scholars focused on the discursive histories of feminism(s) which asks who tells these stories, what purposes they serve and what is included/excluded in the models of feminist (re)generation which tend to dominate both popular and academic accounts of feminisms' histories (Hemmings 2011; Rivers 2017).[1] The

---

[1] Perhaps unsurprisingly given the age(ing) of many women associated with second wave feminist activism, there has been a flourishing of scholarship on Anglo-American feminist activism from the 1970s and 1980s in recent years, with a particular emphasis on the anti-violence movement (e.g. Bevacqua 2000; Graham et al. 2003; Bronstein 2011; Browne 2014; Taylor 2017; Bryan et al. 2018; Jolly 2019; Hague 2021; Robertson 2024). Whilst I am only able to touch on this scholarship in the book (most obviously

popular mediation of feminism has long been a concern for feminist activists as well as media scholars and this provides a helpful context for understanding feminist engagement with—as well as critique of—#MeToo. Women's liberation movement publications from the early 1970s consistently referenced "the media" as a site of possibility—and concern—for feminists. British movement publications often reprinted stories from the national press as sources of information about issues concerning feminists, whilst simultaneously debating the benefits and limitations of the movement in engaging with these same mainstream media organisations. For instance, the first issue of the Women's Liberation Workshop journal *Shrew*, devotes a number of pages to the relationship of the movement to the "bourgeois press" which, it notes in its cover story, "has expressed a great deal of interest in women's liberation" (*Shrew* 1970). On the one hand, it was widely recognised that this kind of engagement could open up the movement to a wider range of women. On the other, media representation was not always positive and feminists were understandably suspicious of journalists' motivations and often frustrated by their insistence on individualising the collective ethos of the movement by constructing "stars" (Mendes 2011; Dow 2014; Sheehan 2016). As such, there has long been a recognition that the discursive construction of feminism has only ever been partly within feminists' control.

These debates point to a recurring concern with who or what feminism represents, with who speaks for feminism or as a feminist, and of the relationship between the individual and (differently situated) collectives and communities. Although this may seem like an obvious point, it is one worth returning to in relation to #MeToo. As is well known, #MeToo began trending after a tweet from US actor Alyssa Milano on 15 October 2017:

> Me Too.
> Suggested by a friend: "If all the women who have been sexually harassed or assaulted wrote "Me Too" as a status, we might give people a sense of the magnitude of the problem.
> (@AlyssaMilano, 15 October, 2017)

in Chapter 4), it is an important inspiration in allowing for a more nuanced account of the relationship of generations of feminism—and feminists—than the media-friendly and individualist story of feminist conflict, which I critique in Chapter 2.

Within just 24 hours, 12 million Facebook posts using the hashtag were written or shared and within 48 hours the hashtag had been shared nearly a million times on Twitter (Lawton 2017). Milano's initial aim for #MeToo was to "give people a sense of the magnitude of the problem". In other words, it was discursive activism, aiming to change what "sexual harassment and assault" means by expanding the understanding of who its victim/survivors are. As a collectively produced story about sexual harassment and assault (Serisier 2018: 101), it has—in many ways—achieved Milano's goal, although, as we will see, a counter-narrative or backlash existed alongside #MeToo virtually from the outset.

It is important to emphasise that #MeToo is indivisible from the media platforms through which it has circulated. For better and for worse, #MeToo is networked feminism: a feminism made possible by the affordances of the social media platforms on which it circulates. The very repetitions of #MeToo are at times read as constituting a movement in and of themselves. For instance, Me Too Rising (https://metoorising.withgoogle.com) is a fascinating resource which maps searches for #MeToo across time and place, from October 2017 to April 2019. However, Me Too Rising is presented as "a visualization of the *movement* from Google Trends": equating online searching for #MeToo with activism. Moreover, points on the map and on the timeline are linked to mainstream news stories about #MeToo in specific locales, thus positioning mainstream media as essential drivers of feminism. There are echoes here of Sarah Banet-Weiser's suggestion that popular feminism "generally materializes as a kind of *media* that is widely visible and accessible" (2018: 9). As Banet-Weiser cautions, the feminisms which become popular—and visible—are those which "do not challenge deep structures of inequities" (*ibid*: 11). These stories may—as Banet-Weiser's analysis of popular feminism demonstrates—do feminist work, but focusing simply on the most visible stories as representative of contemporary feminism is profoundly distorting. Visibility and movement are not synonymous, as the Tufnell Park Women's Liberation Workshop recognised in 1970:

> We can be so written about and give so many interviews that we can be deceived into thinking that there is a movement when all we're doing is dealing with the press and T.V. (Tufnell Park Women's Liberation Workshop 1970: 4)

This is one reason why reading critiques of #MeToo can be a frustrating experience. Important points about the way the #MeToo story has evolved (including, for instance, the centring of economically and racially privileged US women in mainstream media coverage) are used to argue for the limitations of #MeToo as a feminist movement. When this happens, we allow mainstream media to define what feminism is, and miss an opportunity to hold them accountable. In this sense, it is important to investigate #MeToo not only as a facet of digital feminist activism, but also as an object of mainstream media commentary.

Although what was to become #MeToo originated with Milano and her (unnamed) friend, Me Too as a feminist rallying cry and a *movement* did not. The Me Too movement was founded by Tarana Burke in 2006. For Burke, Me Too was an intersectional demand for support and recognition for young women of colour who had experienced sexual abuse, as well as a statement of solidarity (Burke, n.d.). Burke's version of Me Too was not initially visible in Milano's tweet, but Milano did subsequently acknowledge Burke's work, largely as a result of Black feminists amplifying Burke's voice online (Burke 2021). Burke has subsequently become a prominent figure in media debates about #MeToo. However, this should not lead us to the conclusion that these debates have entirely taken on Burke's intersectional demand.

In this book, I, therefore, differentiate between #MeToo and Burke's Me Too, with Me Too standing in for a long, if unevenly intersectional, history of feminist activism around men's violence against women. Although my focus on #MeToo as a moment not a movement reverses the title of Burke's Ted Talk on the issue (Burke 2018), our concerns are similar. In insisting Me Too is a movement, Burke is reinserting a Black feminist history into a mass-mediated narrative which has marginalised it (also Gilmore 2023). In interviews, Burke has—as Serisier (2018: 116) notes—differentiated between #MeToo and "the work", with the hashtag potentially (though not necessarily) creating the space for the work, but not being synonymous with it. This is a distinction between discourse (#MeToo) and activism (Me Too). Discursive activism can, of course, be part of a broader activist project, but activism is never solely discursive. Whilst both the movement/work and the hashtag go by the label "Me Too", as this book is primarily interested in what these mediatised narratives can tell us about wider feminist politics, I want to retain the distinction between the movement (Me Too) and the hashtag and stories with which it is now associated (#MeToo).

Academic publishing on #MeToo—of which this book is obviously part—has also amplified some stories more than others, in ways which have implications for feminist movements and thinking at local, national and transnational levels. Whilst #MeToo's geographic spread has been widely heralded, many researchers have cautioned against #MeToo becoming an origin story for contemporary activism against sexual harassment and assault, instead situating #MeToo in relation to geographically situated histories of feminist (digital) activism. In Chapter 4, I discuss this scholarship in more detail, complicating my 2019 distinction between the moment associated with #MeToo as a hashtag and the longer Me Too movement. Here I argue for the value of looking instead at the *long* #MeToo moment[2] as a way of bringing these different histories together and keeping the relationship of representation and activism in focus.

The impact of the hashtag was (and is) not solely related to the mass disclosures it prompted: women have been speaking out about men's sexual harassment and assault for decades, as I discuss in Chapter 2. Rather what was distinctive about the response to #MeToo was the extent to which some of these disclosures were widely *heard* both within and beyond their immediate contexts. For feminist media scholars, *which* of these stories were—and are—deemed worthy of this attention and belief is significant. Ros Gill and Shani Orgad write:

> …despite the excitement about MeToo's wide appeal and cross-class, cross-ethnicity and cross-race character, its *politics* and *aesthetics* are exclusionary in various problematical ways, echoing similar critiques about previous feminist movements such as SlutWalk (see Black Women's Blueprint 2011; Mendes 2015). Writing in Feministing on her experience as an LGBTQ person and survivor of multiple forms of sexual violence perpetrated within her own community, Jess Fourneir criticized MeToo's "footnoting" of queer experiences, that is, their relegation to the margins of a conversation about pervasive sexual violence that definitely concerns us. The rapper Cardi B spoke powerfully about MeToo's favouring of a particular femininity that is "respectable" (Skeggs 1997) and "believable", leaving out women like herself (woman of colour, previously stripper, hip hop artist) who "do not matter". The overwhelming exclusion of disabled women

---

[2] I first coined the term "the long #MeToo moment" in a PhD supervision with Emma Flynn whose work on #MeToo-adjacent literature and film inspired this rethinking of the temporality of #MeToo (Flynn 2024).

from the MeToo movement has been another important criticism (Flores 2018; Wafula Strike 2018).

(Gill and Orgad 2018: 1319)

I quote Gill and Orgad at length as their examples bear further scrutiny for what they reveal about what #MeToo *is* and the questions this raises about responsibility. Black women protesting against the rhetoric of Slut-Walk could (and did) address their criticisms very directly to organisers of marches and events. As such, they could (and did) address people who were putting themselves forward as doing feminist work, to demand that they think through the implications of organising under this banner (Black Women's Blueprint 2011).

But when we critique #MeToo, who or what are we critiquing?

One obvious point of critique is the erasure of Burke in Milano's initial tweet. The direct and focused critique of Black women online was highly effective in this regard, such that Burke's work *is* now routinely (if unevenly) acknowledged. The articles Gill and Orgad cite are all, in different ways, also concerned with recognition within the #MeToo discourse, but the target of their critique is less immediately obvious. Notably, their critiques were simultaneous with the emergence and circulation of #MeToo and were, in some cases, published in mainstream outlets: Flores in *Teen Vogue* (2018), Wafula Strike in the *Guardian* (2018). Arguably, this speaks to the possibilities of #MeToo in creating spaces for this conversation (also Clark-Parsons 2021) even as, both in personal exchanges and mainstream commentary, these are also challenged and shut down as Fourneir (2017), in particular, argues. Again, this is reminiscent of Banet-Weiser's (2018) work, alerting us to the contradictory presence and erasure of intersectional feminist analysis in and around the #MeToo moment, which points to the limitations of framing intersectionality as a politics of identity and recognition rather than structural critique.

Although this might seem pedantic, these are important issues for feminist analysis and activism as they suggest different sites for action and make different demands in terms of accountability and relationship to wider communities. One of the problems here is the *me* of #MeToo: in Milano's original tweet individuals using the hashtag were asked to share *their own* experiences (*Me*) but to connect with others through the affordances of the hashtag and the acknowledgement of what they share (*Too*). For feminists wanting to build on these experiences to make them part of a *movement*, it is therefore crucial to acknowledge the limitations of the platform and what is, therefore, likely to be missing from the body of evidence gathered under the hashtag #MeToo, as, indeed, Gill and Orgad do. But to present this as a critique of #MeToo runs the risk of making the women sharing their experiences the focus. From here, it is a slippery slope to asserting that some women's testimony is more legitimate and necessary than others.

Evidence relating to the demographics of #MeToo participants—that is, those who responded to the invitation issued by Milano—is limited. Sepideh Modrek and Bozhidar Chaklov (2019) found that white women were disproportionately represented among US-based Twitter users sharing personal experience in the hashtag's first week. This is particularly striking given a 2018 study by the Pew Research Centre found that Black Americans use Twitter more than any other demographic in the US (in Jackson et al 2020: 33). However, Modrek and Chaklov's study is based on geotagged tweets only which make up less than 1% of all #MeToo tweets in the period, and around 4% of all novel tweets in English. As such, what this *might* tell us is that white women disclosing abuse in the US were less concerned about digital surveillance than other groups. There is considerable evidence of the relatively swift uptake of the hashtag across different geographical locations. Focusing on the first 31 hours, Erin Gallagher (2017) notes "I have never seen a hashtag network with so many communities before…. tens of thousands of small groups of people connecting in the #MeToo hashtag", as well as around related hashtags such as the Spanish #YoTambién. In the first year, 29% of #MeToo tweets were in languages other than English (Anderson and Tor 2018) and Sen's 2021 analysis of #MeToo Twitter data for UN Women suggests that 41% of #MeToo Twitter impressions were outside Europe and North America.

At the same time, that #MeToo's spread was so extensive does *not* mean (as has been so often asserted) that it was "global". As Titilope F. Ajayi (2018) writes:

> The majority of international media coverage of #MeToo has been dominated by major news outlets like CNN whose framing of the word "global" has centred on the involvement of certain countries – notably the US, the UK, France and to some extent India and China, with scarcely a mention of Africa and the Middle East.

This is also supported by Sen's analysis (2021: 252) which locates just 2% of #MeToo Twitter impressions in Africa.

There is evidence that the mainstream media stories about #MeToo *did* privilege a very narrow range of experiences and concentrated on mediagenic celebrities and other high-profile figures (De Benedictis et al. 2019). But this does not mean the use of the hashtag was limited in the same way. In the research on #MeToo's first year on Twitter quoted above, for instance, there was a roughly even split between tweets mentioning celebrities or the entertainment industry (15%) and those sharing personal stories (14%) (Anderson and Tor 2018). As such, any critique of the perceived exclusivity of #MeToo needs to focus on media logics or it is too easily appropriated as a critique of individual victim/survivors and a means of re-silencing their stories (Kay 2024; Serisier 2024). Thinking about the limitations of the platform, for instance, opens up questions around digital access and literacy (Mariscal et al. 2019), about audience and surveillance (Megarry 2018) and demands acknowledgement of the policing of women online through abuse which is both racialised and gendered (Amnesty International 2018; Bailey 2021; Young 2022). That differing notions of "respectability" impact on which victim/survivors are constructed as believable is suggested by Cardi B in the Gill and Orgad quote, and has been explored in academic scholarship on believability, visibility and their intersection with race and class (Jackson et al. 2020: 31–64; Williams 2021; Banet-Weiser and Higgins 2023; Wood 2024). As such, it is not specific to the way sexual harassment and abuse are discussed online, but it is clearly part of the context in which individual women decided (not) to post #MeToo or other hashtags of disclosure (Mendes et al. 2019; Jackson et al. 2020: 1–29; Cheema 2023: 4). These notions also shape the way individual testimonies are then taken up and amplified both within and across platforms.

The trajectory of #MeToo as a mainstream media story provides a clear example of how race, wealth, location and celebrity can work to leverage a message whilst erasing its more radical origins. Yet, critiques of the mainstream media story can also work in exclusionary ways. For instance, it is now routinely claimed that the Weinstein case was about white celebrities. The willingness of an—initially singular—white actor (Ashley Judd) to go on the record about Weinstein *was* centrally important in enabling Kantor and Twohey to break the story (Kantor and Twohey 2019). However, the majority of the named women in Kantor and Twohey's 2017 article were *not* famous—either at the time they were assaulted by

Weinstein, or when the *New York Times* article was published. Weinstein routinely targeted "ordinary, unfamous women trying to do their jobs" (Chiu 2019), including young and often poorly paid women who worked in administrative roles within his organisation (Auletta 2022: 121). These women included Zelda Perkins, Lauren O'Connor, Laura Madden and Emily Nestor—who were all named by Kantor and Twohey in 2017—as well as aspiring actors like Ambra Battilana Gutierrez who reported Weinstein to police in New York in 2015. Indeed, it is arguably in *Weinstein's* interests to maintain the fiction that this case was all about white celebrities, as it downplays the significant power differentials which characterised his abusive career. As Lauren O'Connor put it in a memo she wrote whilst working for Weinstein:

> I am a 28 year old woman trying to make a living and a career. Harvey Weinstein is a 64 year old, world famous man and this is his company. The balance of power is me: 0, Harvey Weinstein: 10. (O'Connor in Kantor and Twohey 2019: 135).

Nor did Weinstein only assault white women. Rowena Chiu—Perkins' colleague whose experience is described in the 2017 article, though she is not named in it—has since described the racialised dimension of Weinstein's assault:

> My ethnicity initially marked me as different and inferior. He assured Zelda that he wouldn't harass me because he didn't, as I remember it, "do Chinese or Jewish girls." Then later, he turned around and defined me in terms of sexual exoticism, telling me, just before he tried to rape me, that he'd never had a Chinese girl. (Chiu 2019)

Racial logics shape experiences of abuse as well as the possibilities both of speaking out and of being heard. As feminist critics we need to ensure we do not exacerbate this by making assumptions about the whiteness of disclosure—particularly anonymous disclosure—in ways which further marginalise women of colour. Instead, we need to focus on the algorithms of oppression (Noble 2018) which determine which stories gain prominence on the platform, as well as to the racialised logics of online misogyny (Bailey 2021), the emphasis on celebrity in mainstream media (De Benedictis, Orgard and Rottenberg 2019) *and* the media audiences (including, at times, academics) who see whiteness in anonymity.[3] In other words, it is not #MeToo and related speech which should be our central concern here, but whose speech was (and is) heard and amplified (including in academic work) and under what conditions.

This points to one of the central difficulties in discussing #MeToo: namely, who or what this term now represents. Beyond the parameters of Milano's initial tweet, it is difficult to identify the core characteristics of #MeToo, not least because it has (as a hashtag) been taken up so widely by people who may share little else not just in terms of demographics or location, but also in terms of political philosophy or principles (Loney-Howes 2020). Participating in #MeToo and associated hashtags of disclosure did not *require* a feminist commitment and, indeed, some of its most prominent advocates have distanced themselves—and their speech—from feminisms (Li 2021: 352). As Carol Harrington (2022: 8) puts it: "whilst feminists pioneered practices of speaking out about sexual violence, public accounts of sexual violence can serve a range of political agendas, including conservative, reactionary, and militaristic ones" (also Boyle and Rathnayake 2020; Bedera 2022; Mincheva 2023). The hashtag is part of—but neither synonymous with nor the origins of—a wider movement, including (but again not restricted to) Burke's Me Too. As I will discuss more fully in Chapter 4, #MeToo's interactions with genealogies of feminist activism were (and are) specific to the different locations in which it has been taken up. In this sense, #MeToo needs to be understood not as *initiating* activism where none had previously existed, but as *contributing* to ongoing, context-specific work in ways which were/are often particularly mediagenic (Tambe 2021). In insisting on these distinctions, I want to keep in view the longer (and unevenly intersectional) history of feminist activism against sexual harassment and assault on and offline and also caution against the kind of hyperbole which—given the sheer volume of #MeToo content—has often characterised commentary and critique in this area. We should be particularly wary of claims about its "global" or "worldwide" reach, not only due to

---

[3] For instance, Ashley Noel Mack and Bryan J. McCann (2019: 373) state that the "Emily Doe" raped by Brock Turner is "a White woman". She is not. Chanel Miller has written powerfully of how the erasure of her ethnic identity was part of how she was institutionally "processed" in the aftermath of the attack (Miller 2019: 220). Whilst Miller was still anonymous at the time Mack and McCann's article was published, it is not clear on what basis they made their claim. The assumed whiteness of anonymity in sexual assault reporting is an issue which requires further critical attention.

the exclusions such language performs (of course there are communities where it has not registered or resonated) but also because of the linear model of transmission and influence this suggests. It is on this basis that, in this new edition, I refer to the *long* #MeToo moment as a way of unsettling the origin story to which I contributed in the 2019 edition, whilst still seeking to retain the focus on a temporally located discursive moment linked to—but not synonymous with—longer histories of feminist activism against men's violence.

Weinstein and Beyond

In a book centrally concerned with feminist understandings of sexual violence and critical of mainstream mediations of sexual violence, it may seem contradictory that the only named individual in my title is—still—(Harvey) Weinstein. Feminists in a variety of contexts in and outside of the academy have long questioned how best to represent abusive men, or those accused of abuse, and highlighted the danger of narrativising stories of sexual violence and murder such that perpetrators become celebrities and victims are forgotten (Williamson 2018). These questions are more fully addressed in Chapter 5, but there are a few points I want to make here to set up concerns which I address throughout the book, albeit in rather different ways than in 2019.

First, the ability to speak about—and name—abuse in the public sphere has long been stacked against victim/survivors. For women like Zelda Perkins and Rowena Chiu who were pressurised into signing exhaustive non-disclosure agreements following their complaints about Weinstein, speaking even to a therapist or family member was prohibited (Chiu 2019). Weinstein's threats extended beyond individual women to journalists and publishers: he had the economic power—and the legal and disciplinary power money can buy—to frustrate reporting and threaten reporters (Kantor and Twohey 2019; Farrow 2017b, 2019). Yet, in this book, the "cagey" language I often had to adopt in the first edition has—at least as far as Weinstein is concerned—been replaced with certainty. Harvey Weinstein is a rapist. I am able to state this unequivocally *not* because he raped women (he'd already done that in 2019), or because I believe the women who have spoken out about their experiences (which I did then and do now). I am able to state this in writing because a jury in LA determined that there was sufficient evidence to *prove* that he was guilty of rape. However, that I have had to edit to this paragraph to remove reference to his New York convictions demonstrates the limitations of depending on legal judgement as the basis for writing clearly about men's violence against women.[4] Likewise, the different civil judgements in the Johnny Depp case demonstrate the contingency of legal definitions: as I discuss in more detail in Chapter 4, whilst a UK court ruled that the *Sun's* description of him as a wife-beater was substantially true, a US court determined that Amber Heard defamed Depp when she described herself as "a public figure representing domestic abuse" (Heard 2018). Of course, anyone accused of a crime is entitled to defend themselves, including in a court of law. My point is not to deny that, but rather to stress that speech about sexual harassment and assault is not—by any measure—"free" (Robinson and Yoshida 2023). Access to legal protection is determined by, among other things, wealth and the believability of testimony "is indexed not to facts but to power" (Gilmore 2017: 15; see also Banet-Weiser and Higgins 2023; Gilmore 2023). Against this backdrop, it is perhaps unsurprising that many of the prominent men accused in the immediate aftermath of #MeToo in the US relied on the lack of criminal charges to advance a narrative of "innocence" (Su et al 2022: 12).

After the linguistic gymnastics I sometimes found myself performing in *#MeToo, Weinstein and Feminism* I admit to a certain satisfaction in being able to state—at least for now—that Harvey Weinstein is a rapist. But constructing the "rapist" as a *distinct* category of person goes against much of what decades of feminist research and activism in this field has taught us. In Weinstein's case, it also disguises the, in criminal terms, "lesser" offences which were key to his modus operandi and the immediate response to the *New York Times* reporting under #MeToo. Milano, remember, focused on "sexual harassment and assault". The label "rapist" disguises this more complex reality and reduces his decades-long patterns of abuse to specifically defined incidents. It also risks reconstructing as "not that bad" (Gay 2018) behaviour which was still unacceptable and damaging. As I will discuss in Chapter 5, making connections between

---

[4] In late April 2024, the New York Court of Appeal overturned Weinstein's convictions and ordered a retrial. At the time of writing, it is unclear when that retrial will take place and whether the women Weinstein was charged with assaulting and raping will be willing to testify again. Statements about legal judgments and charges in this book are correct as of 1 May 2024 but—as this example demonstrates—this does not mean they are permanent.

men whose violence is *recognised* as "aberrant" and those men whose abusive interactions are dismissed as "normal" has been a cornerstone of feminist theorising on gender and violence (Kelly 1988; Connell 1995; Boyle 2019). Constructing the person who abuses as a distinct category—whether rapist, abuser or perpetrator—arguably works against this, but is a common feature of both popular and academic writing on men's violence against women, including my own. These terms can function as a form of "othering", making it difficult for victim/survivors to recognise the men who abuse them in these categorical terms. Such dissonance is, perhaps, particularly acute when that man is not *only* the one who has abused them, but is also, for instance, a loved family member or friend, a successful boss, an adored celebrity, or an esteemed political or religious leader. When the abuser is a category of person, it is also easier for men who behave abusively to distance themselves from that identity: he's not *that* kind of person.

As will already be apparent, I have not entirely moved away from referring to perpetrators and abusers. Sometimes it is right and necessary to do so. But ongoing critical reflection about the unintended consequences of our own language must be a feature of feminist media scholarship. As I noted in 2019, reading Catharine MacKinnon's reflections on #MeToo was a real light bulb moment for me:

> Culturally, it is still said "women allege" or "claim" they were sexually assaulted. Those accused "deny" what was alleged. What if survivors "report" sexual violation and the accused "alleges" or "claims" it did not occur, or occur as reported?
> (MacKinnon 2018)

This is such a simple but important point that can have a major impact on the stories we tell about sexual harassment and assault and is a challenge I tried to take up in the first edition and in subsequent work on trial reporting (Boyle and Jessie 2020). Reflecting on my hitherto relatively uncritical use of the term "perpetrator" has been one of the challenges in working on this second edition.

One of the reasons for naming Weinstein in my title in 2019 was to challenge myself (and readers) to think about how to describe what women reported he had done without (at that point) the security of a criminal conviction, and without—even if unconsciously—stacking the discussion against women from the start. As Deb Waterhouse-Watson writes, "while accused persons must be held innocent until proven guilty, a complainant must equally be presumed 'innocent' of fabricating the charge" (2012: 56). This presumption will not always be borne out in any individual case, but neither—of course—is the presumption that women lie/allege and men tell the truth/deny. This is just one of the tried and tested formulations for writing about men's violence against women (and children) which this book seeks to interrogate.

I argued in 2019 that Weinstein had come to occupy a particular place in the public imaginary around #MeToo that bears scrutiny and, in some ways, this is even more marked in 2024. Of course, the Weinstein of my title is a real human—a man who is now imprisoned for rape and sexual assault, and has been publicly accused of many more sexual offences against women than those he has been tried for. But "Harvey Weinstein" has also become a sort of shorthand for referring to men accused of sexual assault in the #MeToo era. The second, more generic, meaning, was first encapsulated in a response to the Kantor and Twohey article which encouraged women to name #MyHarveyWeinstein to call out workplace harassment:

> When did you meet YOUR Harvey Weinstein? I'll go first: I was a 17-yr-old co-op student and he insisted on massaging my shoulders as I typed. (@annetdonahue, 5 October 2017)

This hashtag only worked because Kantor and Twohey *did* name Harvey Weinstein. But notably Donahue did not name her own Harvey Weinstein, and, indeed, Nau et al (2023) suggest that "naming and shaming" *specific* perpetrators was not a common feature of initial responses to Milano.

More than six years on, #MyHarveyWeinstein does not work in quite the same way. When Donahue tweeted, Kantor and Twohey (2017) had identified eight women "paid off" by Weinstein in relation to "sexual harassment" allegations. With the publication of Ronan Farrow's (2017a) report in the *New Yorker* a few days later, the first reports of rape were made. In the months that followed, as many as 150 women came forward to report that they had been abused by Weinstein.[5]

---

[5] *Harvey Weinstein: The Fall of the King of Hollywood*, Sky News, 2019. The full documentary is available here: https://www.youtube.com/watch?v=GESBI9pWWmI (Accessed September 2023).

Unlike nearly all the other public figures named in this book, beyond the first days following Kantor and Twohey's story there has been little public support for Weinstein. Some of the potential reasons for this are explored in Chapter 5, but the extent to which Weinstein has become the standard against which other men accused of abuse are judged (and, hence, absolved in the court of public opinion) has intensified since 2019. If "he's no Harvey Weinstein" had already become a popular defence-of-sorts in 2019, by 2020 Weinstein's legal team was effectively claiming that *he* was no Harvey Weinstein either, that "Harvey Weinstein" had become a caricature—a monster—divorced from the real person (Boyle 2021). This points to the difficult balance between keeping both the structural nature of men's violence against women *and* the responsibility of individual men in view in such highly mediatised contexts.

Burke's simple but powerful statement—Me Too—enables women to speak because it acknowledges that our experiences are shared by others. It situates the individual in the conversation whilst also allowing us to see the bigger picture, thus meaning no one woman should carry the weight of that "Me" alone. The collective voices of women also expose the structural nature of men's violence. Naming Weinstein arguably undercuts this by placing one man in the frame and doing so largely because *so many* women named him. For most victim/survivors, of course, there is little potential for raising a collective voice against an individual perpetrator.

The emphasis on named, high-profile perpetrators is an approach that Burke has been critical of, observing that in the first year after the hashtag went viral there was "an unwavering obsession with the perpetrators—a cyclical circus of accusations, culpability, and indiscretions" (quoted in Rowley 2018). Rose McGowan, one of the most prominent women to speak publicly about Weinstein, also has misgivings: in her book *Brave* (2018: 115), McGowan refuses to name Weinstein and so perpetuate the linking of her name to his, referring to him only as "the monster". At the same time, naming is a means of insisting that individual men *are* responsible for their actions, even within a wider context where these actions are duplicated by other men and condoned by many more. Deborah Cameron (2017) writes: "We cannot put that shame where it belongs— with the perpetrators, not their victims—if we cannot describe the details of what was done and what was said". Although Cameron is referring here to the *what* of men's violence—the details disguised by euphemistic terms such as "inappropriate behaviour" and "sexual misconduct"—her point also applies to the *who*. Keeping Weinstein in frame is partly a reminder that his name *should* now always be yoked to #MeToo (though #MeToo should not always be yoked to him): it is a question of accountability. However, as Burke cautions (Rowley 2018), whilst it is important that men like Weinstein are held accountable, the movement cannot be equated with accused perpetrators. In this book, my focus is men's violence and abuse against women, women's responses, and media representations of victim/survivors. In this context, not naming individual men—particularly those whose abusive behaviour has been extensively, publicly documented—would have a very different meaning. I will argue at different points in this book that naming is linked to consequences (for the perpetrator), recognition (of the victim/survivor's story) and, potentially, to prevention (the aim of the "whisper networks" which women in so many sectors have used to share information and keep one another safe). These are all aspects of what Clare McGlynn and Nicole Westmarland (2019), drawing on interviews with victim/survivors of sexual violence, call "kaleidoscopic justice". Naming can be a form of justice, of asserting our belief in victim/survivors, even in contexts where our language has to be more careful than we might like because certain terms are defined and limited by their legal usage. In short, telling stories about men's violence against women cannot only be about telling women's stories or we risk making men's violence exclusively a women's issue, letting men off the hook.

Considering Weinstein—as I do in a number of the chapters which follow—allows me to critically examine what has become a recurrent theme in writing about celebrity abusers and celebrities alleged to have committed abuse, namely that "everybody knew" about their sexually abusive behaviour before it became news. Chapter 6 offers evidence of some of the contexts in which Weinstein's abusive behaviour in general, and his behaviour towards women in particular, had been publicly acknowledged prior to October 2017. I argue that these stories had a certain cultural value so long as they were not recognised as abuse. However, the repackaging of abuse as, for instance, artistic temperament or standard business practice, has also served a function for Weinstein and those defending him since October 2017, allowing him to argue that the problem is one of interpretation and changing social and sexual mores, not abusive behaviour per se (also Gilmore 2023: 63–70).

Moreover, as the phrase "he's no Harvey Weinstein" suggests, there are limitations in making Weinstein the (anti-)poster boy of the #MeToo moment. Although Weinstein certainly occupied a position of power prior to the Kantor and Twohey story, in many ways, he was always already understood as an outsider in the industry which made him (and which he made). Thus, Weinstein can now be seen as an individual monster without this necessarily leading to questions about the structures that protected him. As such, the focus on Weinstein risks displacing a feminist analysis of the #MeToo moment in ways I discuss in Chapters 5, 6 and 7, comparing media representations of Weinstein with those of other men accused in the same period. Thus, whilst Weinstein remains in my title, I also seek to get beyond Weinstein, or, more accurately, to situate Weinstein in the company of other alleged, accused and convicted abusers to explore the construction of believability in the long #MeToo moment.

Victims, Survivors, Naming and Anonymity

There is considerable debate in feminist scholarship and activism about the use of the terms "victim" and "survivor" to describe those (especially women) who have experienced sexual and other forms of gender-based violence. These debates typically hinge on agency, with the term "survivor" often being preferred as it offers a more agentic identity and the possibility of recognising women's active resistance (Kelly 1988). However, feminists have also cautioned against seeing these terms as binaries and so reinforcing the stigma of victimisation (Jordan 2004: 12) whilst work with survivor-activists points to the ways that "victim" and "survivor" may be embraced—or rejected—for different reasons, depending on context, experience and audience (Loney-Howes 2020: 88–94; Jordan 2022: 12, 17–18). As our knowledge of women's experiences of sexual and other forms of gender-based violence have expanded, we have also come to recognise that survival is not a destination but a process (Kelly et al. 1996; Jordan 2023: 92–93). This makes sense, for instance, of oft-repeated claims that a criminal trial or media coverage may constitute a second victimisation: claims which are highly pertinent in the context of this book.

#MeToo allows us to see that victimisation and survival are moving points on a continuum rather than binary and all-consuming identities (Kelly et al. 1996; Jordan 2023: 92–93). An individual's movement across the continuum is not uni-directional or strictly chronological, such that, for instance, victim *becomes* survivor (Boyle 2019). In this book— as in the first edition—I have therefore used the term victim/survivor throughout as a means of acknowledging that experiences of victimisation and survival are dynamic and contextual. At the same time, it is important to recognise that not all victims survive. Although this book centres Anglo-American #MeToo discourse in the wake of Milano's tweet about sexual harassment and assault, the evidence accumulated under this and related hashtags—such as the Argentinian #NiUnaMenos—has included evidence of femicide.

Even in the context of sexual harassment and assault, the term victim/survivor doesn't always feel right. In October 2020, I tweeted #MeToo but I do not consider myself a victim/survivor because my experiences are so mundane, unremarkable and routine (as I discuss in Chapter 3). As a Twitter user quoted by Rosemary Clark-Parsons (2021: 371) put it: "#MeToo, just like most other women". So are we *all* victim/survivors? That conclusion is arguably in line with the collectivist ethos of the hashtag and is taken up by some critics, including Lisa Lazard (2022: 43), who suggests that by tweeting #MeToo "women self-identified as victims". Yet, there is a danger that this negates the *specific* experiences which lead some people to find identity, belonging and the possibility of healing in the term at the same time as implying the necessity of a victim(ised) identity to prove harm. As Tanya Serisier puts it:

> achieving political effects through stories of suffering can require us to display our trauma and insist that all incidents of sexual violence or harassment are "that bad" rather than asserting that even incidents that don't cause trauma or suffering are, or should be, unacceptable. (Serisier 2020: 171)

These arguments are taken up more fully in Chapters 3 and 7. It's also worth noting that victim/survivor is a gender-neutral term. Of course, there are victim/survivors of all genders. But when we are talking about *specific* groups—and Milano's initial address was explicitly to women—gender-neutral language can disguise structural inequalities.

Whilst #MeToo and other hashtags of disclosure have led many people to publicly identify *as* victims, survivors or victim/survivors, to become what Tanya Serisier (2024) calls a "public survivor" is a choice of a different magnitude. In researching and writing about #MeToo, this is something I continually reflect on. On one hand, I want to acknowledge the emotional and activist labour of #MeToo participants, to make visible the role they have played in advancing understanding of sexual harassment and assault, holding institutions and individuals accountable, and demanding cultural change. A standard way of doing this in academic practice is through citation. Yet to cite a #MeToo story—even one openly shared—is to isolate the story (and the participant) from the broader conversation, remove them from context and permanently link them to that story. When participants retain a degree of control over their stories—when, for instance, they can still delete a post or video—then to cite them without their explicit consent in a book like this one is to give their words a degree of permanence their author may never have intended. To post #MeToo is not to agree to being labelled as a victim/survivor in all contexts in perpetuity. However, this simple statement is in tension with how women's stories are commonly understood: as Serisier puts it "the biographies of women who tell their stories are reduced to the experience and their decision to speak about it" (2020: 168).

In this book I have negotiated this tension by attributing statements (including social media posts) to individuals only when they are public figures or when they have agreed for their words to be used in media over which they do not retain editorial control (such as documentary film or newspaper reporting). For instance, Anne T. Donahue—whose #MyHarveyWeinstein post I quote above—is a writer and comedian and, in the days before Elon Musk's takeover, her Twitter account was verified.[6] In contrast, the Twitter user whose "#MeToo, just like most other women" tweet Clark-Parsons quotes was not a public figure and Clark-Parsons not only removes her username but also makes "minor alterations" to her words "such that…tweets retain their original meanings but cannot be traced back to the authors through a search engine" (Clark-Parsons 2021: 369). My approach mirrors Clark-Parsons' and is broadly in line with the advice of the Association of Internet Researchers (2019).

Where this is arguably more complicated is in relation to legal cases. Whether by convention or by law, complainants in sexual assault cases are—in many but by no means all jurisdictions—often given anonymity in media reporting of trials. When high-profile cases like Weinstein's are covered by media in multiple jurisdictions this can mean that some outlets name survivor-witnesses whilst others don't. Some women also waive a

---

[6] At the time of Donahue's tweet, blue-ticks were a means—albeit imperfect—of identity verification for public figures. This tweet is still visible at the time of writing (February 2023).

right to anonymity (if one does exist) to speak publicly about their experiences, as we have already seen. In that case, where the women have spoken on the record, using their own names, I have followed suit.

OUTLINE OF THE CHAPTERS

The remainder of the book is organised into six substantive chapters and a short conclusion: Chapter 2, 3, 5 and 6 are revised and updated from the first edition; Chapters 4, 7 and 8 are entirely new. Chapters 2, 3 and 4 are centrally concerned with women's #MeToo stories, whilst chapters 5 and 6 focus on men primarily, though not exclusively, those who have been identified as abusive. Chapter 7 returns to women's stories to consider the political and personal implications of privileging testimony in activist, academic and media contexts.

In Chapter 2, I situate the "silence breakers" of the Anglo-American #MeToo moment in a longer Anglo-American feminist history of speaking out about men's violence. This allows me to explore the function of victim/survivor testimony for feminist theory and organising in relation both to histories of feminist consciousness-raising and engagements with mainstream media. I analyse how key moments in the development of the interrelated Weinstein and #MeToo stories were picked up, extended and represented in mainstream media. In updating this chapter for the second edition, I have added a discussion of coverage of Weinstein's criminal trials in New York (2020) and Los Angeles (2022–23). Setting up concerns I will return to throughout the book, I examine how feminism and feminists feature in this coverage. This allows me to highlight the simultaneity of #MeToo and the backlash against its feminist orientations and challenges, whilst also setting up concerns with (proportionate) consequences for perpetrators which are expanded in later chapters.

Chapter 3 is centrally concerned with how feminist theory has advanced our understanding of the *structural* nature of men's violence against women and the pervasive nature of that violence in women's lives. Liz Kelly's formulation of the continuum of sexual violence is the touchstone for this chapter which explores different ways in which #MeToo has rendered the connections between women, between different types of sexual harassment and assault, and between different men, more and less legible. That Milano's original tweet referred to "sexual harassment and assault" is arguably the most significant contribution of the hashtag as it allowed for a focus on the "everyday" nature of what Fiona Vera-Gray (2017), in her study of street harassment, terms "men's intrusions". Whilst Kelly's continuum was always intended to bring those everyday experiences to light, as she notes in a 2012 reflection on the field, the emphasis on criminal justice in much feminist work had meant that whilst the continuum became *theoretically* central, there was actually little empirical (or activist) attention to its less-obviously criminal elements. #MeToo was not the first digital intervention to challenge this: as Loney-Howes et al (2021: 1349) note, some of the earliest examples of "global digital feminist activism" against sexual violence related to street harassment. In many ways, social media are ideal sites for addressing the everyday in a way that supports mass participation and disclosure. However, as this chapter also demonstrates, social media do not always enable the kind of contextually-specific analysis Kelly advocates and can result in people—and experiences—being shoe-horned into narrow categories which risk distorting distinctions and suggesting false equivalences. As a primarily theoretical chapter, this is largely unchanged from the first edition, though here—as throughout—reference is made to more recent scholarship on #MeToo and related hashtags, and details of individual cases are updated.

Chapter 4 is a new chapter which reconsiders what it means to think of #MeToo as a "moment". Whilst arguing for the value of retaining the movement/moment distinction outlined in this chapter, here I situate #MeToo within a longer recent history characterised by popular feminism and popular misogyny: the long #MeToo moment. I explore some of the antecedents which created the conditions for #MeToo's virality in a range of different contexts. In doing so, I consider how we might understand #MeToo in relation to local feminist histories, acknowledging the importance of the moment in shaping public conversations about sexual harassment and assault, even as other achievements remain more nebulous and difficult to measure. Yet, to ask what #MeToo has achieved is, I argue, the wrong question, as it suggests we judge a movement in a moment. It also suggests that the achievements of the movement are entirely within the gift of activists: in contrast, this chapter considers how the backlash against #MeToo was evident from its earliest days and explores what is at stake in the proclaimed "end" of #MeToo. My case study here is the response to the Johnny Depp civil trials relating to media reporting around domestic abuse. I am interested in what the emphasis on legal judgments (whether criminal or civil) achieves *discursively*. This chapter also picks up McGlynn and Westmarland's (2019) concept of kaleidoscopic justice to consider whether #MeToo and discursive activism more broadly has opened up other routes for victim/survivors to achieve justice outside of legal systems which were not designed for them or in their interests.

Where Chapters 2, 3 and 4 are oriented around women's experiences, testimonies and activism, Chapters 5 and 6 are oriented around (alleged) perpetrators and bystanders. Chapter 5 considers what #MeToo has meant for men. This chapter begins with a consideration of male victims of sexual assault, before considering how narratives of male victimisation have also been appropriated by men accused of assault, focusing on the Brett Kavanaugh Supreme Court nomination hearings which took place almost exactly one year after the publication of Kantor and Twohey's *New York Times* article. This is juxtaposed with the way Weinstein has been represented and in exploring this difference I draw both on Kate Manne's (2018) discussion of himpathy, and on broader feminist debates about the "othering" of male perpetrators of gender violence. This chapter has been lightly edited to provide updates on the cases discussed and to bring in some new examples, but remains broadly unchanged from the first edition.

Chapter 6, "The Cultural Value of Abuse" examines the oft-repeated claim about Weinstein and others that "everybody knew" about the way they behaved. It situates this claim in relation to feminist analyses of rape culture, but adds to this a consideration of the cultural (and, to a lesser extent, affective) *value* of men's sexual violence against women in different sectors. This chapter is an edited and expanded version of what was Chapter 4 in the first edition, bringing in new examples of "in plain sight" narratives and teasing out the role communities (in this case, audiences) have to play in responding to sexual harassment and assault. I engage with the question of whether we can—or should—seek to separate the art from the artist and ask whether cancellation might be a component of kaleidoscopic justice.

Chapter 7 brings the book full circle, returning to the importance of victim/survivors' words. It might seem odd then that this chapter is titled *against* testimony, but in using this title I want to suggest the *in*justice of having to keep telling people about sexual harassment and assault as a condition of action. Given the evidence amassed in this book (and in many, many other places), do we really need *more* accounts of men's abuse of women to convince us to do something about it? Whose interests are served by this? In exploring these questions, this chapter first considers the commercial imperative of "breaking the silence" for the news media, interrogating how claims about silence breaking function rhetorically to limit victim/survivor speech. In the long #MeToo moment, accounts of "breaking the story" about celebrity men and about institutional abuse have also proliferated and I consider the feminist potential of these stories in de-centring victim/survivor speech in order to make that speech consequential. This then leads into a discussion of the relationship between experience and expertise, before I finally turn to the #MeToo documentary as a site where the concerns of this chapter come together. Chapter 8 offers a brief conclusion, identifying common concerns which cut across all of the chapters.

This second edition gives a flavour of some of the ways in which the debate about #MeToo has evolved since 2019, but it remains, necessarily, selective not only in its geographical reach but also in its focus on fact-based media. Academic analyses of #MeToo continue to proliferate, shining a light on the possibilities of digital activism in contexts (e.g. Cheema 2023; Yaghoobi 2023) and media forms (e.g. Kornfield and Jones 2021; Flynn 2024) I have not considered in depth here. The appeal of writing a revised and expanded second edition of this book was that to do so is consistent with my concern with feminist *movements*. Just as feminism is in movement, so too is feminist scholarship, and our understanding of phenomena like #MeToo will and must continue to expand and evolve. What #MeToo has achieved is impossible to answer not only because its achievements are not uniform but also because it is by no means over.

References

Ajayi, Titilope F. 2018. #MeToo, Africa and the politics of transnational activism. *Africa is a Country*, 6 July. Available at: https://africaisacountry.com/2018/07/metoo-africa-and-the-politics-of-transnational-activism. Accessed 5 June 2023.

Amnesty International. 2018. *Toxic Twitter—A toxic place for women*, March. https://www.amnesty.org/en/latest/research/2018/03/online-violence-against-women-chapter-1/. Accessed 25 April 2019.

Anderson, Monica and Skye Tor. 2018. *How social media users have discussed sexual harassment since #MeToo went viral*. Pew Research Centre. 11 October. Available at: https://www.pewresearch.org/fact-tank/2018/10/11/how-social-media-users-have-discussed-sexual-harassment-since-metoo-went-viral/. Accessed 2 March 2023.

Association of Internet Researchers. 2019. *Internet research: Ethical guidelines 3.0*. Available at: https://aoir.org/reports/ethics3.pdf. Accessed 5 June 2023.

Auletta, Ken. 2022. *Hollywood Ending: Harvey Weinstein and the Culture of Silence*. New York: Penguin.

Bailey, Moya. 2021. *Misogynoir transformed: Black women's digital resistance*. New York: New York University Press.

Banet-Weiser, Sarah. 2018. *Empowered: Popular feminism and popular misogyny*. Durham: Duke.

Banet-Weiser, Sarah and Kathryn Claire Higgins. 2023. *Believability: Sexual Violence, Media, and the Politics of Doubt*. Cambridge: Polity.

Bedera, Nicole. 2022. Why are so many survivors supporting Johnny Depp? *Harper's Bazaar*, 26 May. Available at: https://www.harpersbazaar.com/culture/politics/a40116993/why-are-so-many-survivors-supporting-johnny-depp. Accessed 5 June 2023.

Bevacqua, Maria. 2000. *Rape on the Public Agenda: Feminism and the Politics of Sexual Assault*. Boston: Northeastern University Press.

Black Women's Blueprint. 2011. An open letter from Black women to SlutWalk organizers. Reprinted in: *Huffington Post*, 27 September 2011. https://www.huffpost.com/entry/slutwalk-black-women_b_980215. Accessed 22 January 2019.

Boyle, Karen. 2019. What's in a name? Theorising the inter-relationships of gender and violence. *Feminist Theory* 20 (1): 19–68.

Boyle, Karen. 2021. Of moguls, monsters and men. In *The Routledge Handbook of the Politics of the #MeToo Movement*, ed. Giti Chandra and Irma Erlingsdóttir, 186–198. London: Routledge.

Boyle, Karen and Brenna Jessie. 2020. How to report sexual assault trials responsibly. *Gender Equal Media Scotland* [Blog] 28 February. https://emcc.engender.org.uk/news/blog/how-to-report-sexual-assault-trials-responsibly/. Accessed 24 March 2024.

Boyle, Karen, and Chamil Rathnayake. 2020. #HimToo and the networking of misogyny in the age of #MeToo. *Feminist Media Studies* 20 (8): 1259–1277.

Bronstein, Carolyn. 2011. *Battling Pornography: The American Feminist Anti-Pornography Movement, 1976–1986*. New York: Cambridge University Press.

Browne, Sarah. 2014. *The Women's Liberation Movement in Scotland*. Manchester: Manchester University Press.

Bryan, Beverley, Stella Dadzie, and Suzanne Scarfe. 2018. *The Heart of the Race: Black Women's Lives in Britain*, 2nd ed. London: Verso.

Burke, Tarana. n.d. The inception. *Me Too*. https://metoomvmt.org/the-inception/. Accessed 2 April 2019.

Burke, Tarana. 2018. *Me Too is a Movement, Not a Moment*. Ted Talk, November. https://www.ted.com/talks/tarana_burke_me_too_is_a_movement_not_a_moment. Accessed 22 January 2019.
Burke, Tarana. 2021. *Unbound: My Story of Liberation and the Birth of the Me Too Movement*. London: Headline.
Cameron, Deborah. 2017. On being explicit. *Language: A Feminist Guide* (Blog). 19 December https://debuk.wordpress.com/2017/12/19/on-being-explicit/. Accessed 20 May 2019.
Cheema, Iqra Shagufta. 2023. *The Other #MeToos*. New York: Oxford University Press.
Chiu, Rowena. 2019. Harvey Weinstein told me he liked Chinese girls. *New York Times*, 5 October.
Clark-Parsons, Rosemary. 2021. "I See You, I Believe You, I Stand With You": #MeToo and the performance of networked feminist visibility. *Feminist Media Studies* 21 (3): 362–380.
Connell, R.W. 1995. *Masculinities*. Cambridge: Polity.
De Benedictis, Sara, Shani Orgad and Catherine Rottenberg. 2019. #MeToo, popular feminism and the news: A content analysis of UK newspaper coverage. *European Journal of Cultural Studies* 22 (5–6): 718–738.
Dow, Bonnie J. 2014. *Watching Women's Liberation 1970: Feminism's Pivotal Year on the Network News*. Urbana: University of Illinois Press.
Farrow, Ronan. 2017a. From aggressive overtures to sexual assault: Harvey Weinstein's accusers tell their stories. *New Yorker*, 10 October.
Farrow, Ronan. 2017b. Harvey Weinstein's army of spies. *New Yorker*, 6 November.
Farrow, Ronan. 2019. *Catch and Kill: Lies, Spies and a Conspiracy to Protect Predators*. London: Fleet.
Flores, Emily. 2018. The #MeToo movement hasn't been inclusive of the disability community. *Teen Vogue*, 24 April. https://www.teenvogue.com/story/the-metoo-movement-hasnt-been-inclusive-of-the-disability-community. Accessed 24 February 2019.
Flynn, Emma. 2024. *Complexity, Complicity and Consent: Representations of Sexual Violence in English and French Literature and Film*. Unpublished PhD thesis. University of Strathclyde.
Fournier, Jess. 2017. #MeToo: don't make trans and queer survivors a footnote. *Feministing*, 31 October. http://feministing.com/2017/10/31/metoo-dont-make-trans-and-queer-survivors-a-footnote/. Accessed 26 February 2019.
Gallagher, Erin. 2017. #MeToo hashtag network visualization. *Medium*. 21 October. https://erin-gallagher.medium.com/metoo-hashtag-network-visualization-960dd5a97cdf. Accessed 17 March 2023.

Gay, Roxanne, ed. 2018. *Not That Bad: Dispatches from Rape Culture*. New York: Harper Perennial.

Gill, Rosalind, and Shani Orgad. 2018. The shifting terrain of sex and power: From the "sexualization of culture" to #MeToo. *Sexualities* 21 (8): 1313–1324.

Gilmore, Leigh. 2017. *Tainted Witness: Why We Doubt What Women Say About Their Lives*. New York: Columbia University Press.

Gilmore, Leigh. 2023. *The #MeToo Effect: What Happens When We Believe Women*. New York: Columbia University Press.

Graham, Helen, Ann Kaloski, Ali Neilson and Emma Robertson, eds. 2003. *The Feminist Seventies*. York: Raw Nerve Books.

Hague, Gill. 2021. *Histories and Memories of the Domestic Violence Movement*. Bristol: Policy Press.

Harrington, Carol. 2022. *Neoliberal Sexual Violence Politics: Toxic Masculinity and #MeToo*. Cham: Palgrave Macmillan.

Heard, Amber. 2018. I spoke up against sexual violence—And faced our culture's wrath. That has to change. *The Washington Post* 18 December. https://www.washingtonpost.com/opinions/ive-seen-how-institutions-protect-men-accused-of-abuse-heres-what-we-can-do/2018/12/18/71fd876a-02ed-11e9-b5df-5d3874f1ac36_story.html. Accessed 16 February 2024.

Hemmings, Clare. 2011. *Why Stories Matter: The Political Grammar of Feminist Theory*. Durham: Duke.

Hooks, Bell. 2000. *Feminism is for Everybody: Passionate Politics*. London: Pluto.

Jackson, Sarah J., Moya Bailey and Brooke Foucault Welles. 2020. *#Hashtag Activism: Networks of Race and Gender Justice*. Cambridge: MIT Press.

Jolly, Margaretta. 2019. *Sisterhood and After: An Oral History of the UK Women's Liberation Movement, 1968–Present*. Oxford: Oxford University Press.

Jordan, Jan. 2004. *The Word of a Woman? Police, Rape and Belief*. Hampshire: Palgrave Macmillan.

Jordan, Jan. 2022. *Women, Rape and Justice: Unravelling the Rape Conundrum*. Abingdon: Routledge.

Jordan, Jan. 2023. *Tackling Rape Culture: Ending Patriarchy*. Abingdon: Routledge.

Kantor, Jodi and Megan Twohey. 2017. Harvey Weinstein paid off sexual harassment accusers for decades. *New York Times*, 5 October.

Kantor, Jodi, and Megan Twohey. 2019. *She Said: Breaking the Sexual Harassment Story That Helped Ignite a Movement*. London: Bloomsbury.

Kay, Jilly Boyce. 2024. The politics of the traumatised voice: Communicative injustice and structural silencing in contemporary media culture. In *The Routledge Companion to Gender, Media and Violence*, ed. Karen Boyle and Susan Berridge, 194–203. London: Routledge.

Kelly, Liz. 1988. *Surviving Sexual Violence*. Cambridge: Polity.

Kelly, Liz, Sheila Burton and Linda Regan. 1996. Beyond victim or survivor: Sexual violence, identity and feminist theory and practice. In *Sexualizing the Social: Power and the Organization of Sexuality*, ed. Lisa Adkins and Vicki Merchant, 77–101. Basingstoke: Macmillan.
Kornfield, Sarah, and Hannah Jones. 2021. #MeToo on TV: Popular feminism and episodic sexual violence. *Feminist Media Studies* 22 (7): 1657–1672.
Lazard, Lisa. 2022. *Sexual Harassment, Psychology and Feminism: #Metoo, Victim Politics and Predators in Neoliberal Times*. Cham: Palgrave Macmillan.
Lawton, Georgina. 2017. #MeToo is here to stay. *Guardian*, 28 October.
Li, Jan. 2021. In the name of #RiceBunny: Legacy, strategy, and efficacy of the Chinese #MeToo movement. In *The Routledge Handbook of the Politics of the #MeToo Movement*, ed. Giti Chandra and Irma Erlingsdóttir, 343–359. London: Routledge.
Loney-Howes, Rachel. 2020. *Online Anti-Rape Activism: Exploring the Politics of the Personal in the Age of Digital Media*. Bingley: Emerald Publishing.
Loney-Howes, Rachel, Kaitlynn Mendes, Diana Fernándes Romero, Bianca Fileborn, and Sonia Núñez. Puente. 2021. Digital footprints of #MeToo. *Feminist Media Studies* 22 (6): 1345–1362.
MacKinnon, Catharine. 2018. #MeToo has done what the law could not. *New York Times*, 4 February.
Mack, Ashley Noel, and Bryan J. McCann. 2019. Recalling Persky: White rage and intimate publicity after Brock Turner. *Journal of Communication Inquiry* 43 (4): 372–393.
Manne, Kate. 2018. *Down Girl: The Logic of Misogyny*. New York: Oxford University Press.
Mariscal, Judith, Gloria Mayne, Urvashi Aneja, and Alina Sorgner. 2019. Bridging the gender digital gap. *Economics: the Open-Access, Open-Assessment E-Journal* 13 (9): 1–12.
McGlynn, Clare, and Nicole Westmarland. 2019. Kaleidoscopic justice: Sexual violence and victim-survivors' perceptions of justice. *Social and Legal Studies* 28 (2): 179–201.
McGowan, Rose. 2018. *Brave*. London: HQ.
Megarry, Jessica. 2018. Under the watchful eyes of men: Theorising the implications of male surveillance practices for feminist activism on social media. *Feminist Media Studies* 18 (6): 1070–1085.
Mendes, Kaitlynn. 2011. *Feminism in the News: Representations of the Women's Movement Since the 1960s*. London: Palgrave.
Mendes, Kaitlynn, Jessica Ringrose and Jessalynn Keller. 2019. *Digital Feminist Activism: Girls and Women Fight Back Against Rape Culture*. Oxford: Oxford University Press.
Miller, Chanel. 2019. *Know My Name: A Memoir*. London: Viking.

Mincheva, Dilyana. 2023. #DearSister and #MosqueMeToo: Adversarial Islamic feminism within the Western-Islamic public sphere. *Feminist Media Studies* 23 (2): 525–540.

Modrek, Sepideh and Bozhidar Chakalov. 2019. The #MeToo movement in the United States: Text analysis of early twitter conversations. *Journal of Medical Internet Research* 21 (9): e13837.

Nau, Charlotte, Jinman Zhang, Anabel Quan-Haase and Kaitlynn Mendes. 2023. Vernacular practices in digital feminist activism on twitter: Deconstructing affect and emotion in the #MeToo movement. *Feminist Media Studies* 23 (5): 2046–2062.

Noble, Safiya Umoja. 2018. *Algorithms of Oppression: How Search Engines Reinforce Racism*. New York: New York University Press.

Rivers, Nicola. 2017. *Postfeminism(s) and the Arrival of the Fourth Wave: Turning Tides*. Cham: Palgrave Macmillan.

Robertson, Charlotte James. 2024. *Working in Between: Women's Aid and Networks of Anti-Domestic Abuse Activism in the UK, 1971–1996*. Unpublished PhD thesis. University of Glasgow and University of Strathclyde.

Robinson, Jennifer, and Keina Yoshida. 2023. *How Many More Women? The Silencing of Women by the Law and How to Stop It*. London: Endeavour.

Rowley, Liz. 2018. The architect of #MeToo says the movement has lost its way. *The Cut*, 23 October. https://www.thecut.com/2018/10/tarana-burke-me-too-founder-movement-has-lost-its-way.html. Accessed 10 June 2019.

Sen, Purna. 2021. #MeToo: Anger, denouncement, and hope. In *The Routledge Handbook of the Politics of the #MeToo Movement*, ed. Giti Chandra and Irma Erlingsdóttir, 249–268. London: Routledge.

Serisier, Tanya. 2018. *Speaking Out: Feminism, Rape and Narrative Politics*. Cham: Palgrave Macmillan.

Serisier, Tanya. 2020. Speaking out, public judgments, and narrative politics: Researching survivor stories and (not) telling my own. In *Me Too, Feminist Theory, and Surviving Sexual Violence in the Academy*, ed. Laura A. Gray-Rosendale, 167–180. Lanham: Lexington Books.

Serisier, Tanya. 2024. Public survivors: The burdens and possibilities of speaking as a survivor. In *The Routledge Companion to Gender, Media and Violence*, ed. Karen Boyle and Susan Berridge, 204–212. London: Routledge.

Sheehan, Rebecca J. 2016. "If we had more like her we would no longer be the unheard majority": Germaine Greer's reception in the United States. *Australian Feminist Studies* 31 (87): 62–77.

Shrew. 1970. Bourgeois press. *Shrew* 1: 1–3.

Su, Chiaoning, Rebecca Mercado Jones and Valerie Palmer-Mehta. 2022. The hall of shame: Reconstructing dominant masculinities in the *New York Times*' representation of US #MeToo offenders' apologias. *Communication Review* 25 (1): 1–29.

Tambe, Ashwini. 2021. Afterword. "Walking alongside many #MeToos." *Feminist Formations* 33 (3): 351–359.
Taylor, Keeanga-Yamahtta., ed. 2017. *How We Get Free: Black Feminism and the Combahee River Collective*. Chicago: Haymarket Books.
Tufnell Park Women's Liberation Workshop. 1970. Final word on the media. *Shrew* 1: 4–5.
Vera-Gray, Fiona. 2017. *Men's Intrusion, Women's Embodiment: A Critical Analysis of Street Harassment*. London: Routledge.
Wafula Strike, Anne. 2018. Disabled women see #MeToo and think: What about us? *Guardian*, 8 March.
Waterhouse-Watson, Deb. 2012. Framing the victim: Sexual assault and Australian footballers on television. *Australian Feminist Studies* 27 (71): 55–70.
Williams, Sherri. 2021. Revisiting digital defense and Black feminism on social media. *Feminist Media Studies* 21 (8): 1373–1377.
Williamson, Terrion L. 2018. What does that make you? Public narration and the serial murders of Black women. In *Where Freedom Starts: Sex, Power, Violence, #MeToo*, A Verso Report: 42–48.
Wood, Helen. 2024. Class, victim credibility and the Pygmalion problem in real crime dramas *Three Girls* and *Unbelieveable*. In *The Routledge Companion to Gender, Media and Violence*, ed. Karen Boyle and Susan Berridge, 251–260. London and New York: Routledge.
Yaghoobi, Claudia, ed. 2023. *The #MeToo Movement in Iran: Reporting Sexual Violence and Harassment*. London: IB Tauris.
Young, Kalima. 2022. *Mediated Misogynoir: Erasing Black Women's and Girls' Innocence in the Public Imagination*. London: Lexington Books.

CHAPTER 2

Silence Breaking

INTRODUCTION

In December 2017, *Time* magazine named "The Silence Breakers"—the women (and some men) speaking out about sexual harassment in workplaces—their "person" of the year. In the editorial explaining this choice, *Time*'s Editor-in-Chief identifies the "individual acts of courage" which initiated what was to become "a hashtag, a movement, a reckoning" (Felsenthal 2017). In this way, Felsenthal identifies both the individual and collective importance of "the silence breakers". But the conclusion of his editorial also gestures towards some of the tensions which are inherent in the silence breaking metaphor, acknowledging that 2017 was not the year when these women necessarily broke their silence, but rather when "open secrets" and "moving whisper networks" moved onto social media and "push[ed] us all to stop accepting the unacceptable".

The *Time* story is a useful entry into the concerns of this chapter as it simultaneously highlights the power—and limitations—of speech, the importance of both social media and legacy media in giving voice, and prompts the question as to whether it is the *silence* which has been broken or a cultural inability to *listen* to victim/survivor speech. Actor Ashley Judd—one of the first women to publicly name Harvey Weinstein as an abuser—is quoted in the opening paragraphs of the *Time* story making exactly this point: "I started talking about Harvey the minute that it happened" (Zacharek et al. 2017). Judd had been talking about

© The Author(s), under exclusive license to Springer Nature Switzerland AG 2024
K. Boyle, *#MeToo and Feminism*,
https://doi.org/10.1007/978-3-031-67314-6_2

Weinstein since 1997 within her own networks, but it was her inclusion in Jodi Kantor and Megan Twohey's *New York Times* exposé, alongside other women who reported experiencing or witnessing Weinstein's abuse, that propelled her speech into the public realm. In other cases that have since achieved similar prominence, scholars have noted that even when speech against prominent men had already existed in the public realm, the context provided by #MeToo allowed that speech to be heard differently (e.g. Sreedharan et al. 2020: 132).

Notably, part of the reason that Weinstein's sexually abusive behaviour had not previously been made public—at least in a way that allowed the behaviour to be seen as problematic—was the inclusion of non-disclosure agreements in Weinstein's settlements with those women who did raise complaints about his behaviour or seek legal redress. Weinstein was also notoriously litigious, and his influence with editors and broadcasters frustrated reporting (Farrow 2019; Auletta 2022). In this context, that investigative journalism was the genre in which the story could finally be publicly told is significant and Kantor and Twohey's piece (2017), and subsequent reporting by Ronan Farrow (2017a, 2017b), are at pains to establish the corroborating evidence their stories are built on. As lawyers Jennifer Robinson and Keina Yoshida (2023) demonstrate, the legal, financial and, sometimes, physical risks to survivors, journalists and publishers in speaking out about sexual violence—particularly when it involves wealthy, powerful men—are considerable. Media stories are, rarely, therefore, as simple as the "he said, she said" formula which is routinely used to cast doubt on survivor speech: what "she said" rarely stands alone (Tuerkheimer 2021). Farrow (2017a) also acknowledges the motivations of the women in speaking to him ("because they hoped to protect other women in the future"), as well as the cultural conditions which enabled them to speak out, including the slew of stories about public figures which preceded the Weinstein case (see Chapter 4). Speech begets speech, but it is the *mediation* of that speech—and, crucially, its (perceived) corroboration—which is key to its success. Moreover, it is significant that the *Time* editorial positions silence breaking as generative of a reckoning, opening up questions about what this speech should mean for perpetrators which I pick up later in the book.

The "silence breakers" in the *Time* article are not all linked to the Weinstein exposé however, and I want to briefly discuss the initiators of Me Too and #MeToo to demonstrate some rather different forms and functions of speech which are collapsed in the term "silence breakers".

In the story Tarana Burke (n.d) tells of the Me Too movement's origins, it is her failure to listen and to speak in response to a young Black girl's disclosure of sexual assault which inspires her activism. Burke painfully acknowledges that she "wanted no part" of the girl's disclosure. Although she redirected the girl, Heaven, to another counsellor, she acknowledges that her failure to listen haunts her: "The shock of being rejected, the pain of opening a wound only to have it abruptly closed again—it was all on her face". Burke continues:

> I watched her walk away from me as she tried to recapture her secrets and tuck them back into their hiding place. I watched her put her mask back on and go back into the world like she was all alone and I couldn't even bring myself to whisper....me too.
> (Burke, n.d.)

Burke's powerful writing forces us to recognise the emotional costs of both speaking out and listening, acknowledging the power and difficulty of solidarity. What Burke identifies as an interpersonal failure is, however, transformed into activism which has both therapeutic and advocacy functions "specific to the needs of different communities" (me too, n.d.). This is what Burke (2018) refers to as "the work" and I will argue that there are resonances, as well as dissonances, here with accounts of speaking out as the privileged site through which feminist analysis of sexual violence was developed through the 1970s. Crucially, for both Burke and those involved in the 1970s speak outs, speech is not a political end in itself but rather initiates the development of a public-facing, structural, political analysis.

Compare this with Alyssa Milano's tweet in the aftermath of the Weinstein revelations which, as detailed in Chapter 1, initiated #MeToo. It is the orientation and function of Milano's speaking out which interests me here. Like Burke, Milano positions herself *within* a community of victim/survivors through her statement "me too" and (again like Burke) does not give details of her own experience. Rather, this is a jumping off point for establishing commonalities with other "women who have been sexually harassed or assaulted". Milano's address is not solely to victim/survivors, as the explicit intent of these speech acts is to "give people a sense of the magnitude of the problem" (@AlyssaMilano, 15 October 2017). As Rosemary Clark-Parsons (2021: 369) notes, that #MeToo was a complete statement in itself allowed participants to "stand in solidarity with other survivors without necessarily having to describe traumatic experiences" and this was no doubt instrumental to its success in achieving Milano's initial stated aim. This is speaking out as awareness raising: the speaking *is* the work which unites women whose experiences—as well as their understanding of those experiences and motivations for speaking out—are otherwise very different. Whilst the emotional work of online disclosure is a growing theme in feminist scholarship (e.g. Mendes et al. 2019), questions about whether speaking out is in itself a transformative political practice have concerned feminist activists and scholars for some time (e.g. Alcoff and Gray 1993; Armstrong 1996; Serisier 2018; Alcoff 2018) and remain highly relevant in relation to #MeToo.

These stories therefore set up some of the central concerns of this chapter. I begin by situating the "silence breaking" of the #MeToo moment in relation to a longer history of feminist speak outs and the activism, research and theory which these speak outs generated. As well as raising questions about speech and the collective, this also raises fundamental questions about knowledge in light both of the repeated claims that "everybody knew" about Weinstein's behaviour and the ahistorical media representations of #MeToo which divorce the hashtag from feminist knowledge, activism and research. I then move on to consider online affordances: how do these stories gain traction on and through social media? In the final section, I return to legacy media to explore how reporters and commentators have tried to make sense of this explosion of sexual harassment discourse on and offline. I explore how contemporary speak outs are—and are not—understood in relation to feminism and feminists, by examining the discursive construction of feminism and feminists in news coverage of selected points of the Weinstein story.

Speaking Out

Personal stories about rape and other forms of sexual violence are the foundation on which feminist theory and activism to end men's violence against women are built. As Tanya Serisier (2018: 4) notes in her impressive account of feminism, rape and narrative politics:

> feminist anti-rape politics is founded on the belief that producing and disseminating a genre of personal experiential narratives can end sexual violence. It is a belief, in the words of the well-known slogan, that

"breaking the silence" through telling personal stories can and will "end the violence".

As Serisier acknowledges, the feminist project of speaking out is not an end in itself, rather it is a step towards challenging, and ultimately ending, men's violence against women. But for speech to have an impact it has to be heard. It was through telling stories of their own experiences *and* listening to those of other women—in consciousness-raising groups and larger "speak outs"—that feminists were able to understand the common structure of their experiences. This understanding allowed them to build an analysis of sexual and other forms of men's violence, as well as to develop strategies to support women and challenge that violence. At the same time, in emphasising the common character in women's experiences, important differences between women were neglected in this foundational analysis (Richie 2012: 65–98).

The history of the feminist anti-rape movements in the US (Bevacqua 2000: 18–65) as well as similar movements in the UK (e.g. Maitland 2009; Browne 2014: 140–177; Scottish Women's Aid 2017; Hague 2021) are thus intimately bound up with the process of speaking out and consciousness-raising. These and other feminist anti-violence movements broke the silence decades ago. In this sense, the #MeToo moment with its outpouring of victim/survivor testimony is not new, yet this longer history of feminist speech is largely absent from popular understandings of #MeToo (as I demonstrate later in this chapter). If the feminist past is not readily accessible, and feminist organisations in the present are struggling to maintain profile as well as funding, then it is hardly surprising if we seem to be reinventing the wheel. This is not simply about telling the same, or similar, stories again, but rather about divorcing these stories from the work of activist and advocacy organisations founded during the second wave whose work continues in the #MeToo moment. This creates schisms rather than connections with feminism's knowledge base, creating conditions for generational conflict to flourish.

It is worth pausing on the term consciousness-raising to consider its relationship to speaking out. Whilst speaking out assumes the primacy of experience, consciousness-raising suggests that a feminist understanding of that experience has to be built. This might be about naming or making public experiences which had previously been unspeakable or invisible. But it can also be about re-interpreting experiences which have long had a public character but have been understood only from a male point of view. This can mean making visible *as violence* experiences which have not previously been understood in this way. An obvious example here would be rape within marriage, which only became illegal in England and Wales in 1991, and Scotland in 1989, a husband's "right" to his wife's body having previously over-ridden her right to bodily autonomy. That said, violence does not have to be recognisably criminal for it to contribute to gender inequality, nor has feminist theory or activism concentrated solely on criminal justice.

This intertwining of speech with process is encapsulated in a history project marking the fortieth anniversary of Scottish Women's Aid—entitled, appropriately enough, *Speaking Out*. In the anniversary publication, we are told:

> Ultimately, Women's Aid in Scotland aims to "break the silence" – to raise awareness of domestic abuse among the public and policy makers, to change attitudes and promote women's equality and children's rights, to campaign for responses which actively prevent violence against women, and to bring an end to domestic abuse altogether. (Scottish Women's Aid 2017: 6)

This suggests the ongoing centrality of victim/survivor experience to the movement, but also highlights the expertise within the organisation itself, built from decades of speaking, listening and acting. There are echoes here with Burke's (2018) argument that speaking out creates the conditions for the work, but is not, or not always, the work in itself.

Work is an important word in relation to consciousness-raising as it helps us to understand the commitment and organisation it required (e.g. Women's Liberation Workshop 1971/72). This work was typically conducted in small, women-only groups and the work of these groups was not only emotional, but organisational, practical and theoretical (Hanisch 2010). Consciousness-raising demanded a considerable commitment of time and energy and was central to feminist theorising and activism in both the UK and US (Megarry 2018a; Bevacqua 2000). As Jalna Hanmer put it, the consciousness-raising groups *were* the movement.[1]

---

[1] Transcript and audio of excerpts of 2010 oral history with Jalna Hanmer for the Sisterhood and After project, available at: https://www.bl.uk/collection-items/jalna-hanmer-consciousness-raising-groups.

In the US in particular, larger speak outs were also an important building block for activism and attracted wider public attention (Brownmiller 1975/1986; Armstrong 1987, 1996; Bevacqua 2000: 54–57). Whilst these made different demands on participants (not least in terms of the longevity of commitment), what the consciousness-raising groups and speak outs shared was the political use to which they put personal narratives, encapsulated in the second-wave slogan "the personal is political". Speak outs, conferences and movement publications provided some of the spaces for developing and sharing insights beyond the small group (Beins 2017; McKinney 2015; Bevacqua 2000). But, as Megarry (2018a, 2018b) argues, the closed nature of the groups was important in creating a space where women could develop an analysis free from male surveillance, something which she argues is missing from feminist attempts to build solidarity in digital networks. However, it is also important to note that consciousness-raising did not remain enclosed within the movement, but rather led to outward-facing activities from protests and campaigns to the establishment of services, and (sometimes fraught) attempts to engage with mainstream institutions, including the media (Dow 2014).

I want to turn here to Louise Armstrong's reflections on what this mass mediation did to the movement, specifically, in her case, the incest survivors movement. Armstrong's book *Kiss Daddy Goodnight*—published in 1978—was modelled on the speak out, placing her own experiences alongside those of other women although, as Serisier (2018: 188–189) notes, Armstrong's narrative is deliberately selective and fails to account for race and class. Both in the Introduction to the 10th anniversary re-printing of *Kiss Daddy Goodnight* (Armstrong 1987) and subsequently in *Rocking the Cradle of Sexual Politics: What Happened When Women Said Incest* (1996), Armstrong reflects on the gap between what she intended speaking out to achieve and what happened next:

> "Well", people say to me, "But at least we're talking about it now."
> Yes. But it was not our intention merely to start a long conversation. Nor did we intend simply to offer up one more topic for talk shows, or one more plot option for ongoing dramatic series. We hoped to raise hell. We hoped to raise change. What we raised, it would seem, was discourse. And a sizable problem-management industry. Apart from protective service workers, we have researchers, family treatment programs, prevention experts, incest educators....It was not in our minds, either, ten years ago, that incest would become a career option.

It in no way impugns the motives of those professionals who are dedicated to helping victims and survivors to suggest that the institutionalization of the problem does not augur its solution. (Armstrong 1987: ix)

Specifically, Armstrong is critically reflective of how the media engaged with "the World's First Walking, Talking Incest Victim", as she ironically labels herself (1996: 2). For the media, she argues, making this story public was the beginning and end of the narrative: speaking out became an end in itself: the personal is the public (*ibid*: 3).

This publicising of the personal was central both to the #MeToo hashtag and to the way it was taken up in mainstream media, legitimating invasive personal questioning of women with any kind of public profile. For instance, actor Uma Thurman was asked the sexual harassment question in an interview with *Access Hollywood*. In, politely, refusing the question, Thurman responded:

> I don't have a tidy soundbite for you, because I've learned – I'm not a child, and I've learned that when I've spoken in anger I usually regret the way I express myself. So I've been waiting to feel less angry. And when I'm ready, I'll say what I have to say.
> (Thurman, in Evans 2017)

Interviewed outside a theatre where she had begun previews for her debut Broadway performance, the line of questioning arguably constituted a form of harassment in itself: here is a woman whose job requires that she engage with the media, being asked not about her professional role but rather about sexualised and traumatic personal experiences (also Serisier 2020; Boyle 2022). And she has to play nice. As Soraya Chemaly (2018: 196–197) notes, Thurman made visible the tone policing she had to perform in that moment and her keen awareness of the precariousness of her position and how her emotions can be (and had been) used against her, despite her relative privilege in terms of race, profession and wealth (Orgad and Gill 2019).

Whilst the dynamics of disclosure in the #MeToo moment will have been different for women with a less public platform, Armstrong's experience points to the way in which noise can perform a similar function to silence in the way the media engages with women's experiences of male violence: distracting, diverting, distorting, disenfranchising. In an analysis which has clear parallels with the way a number of celebrity abuse stories have unfolded, Armstrong notes that when stories of child sexual abuse were, finally, believed, they were recast as common sense, something that everybody (in particular, non-abusing mothers) knew. If everybody knew, then the responsibility was no longer with the perpetrator alone, and this had concrete repercussions for non-abusing mothers and their relationships with their children. As I will explore in Chapter 6, questions about the broader cultural investment in these narratives are important ones. At the same time, this wider cultural complicity can be quickly gendered so that women's knowledge (or failure to know) is what is at stake. This is true not only in relation to women who could (or should) have witnessed, but also in relation to victim/survivors themselves. If everyone knew about Weinstein, then why did she go into a hotel room alone with him? The imperative to speak out is thus curiously linked to the assumption that everybody *already* knows.

Yet, the stories which mainstream media want to tell about these personal experiences are, as Armstrong also notes (1996: 38), personal ones. Without a feminist analysis (a feminist consciousness), the personal *remains* personal, as speaking publicly is constructed as part of a personally therapeutic process. This is in sharp contrast to the political character of consciousness-raising which was antithetical to therapy: consciousness-raising does not see the victim/survivor as the problem which needs to be fixed, rather it ascribes this role to society (Armstrong 1996: 11).[2] This is significant for an understanding of the #MeToo moment as it demands that we think critically about what it means to tell personal stories in a highly mediated context and invites us to think not only about who benefits from these tellings but also who has the opportunity to be heard and in what capacity (Kay 2020, 2024; Serisier 2024).

Breaking the silence only gets us so far. For the stories to have political potential a first—but by no means sufficient—condition is to be able to link women's stories in a *collective* telling. The affordances of social media extend the possibilities of these links, potentially globally. At the same time, some critics are cautious about the political potential of social media platforms in general and "hashtag feminism" has become the focus of considerable scholarly attention. It is to the debates raised in this work

---

[2] See Vera-Gray (2020) for an exploration of how that tension between "therapy" and the cultural, social and structural dimensions of rape plays out within the contemporary Rape Crisis movement in England and Wales.

and the implications for how we might think of both the Weinstein case and #MeToo that I now turn my attention.

Speaking Out Online

How feminism operates in digital spaces is the focus of a growing scholarly literature (e.g. Fotopoulou 2016; Mendes et al. 2019). For some critics, it is feminism's embeddedness in everyday digital spaces which is its greatest potential, creating an open-access feminism which brings people to the movement, sometimes for the first time (Rentschler and Thrift 2015; Mendes et al. 2019; Blevins 2018; Desborough 2018). This has been particularly important for communities marginalised *within* feminist movements and there is a growing literature on the potential of the digital for Black feminist organising in particular (Loza 2015; Conley 2017; Jackson 2015; Jackson et al. 2019, 2020; Bailey 2021; Williams 2021).

In contrast, Megarry (2018a, 2018b) is pessimistic about the potential of social media to replicate consciousness-raising groups, specifically because social media interactions take place under male surveillance. Differential access and digital literacy also generate and sustain divisions between feminists, particularly generational ones (Fotopoulou 2016: 44–47), whilst the necessity of maintaining a digital presence is even more challenging for feminist organisations facing funding cuts and increased precarity (*ibid.* 39, 54).

The digital has created new possibilities for those perpetuating sexual and gender-based violence and harassment as well as for those resisting it. Indeed, scholars have documented the relatively routine experiences of gendered, sexualised and racialised abuse in online spaces and using digital technologies, compounding the sense that the inequities of the digital world are an extension of those women, and particularly minority women, experience offline (e.g. Megarry 2014; Mantilla 2015; Jane 2017; Powell and Henry 2017; McGlynn et al. 2017; Powell et al. 2020; Vickery and Everbach 2018; Lumsden and Harmer 2019; Bailey 2021).

It is therefore not surprising that what this means for feminists who use online spaces to challenge men's violence has been a topic of recurring concern. Since the first edition of this book, there has been an explosion of writing in this field, much of it centred on #MeToo specifically (e.g. Fileborn and Loney-Howes 2019; Lazard 2020; Loney-Howes 2020; Phipps 2020; Chandra and Erlingsdóttir 2021; Alcade and Villa 2022;

Harrington 2022). This work is considered in more detail in Chapter 4, where it is placed alongside scholarship on other hashtags of disclosure and solidarity as part of my consideration of the scope of #MeToo. Here, it is sufficient for my purposes to highlight some recurring themes in the literature on speaking out online. Most obviously, these studies point to the ways in which personal experiences are linked with hashtags to become part of a curated conversation providing a link to other survivors and, so, an expectation of belief (e.g. Alaggia and Wang 2020). Victim/survivors' motivations for disclosing online are varied but can include: speaking back to victim-blaming discourses; the importance of being heard and believed (often for the first time) as part of a networked survivor community; affective solidarity; advice-seeking or giving; and disclosure as exposure, awareness raising or educating others (Skalli 2014; Loney-Howes 2018; O'Neill 2018; Crawley and Simic 2018; Mendes et al. 2019; Gundersen and Zaleki 2021). The extensive media coverage of #MeToo had concrete implications for many victim/survivors, not only those who were most visible in public discourse. For instance, the Rape Crisis network in England and Wales received a 28% increase in calls in the two weeks after the Weinstein story broke (Moss 2018); whilst, in the US, the Rape, Abuse and Incest National Network reported a 23% rise in calls to their crisis hotline in October-December 2017 compared to the same period in 2016 (Seales 2018). There is also some evidence that in countries where #MeToo achieved the greatest prominence, there was an increase in sexual assault reporting to the police that cut across socio-economic and racial groupings (Levy and Mattson 2023).

For victim/survivors speaking out and those listening in, however, these largely positive aspects have to be weighed against the retraumatising potential of wall-to-wall coverage of sexual assault which can result in victim/survivors feeling pressurised to disclose (Muller 2018, Clark-Parsons 2021; Strauss Swanson and Szymanski 2020; Maier 2023). Moreover, whilst some women describe the relative "safety" of specific platforms as spaces of disclosure, "the ability to harness and reap the benefits of online disclosure is largely uneven" (Mendes et al. 2019: 67), not least because of the emotional labour involved and the potential of abusive responses, which can themselves replicate elements of the original experience of abuse, harassment or discrimination in ways that are gendered, sexualised and racialised. Indeed, even in the earliest days of #MeToo's virality, it was clear that whilst the hashtag enabled *survivors* to find each other and supporters to express empathy (Liu 2023), it also opened up spaces for detractors to attack survivors' credibility and motivations (Bogen et al 2021), with concrete repercussions for other survivors witnessing this online (Anderson and Overby 2021). All of this combines to produce sometimes contradictory affective engagements, encapsulated in the subtitle of Aristea Fotopolou's book on *Feminist Activism and Digital Networks: Between Empowerment and Vulnerability* (2016).

It is also important to acknowledge that not all stories go viral. The costs of *not* being heard when speaking out at a time of heightened attention to sexual violence have not yet been adequately reckoned with.[3] However, the extent to which both algorithmic bias and the selective attention of mainstream media result in the amplification of some survivors' voices (predominately white, often celebrity and Anglo-American) at the expense of others is recognised (Serisier 2018; Alcoff 2018; Jackson et al. 2019, 2020; Kay 2020; Phipps 2020). For instance, the story of #YesAllWomen—a hashtag started by Muslim feminist Kaye M in response to #NotAllMen—reveals processes of co-option, whitewashing and abuse, as well as solidarity and political engagement (Serisier 2018; Kaye M 2015). Serisier and Kaye M detail how, for some white feminists, the intersectional demand of Kaye M's #YesAllWomen was a distraction from a gendered analysis, so that rather than amplifying Kaye M's message they co-opted it, and even attacked its originator. At the same time, Kaye M faced a racialised misogynist backlash. Kaye M's own account of this period (2015) reveals the emotional costs of #YesAllWomen both in terms of bearing witness to the accounts of abuse women shared using the hashtag, and in terms of her sudden hypervisibility and the equally sudden (and swift) personal threat this engendered.

Kaye M's account is a cautionary one in terms of the hidden costs of the economy of visibility (Banet-Weiser 2018a) where people posting in a personal capacity have no institutional support or resources to deal with a racialised, gendered backlash on a platform which is notoriously ineffectual in policing racialised, gendered threats. The emotional labour and vulnerability to abuse involved in being online—particularly for women of colour—is increasingly recognised (Loza 2015; Hackworth 2018; Madden et al. 2018; Bailey 2021), and, as Kaye M's account

---

[3] Author Hilary McCollum spoke powerfully about this issue in relation to the lack of critical and commercial engagement with her memoir at the "Writing through sexual violence" event organised by London Metropolitan University, 24 May 2022. See also Dougherty (2019).

demonstrates, this places significant restrictions on the potential of activist engagement with the platform. The lack of gatekeepers for a platform like Twitter/X means that it has a certain democratic potential, particularly when juxtaposed with the institutional biases of mainstream media (Williams 2015, 2016). Yet, when marginalised voices do achieve the prominence promised by the democratic mythology of the platform, they do so without the institutional support or material advantage that those speaking from more secure positions may enjoy (Bailey and Trudy 2018). I certainly do not want to overstate the potential of institutional support here: many institutions which require and profit from their employees' social media use have yet to take responsibility for the different ways this impacts on women and other marginalised employees (Vera-Gray 2017; Everbach 2018; Gardiner 2018; Olson and LaPoe 2018; Savigny 2020). Moreover, the increasing precarity of labour—particularly, but by no means exclusively, in media and cultural industries—means that fewer and fewer workers enjoy labour protections of this kind (Jane 2018). Nevertheless, dealing with a social media pile on as an individual, as Kaye M describes, is a very different experience to dealing with a social media pile on when speaking on behalf of an organisation: as women who have dealt with both attest.[4] The limited protections that Twitter did provide—such as blocking—are also increasingly under threat since Elon Musk's take over, and renaming, of the platform.

Questions around acknowledgement, ownership, leadership and community also arise in Tarana Burke's reflections on #MeToo. Thanks to the interventions of Black women online, Burke's activism has now become part of the mainstream narrative around #MeToo (Burke 2018), and her leadership is also widely recognised within online feminist networks (Xiong et al. 2019: 16). Yet, she has also reflected on the roles in which she has been cast by mainstream media:

> While it's true that I have been widely recognized as the "founder" of the movement – there is virtually no mention of my leadership. Like I just discovered something 12 years ago and in 2017 it suddenly gained value. #metooMVMT #metoo

---

[4] This argument is indebted to panellists at the "Violence Unseen" discussion which I chaired at the University of Strathclyde, 25 March 2019: Lily Greenan, Brenna Jessie, Claire Heuchan and Anni Donaldson. See also: Edwards et al (2020); Mendes et al. (2019: 88–89); Towers (2024).

(@TaranaBurke, 21 February 2018)

What is at stake in these representations is therefore not her breaking of the silence, but rather the amplification of her message through its celebrification and extension beyond the minoritised girls who have been the primary focus of Burke's work. Burke's experience highlights the ways in which an increased mainstream profile can come at the cost of the flattening out of the intersectional specificities and demands of the work. She describes this as being "acknowledged and erased": mainstream media gives voice to survivors whilst distorting their analysis and restricting their authority (Alcoff and Gray 1993; Armstrong 1996; Serisier 2018: 102). Burke's account suggests that "the work" gets lost in accounts which seize on the *person* of the "founder" rather than the continuing *activism* of a "leader".

One of the key tensions I want to get at here, then, is that whilst the affordances of social media enable connection, these are easily decontextualised. This facilitates the misremembering of feminism's pasts, particularly as this relates to the long-standing contributions and challenges of feminists of colour (Hemmings and Brain 2003; Collins and Bilge 2016: 63–113; Loza 2015; Bailey 2021). It is not only feminism's pasts which are erased here, but—importantly—the longevity of, and expertise acquired within, *ongoing* movements. Whilst high-profile activities such as TimesUp! did, initially at least, acknowledge and seek to support this ongoing work, as I will demonstrate in the next section, this has not typically been part of the mainstream media narrative.

What's Feminism Got To Do With It?

The sexual harassment and assault story that began with the Weinstein articles in the *New York Times* and *New Yorker* is, in obvious ways, a story about gender inequality. Twohey, Kantor and Farrow's stories—expanded in their later book-length accounts (Kantor and Twohey 2019; Farrow 2019)—reveal Weinstein's systematic abuse of women over whom he held a degree of professional as well as physical power, as well as the structures within the industry which enabled his behaviour. However, mainstream understandings of the place of feminism in this story have been ambivalent and contradictory at best and that ambivalence has remained in later reporting of the Weinstein case.

Time magazine's *Person of the Year* issue with which I opened this chapter is emblematic of these tensions.[5] This story engages with and reflects upon the feminist-informed process of speaking out, centring the experiences of survivors and connecting the experiences of the economically and racially privileged women of the entertainment industry with those of minority women whose economic status is more precarious. What unites these women (and two men)—Hollywood actors, strawberry pickers, hotel housekeepers, engineers, lobbyists—is their experience of workplace sexual harassment from men and the fact that they have spoken out about it, albeit with different degrees of publicity and anonymity.

In some ways, this is a quintessentially feminist story. Yet, feminism is an oblique presence in the article:

> Like the "problem that has no name", the disquieting malaise of frustration and repression among postwar wives and homemakers identified by Betty Friedan more than 50 years ago, this moment is born of a very real and potent sense of unrest.
>
> (Zacharek et al. 2017)

Friedan's *The Feminine Mystique* (1963) is widely understood to be foundational to the growth of white, liberal feminism in the US, though Friedan herself was critical of the focus on men's violence against women in feminist activism in the years that followed (Bevacqua 2000: 6). The article provides this link to a very select white, liberal feminist past, divorcing #MeToo both from the specific history of feminist activism against men's violence and from an intersectional feminist present. Notably, the word "feminist" is used only twice and is associated with suspicion (feminists supported Bill Clinton despite sexual harassment allegations against him) or disavowal (the women coming forward do not see themselves as feminists) (Serisier 2018: 93). Moreover, whilst the article privileges the voices of survivors, the other experts cited specialise in social movements, workplace training and organisational psychology, not

---

[5] Catherine Mayer, co-founder of the Women's Equality Party in the UK, reveals an additional contradiction in *Time*'s championing of the "silence breakers". Also in 2017, Mayer brought a sex and age discrimination case against *Time* (Mayer 2018). That "the traffic in feminism" (Banet-Weiser and Portwood-Stacer 2017) can be profitable for the very mainstream media companies feminists might rally against in other contexts is one of the central contradictions of the current climate (Mendes et al. 2019: 31).

in men's violence against women or gender inequality.[6] Although Tarana Burke is featured, she is *not* visible on the cover, and the intersectional challenge of her Me Too movement is watered down to "a non-profit that *helps* survivors of sexual violence" and encourages "young women to *show solidarity* with one another" (Zacharek et al. 2017, emphasis added). Support for survivors is an important part of activist work. However, as discussed above, the feminist speak out tradition—in seeking to build a structural, political analysis and to change social reality—is at odds with a *purely* therapeutic tradition (Armstrong 1996: 11) and building solidarity is its starting point, not its destination. The reframing of Burke's work undermines the expertise gathered from working with young women of colour, instead emphasising first-person survivor testimony.

The *Time* story thus encapsulates the "double entanglement" which feminist cultural theorist Angela McRobbie (2009) argues has characterised mainstream media's engagements with feminism since the 1990s. Feminism is "taken into account" as the ground on which this story is built, at the same time that the contemporary relevance of feminism is disavowed. The #MeToo moment as represented in this *Time* story is one in which feminism is notably absent as a *continuing* presence, a body of *knowledge* and a social *movement*. It is the movement with no name, and thus no history.

"The Silence Breakers" is far from an isolated example of this "double entanglement". In the remainder of this section, I analyse news coverage relating to four key moments in the Weinstein coverage moving beyond the initial "silence breaking" to consider how feminism and feminists function in a long-running story of this kind. Starting in October 2017 (with the publication of Kantor and Twohey's story), I move on to January 2018 and the first awards season of the #MeToo era which coincided with the launch of TimesUp!, before fast-forwarding to Weinstein's criminal trials in New York (January–February 2020) and Los Angeles (October–December 2022). I consider how feminism—and feminists— do (and do not) feature as a *named* presence in the media coverage and note inconsistent and uneven progress as certain of the challenges posed by #MeToo are mainstreamed, alongside a simultaneous backlash. Whilst Weinstein himself becomes less newsworthy as time goes on—with his

---

[6] The marginalisation of feminist expertise has also been identified in Ange Barton's work on four decades of rape reporting in Aotearoa New Zealand (see Jordan 2023: 106–107).

LA trial in 2022 generating only around a third of the coverage of his New York trial in 2020—it is notable that the Weinstein story remains a reference point in both news and cultural commentary. Throughout this section, I work with a corpus of English-language news publications identified through searching the Nexis database for articles which use the words Weinstein *and* feminist *or* feminism in each of the key periods.[7] The search results were refined through manual exclusion of duplicates, teasers and translations to produce the final corpus of 832 stories. Although my analysis is qualitative,[8] it is worth noting at the outset that the link with feminism is made in a tiny fraction of all the stories which mention Weinstein: less than 2% of all stories across the four periods studied.

The construction of feminism as a site of suspicion is present at the very beginning of the Weinstein story. Partly this is a result of the central role played by lawyer, Weinstein adviser, and "fake feminist"[9] Lisa Bloom. Bloom was prominently and strategically deployed by Weinstein's team in the first days after the publication of Kantor and Twohey's story to indicate the producer's willingness to change as well as to front his denials of criminal wrongdoing. In the media coverage, this establishes

---

[7] The key periods were: 5–31 October 2017 (244 stories); 1–31 January 2018 (394 stories); 6 January–24 February 2020 (138 stories); and 10 October–19 December 2022 (56 stories). For both the New York and LA trials I focused on the period from day one of the trial until the day after the verdict.

[8] Following the approach I adopted in a previous project mapping the development of the Jimmy Savile sexual abuse news story (Boyle 2018), this stage of the research deployed a qualitative, inductive approach to the material based on close reading. This allowed me to chart the development of the Weinstein story, noting both the language used to describe claims at different stages in the story and the role feminism—and feminists—played in the telling of these stories. It is worth noting here that the corpus amounted to literally thousands of pages of text: very few of the articles were short news items, most were longer opinion pieces and the corpus also includes a number of transcripts from current affairs programmes on US television. My intent in this chapter is to note patterns in the coverage which I hope will prove suggestive for future research examining the discursive construction of feminism in the reporting of feminist issues in mainstream media.

[9] Bloom is dubbed a "fake feminist" repeatedly on Fox News' *Tucker Carlson Tonight*. See, for example, the broadcasts on 18 October, 21 October, 27 October and 28 October 2017, all available on the Nexis database.

feminism up as a site of suspicion (something that can be faked by privileged women like Bloom) with the added frisson of generational feminist conflict (Bloom's mother is the feminist lawyer Gloria Allred).[10]

Bloom's involvement with Weinstein was relatively short-lived and whilst I do not want to downplay the significance of her purportedly feminist "alibi" for the man accused of serial rape and sexual assault, it is notable that high-profile male lawyers involved in celebrity sexual assault cases have taken roles with alleged perpetrators as well as with victim/survivors with little pushback.[11] In my corpus, though, Bloom's significance is not as a lawyer, but as a "feminist" and she is not the only suspect feminist to appear in the initial reporting of the Weinstein case: Hillary Clinton and Meryl Streep are also routinely characterised in this way. In these stories, their feminism is cast as hypocritical and opportunistic in light of their association with Weinstein and their failure to issue immediate public statements following the *New York Times* story. Whilst there are, obviously, legitimate questions to be posed about complicitly, what is frustrating about much of this coverage is the way it sets up these straw-feminists without offering any feminist alternatives (e.g. Crispin 2020). As such, the straw-feminist comes to stand for all feminism.

Later reports of feminist "hypocrisy" within the corpus often take their cue from Rose McGowan's Twitter feed and her personalised critiques of individual women. This demonstrates the inextricability of old and new platforms and the appeal of sexual assault stories which pit women against women—particularly when those women are celebrities—decentring perpetrators. This construction of feminism as hypocritical and opportunistic is reinforced by reference to Weinstein's own self-promotion as a feminist, with many stories following the lead established by Kantor and Twohey in mentioning his acts of feminist "philanthropy", support for feminist filmmaking and participation in feminist protest. Weinstein's October 2017 statement in response to Kantor and Twohey's reporting cements this relationship, making reference to his foundation

---

[10] Allred has represented a number of sexual assault survivors in high-profile cases, including those (allegedly) assaulted by Donald Trump and Bill Cosby. She also represented survivors involved in Weinstein's criminal trials in 2020 and 2022.

[11] To give just one example, David Boieswho was on Weinstein's legal team for decades (Auletta 2022)—also represented Virginia Roberts Guiffre, the woman who sued Prince Andrew in civil court in New York. Guiffre claims that she was trafficked by Jeffrey Epstein and forced to have sex with Prince Andrew.

giving scholarships for women directors at USC (Weinstein 2017). His reluctance to let go of this self-serving, feminist-philanthropist alibi is evidenced in an interview with the *New York Post* prior to his New York trial (Rosenberg 2019). Whilst the *New York Post* interview was widely criticised, what is interesting for my purposes here is the way the Weinstein-feminism connection is used not only to discredit him but, more worryingly, to discredit feminism and feminists. In other words, Weinstein is a stain on feminism.

Casting feminism as a site of suspicion in this way depends on feminism being equated with the behaviour of individuals who call themselves feminists. The Weinstein case and #MeToo more generally have, in this way, become battlegrounds for the meaning and relevance of feminism. An early example of this was the letter to *Le Monde,* published the day after the 2018 Golden Globes and signed by one hundred French women—including, most famously, actor Catherine Deneuve—decrying the #MeToo moment as a "witch hunt", characterised by "puritanism", which "chains women to the status of eternal victim".[12] Other prominent denouncements of #MeToo that attracted considerable media attention in early 2018 include a *New York Times* article in which Daphne Merkin (2018) claims that "we seem to be returning to a victimology paradigm for young women", and Germaine Greer's much-reported comment that women "spread their legs" for Weinstein to land movie roles. The ways in which the arguments of these women are taken up in my corpus demonstrate the limitations of framing feminism as an individual quality (you are or are not a feminist) and an opinion (held by feminist individuals). Merkin, Greer, Deneuve and others are constructed as *opposing* #MeToo, prompting online responses that are vitriolic, ageist and—crucially—personalised. Actor Asia Argento, who went public about Weinstein in October 2017, suggested of Deneuve and her co-signatories that "their interiorized misogyny has lobotomized them to the point of no return" (McKay 2018), whilst Katie Way—whose article on Aziz Ansari I will return to—described TV-anchor Ashleigh Banfield as a "burgundy-lipstick, bad-highlights, second-wave feminist" in a message which Banfield read on air.[13] This is feminism as a generational catfight,

---

[12] A full English translation of the letter can be found here https://www.worldcrunch.com/opinion-analysis/full-translation-of-french-anti-metoo-manifesto-signed-by-catherine-deneuve. Accessed 20 May 2019.

[13] *Primetime Justice With Ashleigh Banfield*, CNN, 16 January 2018.

or "intergenerational feminist soap opera" (Rivers 2017: 42–43). This catfight *becomes* the story, hinging on opinion and personalised rebuke, whilst feminist *expertise*—such as that forged in more than four-decades of work in anti-rape movements—remains invisible.

This serves the agenda of accused men well. For instance, in October 2017 Weinstein made a statement to the *New York Times* claiming he came of age in the 1960s and 1970s "when all the rules about behaviour and workplaces were different" (Weinstein 2017). Variations of this "different times" excuse are in evidence in the non-apologies of many men whose historic abuses of women have been reported since the Weinstein story (Su et al. 2022). In arguing that generational catfights play into this "different times" narrative I am not suggesting that we should hang on to a romanticised view of feminisms' pasts or ignore their exclusions. However, we need to be alert to the way in which the catfight operates in mediated contexts where alternative (and collective) accounts of feminism are missing and feminist expertise is consistently marginalised. Thus Weinstein can gamble that his account of the 1960s and 1970s is a credible one as feminists of that period are, within the mainstream narrative, either invisible or themselves misogynist. In that context, how could he possibly have known any better?

Feminist conflict is also central to the 2020 stories in ways which both parallel and diverge from the earlier period. Stepping into Bloom's shoes is Donna Rotunno, Weinstein's victim-blaming lawyer whose self-description as the "ultimate feminist" is repeatedly cited and debated within the corpus. Weinstein's first criminal trial played out against the backdrop of awards season and, in the stories I have analysed, this allows for sometimes quite sophisticated discussions about the tensions inherent in a corporatised celebrity feminism to emerge. Rose McGowan is again at the forefront of many of these stories and this time Natalie Portman is in her line of fire, for wearing a cape to the Academy Awards ceremony embroidered with the names of snubbed female directors. In comments made on Facebook—and widely reported in mainstream news outlets—McGowan challenged the characterisation of Portman as "brave", described "Portman's type of activism" as "deeply offensive to those of us who actually do the work" and called on Portman to "walk the walk" noting how few female directors she had actually worked with as an actor and producer (Rose McGowan, 12 February 2020). However, this story never took off in the way the Deneuve story did for two reasons. First, Portman's response to McGowan was to agree with the substance of her comments, agreeing that she was not brave—"Brave is a term I more strongly associate with actions like those of the women who have been testifying against Harvey Weinstein the last few weeks, under incredible pressure"—and to open up a wider conversation about film production practices (Kilkenny 2020). Second, McGowan then partially backtracked, writing on Twitter (in a now deleted post) that "by critiquing someone personally, I lost sight of the bigger picture". Whilst there are not as many stories about the agreement in my corpus as there are about the conflict, that the agreement was news *at all* is, arguably, a sign of progress.

Another striking comparison between 2018 and 2020 is the reporting of another French conflict over the meaning and significance of sexual assault. Director and convicted rapist Roman Polanski received multiple nominations at the 2020 Césars prompting an open letter, signed by more than 200 film industry personnel, calling for "profound reform" of the Académie des Césars (Dodman 2020). Depressingly, this and other well-reported feminist protests did not stop Polanski from winning the César for Best Director, with actor and sexual assault survivor Adèle Haenel walking out angrily at the announcement. As this example perhaps suggests, the mainstream visibility of feminist protest is also evidence of the lack of change, here represented by the endurance of victim blaming (in Rotunno) and rape apologism in the film industry (in relation to the Césars): popular feminism and popular misogyny remain inextricably linked (Banet-Weiser 2018a).

Reflecting on media requests received by Scottish feminist organisation Engender in the first days after #MeToo went viral, Alys Mumford (2017) notes this tendency of media organisations to frame the debate around conflict and, specifically, the authenticity and believability of women. Believability—as my examples above suggest—is not, however, solely an issue of *victim* believability, but here relates to the contested nature of *all* women's speech about sexual assault. This not only personalises the issue and promotes victim blaming, but also means that many feminist organisations cannot and will not take part in these debates because they are based on a false premise. I have heard from other colleagues in feminist organisations that their media requests peaked when the story could be framed as a question as to whether #MeToo had "gone too far". In other words, the media did not want to draw on these organisations' decades of experience working with women, but rather to construct a debate about men's "victimisation". This approach mirrors that taken by some accused men and their defenders. Part of Weinstein's defence in 2020, for instance, was to argue that he had become the victim of indiscriminate speech (Boyle 2021). This was also part of Polanski's approach to the 2020 César controversy. In a particularly bizarre statement, Polanski blamed Weinstein for his ostracisation, suggesting the producer had tried to brand him as a "child rapist" in order to stop him winning an Oscar in 2003 for *The Pianist*. In so-doing, he sought to align himself with Weinstein's victims whilst repositioning victims of child sexual abuse—like Haenel and the woman Polanski was convicted of raping when she was 13—with the abusive Weinstein. Whilst the 2020 stories I analysed are (rightly) sceptical of the self-serving nature of these claims, that the limited space given to feminism in Weinstein coverage is taken up by such issues underlines my central point here that feminism is *contested* in a speech about sexual violence.

My corpus also provides evidence of the immediacy of the #MeToo backlash: the question as to whether #MeToo has "gone too far" is there almost from the outset. One of the highest profile stories of this kind followed on from the Babe.net story about a "bad date" with comedian Aziz Ansari in which a young woman, pseudonymously referred to as "Grace", recounted a night with the actor which left her feeling "violated" after he "ignored clear non-verbal cues" (Way 2018). This story generated considerable mainstream coverage about the purported excesses of #MeToo, primarily in opinion pieces. Whilst these stories often make use of a feminist language around meaningful consent, power and sexual pleasure, the genre of opinion writing privileges personal morality and judgement. Ansari's publicly *feminist* persona prior to the *Babe* story is also important: if Ansari (like Weinstein) can also present himself as a feminist, then this justifies the suspicion of feminism as a self-serving ideology which circulates in mainstream media discourse. When everyone is, or can be, a feminist, feminist knowledge—built from experience, activism, research—is rendered largely irrelevant.

Yet, in all the periods I examined, there are also articles which are positive and unapologetic about the necessity of feminist analysis. The term "sexism" is fairly widely used; "gender inequality" is understood as the wider context for sexual harassment; and terms like "rape culture" (Gay 2017), "patriarchy" (Allan 2017; Waddell 2020) and "intersectionality" (Garcia 2017; Asmelash 2022) are used. In these kinds of stories Weinstein is understood *in context*—for instance, with reference to other sexual harassment and assault stories, such as the Access Hollywood tape and the cases against Bill Cosby and Roger Ailes. That the #MeToo moment gives a heightened visibility to feminism—and, specifically, to feminist *action*—is nicely encapsulated in the *Washington Post*'s list predicting what is "in" and "out" in 2018, which signals a shift from feminism as an accessory (feminist tees are "out") to feminism in action (feminist lawmakers are "in") (Contrera and Mason 2018). Much of the commentary generated by the launch of TimesUp! alongside the Golden Globes protest in January 2018—where women dressed in black as a protest against sexual harassment in the industry, and Hollywood stars brought gender and racial justice activists with them to the ceremony—is centrally *about* feminist issues and strategies. There is, for instance, considerable discussion about the possibilities and challenges of intersectional feminist politics and practice, and how, or whether, a movement led by economically and racially privileged actors can foster change. Interestingly, this moves beyond passing judgement on individual feminists (as in the stories discussed previously), to think critically about activist practice.

The most insightful writing links women's experiences of sexual harassment with gender inequality, particularly in reporting on the Women's March where harassment is often discussed alongside other issues including employment, political representation and reproductive rights. However, the coverage of the activists on the Golden Globes red carpet demonstrates some of the limitations of these moments of heightened visibility. In a statement released through TimesUp!, the Golden Globes protest is described as an attempt to expand the conversation beyond Hollywood and connect the #MeToo moment to broader inequalities. This approach is described as inspired by the statement of solidarity with women in Hollywood from Alianza Nacional de Campesinas—an organisation working on behalf of female farmworkers across the US (TimesUp!, n.d.). But the very collectivity and solidarity which TimesUp! centres, allows the *specific* work of the activists on the red carpet—and the organisations they represent—to be widely ignored. They are namechecked, but the engagement does not go further than that. This failure to tap into feminist expertise—even when so prominently on display—is notable.

Encouragingly, this kind of expertise is at least marginally more evident in the 2020 corpus with campaigners, academics and politicians not only labelled as feminist but given opportunities to present feminist analyses. Admittedly, this is in a very small proportion of the overall stories mentioning Weinstein during his New York trial but does nonetheless allow for the trial to be situated in a broader context such that its relative *a*typicality is apparent. Moreover, feminist activism has an enhanced presence in this reporting that is not tied to individuals. This is, in large part, down to the performance of the Chilean feminist anti-rape protest "Un Violador en tu Camino" ("A Rapist in Your Path") outside the New York courthouse. Un Violador en tu Camino was first performed in Chile in 2019 by feminist collective Las Tesis and is a collective performance involving choreographed movement and lyrics informed by feminist anthropologist Rita Segato's arguments about the political and structural nature of rape (Serafini 2024). Interestingly, some mainstream coverage of the New York protest name-checks both Las Tesis and Segato, whilst also providing local activists with the opportunity to situate the significance of Weinstein's trial in relation to broader histories of injustice and protest (e.g. Barbara 2020; Hinsliff 2020). This reporting thus chips away at the dominant—and much criticised—narrative that situates #MeToo as originary and transnational influence emanating *outwards* from the US.

By 2022, the interest in both Weinstein *and* feminism appears to be on the wane: indeed, this argument is made by some commentators (including Weinstein himself) in relation to the perceived box-office "failure" of *She Said* (dir. Maria Schrader 2022), the film based on Kantor and Twohey's (2019) account of breaking the Weinstein story (Newland 2022). However, October 2022 also provides a moment for "taking stock", five years after Kantor and Twohey's first story and Milano's tweet. Some of these stories offer a nuanced account of what has (and has not) and can (and cannot) be achieved by #MeToo, gesturing to the longer feminist project of challenging and changing men's violence (e.g. Asmelash 2022). In this respect, the decreased media attention is not necessarily a bad thing as it allows for more thoughtful and nuanced accounts to emerge than in the initial periods when feminism is more typically presented as a moralising opinion, a "hot take" on a controversial issue (Banet-Weiser 2018b), or, more sinisterly, a site of suspicion or barrier to progress.

Of course, it is possible—and strategically desirable at times—to do feminist work without using the word "feminism". I was curious to establish whether long-standing organisations working against sexual violence were more widely represented than my initial searches suggested, so, I conducted a further search for Weinstein stories which mentioned either the Rape, Abuse and Incest National Network (RAINN) (the largest anti-sexual violence organisation in the US) or rape crisis (a term used fairly internationally by feminist organisations). Of the nearly 17,000 stories on the Nexis database mentioning Weinstein in October 2017, only 82 articles mention these leading organisations, and in January 2018 there are only 28 mentions (in 8810 stories). Notably, twenty per cent of these stories[14] are about prominent figures making guilt-money donations to offset the way they have profited from their connections with Weinstein or Woody Allen. Although good practice guidelines for responsible reporting of men's violence against women suggest signposting to support organisations (Zero Tolerance 2018; NUJ 2013), my initial searches for Weinstein and feminism/feminist produced not a single direct reference to sources of support, and only 17 stories in the RAINN/ rape crisis 2017–2018 corpus include helplines or other links to support. Interestingly, if surprisingly, the only publications to list helplines on more than one occasion are *Hollywood Life* (an online entertainment magazine) and *New Musical Express* (a UK print-based publication). When I repeated this search in 2020 and 2022, I found that a number of news outlets—notably, the *Guardian*, *Huff Post* and *Newsweek*— gave helpline information in their Weinstein trial reporting. Whilst this is an encouraging development, it is clearly still a minority practice (featuring in only 36 stories out of just over 18,000 which mentioned Weinstein) nor is it uniformly adopted by these outlets. Disappointingly, for instance, both the *Guardian* and *Huff Post* did not carry this practice forward to their reporting of the LA trial in 2022. These findings chime with work I undertook with Rape Crisis Scotland around responsible reporting of sexual assault trials where we could find little consistent practice and journalists repeatedly told us that they were discouraged from giving helpline information in case this was deemed prejudicial (Boyle et al. 2023: 120).

This analysis therefore reveals something of the messiness of the discursive construction of feminism in relation to the Weinstein case, echoing McRobbie's arguments about the "double entanglement" whereby feminism is that which is taken into account in order to be moved beyond or, as I have suggested here, otherwise contested. Admittedly, feminism is now considerably more popular than when McRobbie was writing in 2009 (Banet-Weiser 2018a), and I found many articles which were forthright in their feminist analysis (e.g. Bennett 2018; Funnell 2018; Frances-White 2020). Interestingly, Sara De Benedicitis, Shani Orgad and Catherine Rottenberg's (2019) analysis of the first six months of coverage

---

[14] $N = 22$, with eight stories in October, and fourteen in January following this pattern.

of #MeToo in the UK press suggests that the majority of coverage was *positive* in its orientation, suggesting a certain mainstreaming of a feminist perspective. What my analysis adds to their account is evidence of the continued marginalisation of feminist activists, organisations and researchers who could put this case in a broader, evidence-based context. To the extent that feminism—under that name—thrives in mainstream contexts, it is primarily as an individual opinion which also makes it open to personalised rebuke.

Conclusion

The principle of the feminist speak outs was to give personal stories a political character through understanding their commonalities with other personal stories. At one level, #MeToo has been phenomenally successful in achieving this and I do not want to downplay either the personal bravery or political importance of those who have taken on formal and informal leadership roles, or of the individual women and men who have disclosed their experiences in this context. However, as Jessica Megarry argues (2018a, 2018b), the indiscriminate audience for a social media status means that the act of speaking out is—in some ways—divorced from the intellectual, political and organisational work, the commitment of time and energy involved in listening as well as speaking, which feminist consciousness-raising demanded. As these stories migrate from social media to mainstream media, women's control of their narratives is limited and the stories depoliticised. Feminism is no longer the movement which gives rise to these disclosures, supports women and develops knowledge, policy and analysis, but is recast as a moralising opinion, a hot take (Banet-Weiser 2018b). This decontextualisation allows for the feminist story of sexual harassment and violence in the context of gender inequality to be recast as a story about feminist (and feminists') infighting. Whilst personal silences are broken, political silences can be paradoxically reinforced.

However, it is possible to temper this somewhat pessimistic conclusion with the benefit of some hindsight. It is not simply the case that, to paraphrase Louise Armstrong (1987: ix), the Weinstein reporting and subsequent coverage of #MeToo has "merely start[ed] a long conversation", though the sustained (albeit waning) coverage over a 5-year period provides evidence that it has certainly done that. As I will argue in later chapters, it has also—in some contexts, for some victim/survivors and for some perpetrators—supported concrete and meaningful change.

References

Alaggia, Ramona and Susan Wang. 2020. 'I never told anyone until the #MeToo Movement": What can we learn from sexual abuse and sexual assault disclosures made through social media? *Child Abuse and Neglect* 103: 1044312.
Alcade, M. Cristina. and Paula-Irene. Villa, eds. 2022. *#MeToo and Beyond: Perspectives on a Global Movement*. Lexington: University Press of Kentucky.
Alcoff, Linda Martín. 2018. *Rape and Resistance: Understanding the Complexities of Sexual Violation*. Cambridge & Medford: Polity.
Alcoff, Linda Martín and Laura Gray. 1993. Survivor discourse: Transgression or recuperation. *Signs* 18 (2): 260–290.
Allan, Drew. 2017. We must strive to overcome this world of boorish excess. *The Herald* (Glasgow), 17 October.
Anderson, Gwendolyn D. and Rebekah Overby. 2021. The impact of rape myths and current events on the well-being of sexual violence survivors. *Violence against Women* 27 (9): 1379–1401.
Armstrong, Louise. 1987. *Kiss Daddy Goodnight: Ten Years Later*. New York: Pocket Books.
Armstrong, Louise. 1996. *Rocking the Cradle of Sexual Politics: What Happened When Women Said Incest*. London: The Women's Press.
Asmelash, Leah. 2022. In 5 years of #MeToo, here's what's changed—And what hasn't. *CNN Wire*, 27 October.
Auletta, Ken. 2022. *Hollywood Ending: Harvey Weinstein and the Culture of Silence*. New York: Penguin.
Bailey, Moya. 2021. *Misogynoir Transformed: Black Women's Digital Resistance*. New York: New York University Press.
Bailey, Moya, and Trudy. 2018. On misogynoir: Citation, erasure, and plagiarism. *Feminist Media Studies* 18 (4): 762–768.
Banet-Weiser, Sarah. 2018a. *Empowered: Popular Feminism and Popular Misogyny*. Durham, NC: Duke University Press.
Banet-Weiser, Sarah. 2018b. Popular feminism: Feminist flashpoints. *LA Review of Books*, 5 October. https://lareviewofbooks.org/article/popular-feminism-feminist-flashpoints/#!. Accessed 1 April 2019.
Banet-Weiser, Sarah and Laura Portwood-Stacer. 2017. The traffic in feminism. *Feminist Media Studies* 7 (5): 884–888.
Barbara, Vanessa. 2020. Latin America's Radical Feminism is Spreading. *New York Times*, 28 January.

Beins, Agatha. 2017. *Liberation in Print: Feminist Periodicals and Social Movement Identity*. Athens: University of Georgia Press.
Bennett, Catherine. 2018. When feminists insult each other chauvinists cheer. *The Observer*, 28 January.
Bevacqua, Maria. 2000. *Rape on the Public Agenda: Feminism and the Politics of Sexual Assault*. Richmond: Northeastern University Press.
Blevins, Katie. 2018. Bell hooks and consiousness-raising: Argument for a fourth wave of feminism. In *Mediating Misogyny: Gender, Technology & Harassment*, ed. Jacqueline Vickery and Tracy Everbach, 91–108. Cham: Palgrave Macmillan.
Bogen, Katherine W., Kaitlyn K. Bleiweiss, Nykia R. Leach, and Lindsay M. Orchowski. 2021. #MeToo: Disclosure and response to sexual victimization on Twitter. *Journal of Interpersonal Violence* 36 (17–18): 8257–8288.
Boyle, Karen. 2018. Hiding in plain sight: Gender, sexism and press coverage of the Jimmy Savile case. *Journalism Studies* 19 (11): 1562–1578.
Boyle, Karen. 2021. Of moguls, monsters and men. In *The Routledge Handbook of the Politics of the #MeToo Movement*, ed. Giti Chandra and Irma Erlingsdóttir, 186–198. London: Routledge.
Boyle, Karen. 2022. Has it happened to you? *Gender Equal Media Scotland* [blog], 17 May. Available at: https://emcc.engender.org.uk/news/blog/has-it-happened-to-you/. Accessed 27 September 2023.
Boyle, Karen, Brenna Jessie and Megan Strickland. 2023. Rape in the news: Contemporary challenges. In *Rape—Challenging Contemporary Thinking—10 Years On*, ed. Miranda A.H. Horvath and Jennifer M. Brown, 113–127. London: Routledge.
Browne, Sarah. 2014. *The Women's Liberation Movement in Scotland*. Manchester: Manchester University Press.
Brownmiller, Susan. 1975/1986. *Against Our Will: Men, Women, and Rape*. London: Pelican Books.
Burke, Tarana. 2018. *Me Too is a Movement, Not a Moment*. Ted Talk, November. https://www.ted.com/talks/tarana_burke_me_too_is_a_movement_not_a_moment. Accessed 22 January 2019.
Burke. Tarana. (n.d.). The inception. *Me Too*, https://metoomvmt.org/the-inception/. Accessed 2 April 2019.
Chandra, Giti, and Irma Erlingsdóttir, eds. 2021. *The Routledge Handbook of the Politics of the #MeToo Movement*. London: Routledge.
Chemaly, Soraya. 2018. *Rage Becomes Her: The Power of Women's Anger*. London: Simon and Schuster.
Clark-Parsons, Rosemary. 2021. "I See You, I Believe You, I Stand With You": #MeToo and the performance of networked feminist visibility. *Feminist Media Studies* 21 (3): 362–380.
Collins, Patricia Hill, and Sirma Bilge. 2016. *Intersectionality*. Cambridge: Polity.

Conley, Tara L. 2017. Decoding black feminist hashtags as becoming. *The Black Scholar* 47 (3): 22–32.
Contrera, Jessica and Everdeen Mason. 2018. The list 2018. *Washington Post*, 1 January.
Crawley, Karen, and Olivera Simic. 2018. Telling stories of rape, revenge and redemption in the age of the TED talk. *Crime, Media, Culture*. https://doi.org/10.1177/1741659018771117.
Crispin, Jessa. 2020. Hillary Clinton is still trying to sell herself as a feminist icon. Don't buy it. *Guardian*, 24 January.
Desborough, Karen. 2018. The global anti-street harassment movement: Digitally-enabled feminist activism. In *Mediating Misogyny: Gender, Technology & Harassment*, ed. Jacqueline Vickery and Tracy Everbach, 333–351. Cham: Palgrave MacMillan.
De Benedictis, Sara, Shani Orgad, and Catherine Rottenberg. 2019. #MeToo, popular feminism and the news: A content analysis of UK newspaper coverage. *European Journal of Cultural Studies* 22 (5–6): 718–738.
Dodman, Benjamin. 2020. The "French Oscars", under fire, brace for a Polanski showdown. *France 24*, 12 February.
Dougherty, Cyra P. 2019. *The Anatomy of Silence*. Dorset: Red Press.
Dow, Bonnie J. 2014. *Watching Women's Liberation 1970: Feminism's Pivotal Year on the Network News*. Urbana: University of Illinois Press.
Edwards, Lee, Fiona Philip, and Ysabel Gerrard. 2020. Communicating feminist politics? The double-edged sword of using social media in a feminist organisation. *Feminist Media Studies* 20 (5): 605–622.
Evans, Greg. 2017. Uma Thurman on sexual harassment: "when I'm ready, I'll say what I have to say". *Deadline Hollywood*, 4 November. https://deadline.com/2017/11/uma-thurman-access-hollywood-sexual-harassment-harvey-weinstein-1202201978/. Accessed 3 April 2019.
Everbach, Tracy. 2018. 'I realized it was about them....not me': women sports journalists and harassment. In *Mediating Misogyny: Gender, Technology & Harassment*, ed. Jacqueline Vickery and Tracy Everbach, 131–149. Cham: Palgrave MacMillan.
Farrow, Ronan. 2017a. From aggressive overtures to sexual assault: Harvey Weinstein's accusers tell their stories. *The New Yorker*, 10 October.
Farrow, Ronan. 2017b. Harvey Weinstein's army of spies. *The New Yorker*, 6 November.
Farrow, Ronan. 2019. *Catch and Kill: Lies, Spies and a Conspiracy to Protect Predators*. London: Fleet.
Felsenthal, Edward. 2017. The choice. *Time*, December.
Fileborn, Biana, and Rachel Loney-Howes, eds. 2019. *#MeToo and the Politics of Social Change*. Cham: Palgrave Macmillan.

Fotopoulou, Aristea. 2016. *Feminist Activism and Digital Networks: Between Empowerment and Vulnerability*. London: Palgrave Macmillan.
Frances-White, Deborah. 2020. Why feminism in the 2020s needs to be uncomfortable. *Telegraph* (Women), 15 January.
Friedan, Betty. 1963. *The Feminine Mystique*. New York: WW Norton & Co.
Funnell, Nina. 2018. Q&A what were you thinking? *The Age*, 25 January.
Garcia, Sandra E. 2017. The woman who created #MeToo long before hashtags. *New York Times*, 21 October.
Gardiner, Becky. 2018. "It's a terrible way to go to work": What 70 million readers' comments on the *Guardian* reveal about hostility to women and minorities online. *Feminist Media Studies* 18 (4): 592–608.
Gay, Roxanne. 2017. Dear men: it's you, too. *New York Times*, 19 October.
Gundersen, K.K., and Kristen L. Zaleski. 2021. Posting the story of your sexual assault online: A phenomenological study of the aftermath. *Feminist Media Studies* 21 (5): 840–852.
Hackworth, Lucy. 2018. Limitations of "just gender": The need for an intersectional reframing of online harassment discourse and research. In *Mediating Misogyny: Gender, Technology & Harassment*, ed. Jacqueline Ryan Vickery and Tracy Everbach, 51–70. Cham: Palgrave Macmillan.
Hague, Gill. 2021. *Histories and Memories of the Domestic Violence Movement*. Bristol: Policy Press.
Hanisch, Carol. 2010. Women's liberation consciousness-raising: then and now. *On the Issues* Spring. https://www.ontheissuesmagazine.com/2010spring/2010spring_Hanisch.php. Accessed 2 April 2019.
Harrington, Carol. 2022. *Neoliberal Sexual Violence Politics: Toxic Masculinity and #MeToo*. Cham: Palgrave Macmillan.
Hemmings, Clare, and Josephine Brain. 2003. Imagining the feminist seventies. In *The Feminist Seventies*, ed. Helen Graham, Ann Kaloski, Ali Neilson and Emma Robertson, 11–24. York: Raw Nerve Books.
Hinsliff, Gaby. 2020. "The rapist is you!'" why a Chilean protest chant is bring sung around the world. *Guardian*, 3 February.
Jackson, Sarah J. 2015. (Re)imagining intersectional democracy from black feminism to hashtag activism. *Women's Studies in Communication* 39 (4): 375–379.
Jackson, Sarah J., Moya Bailey and Brooke Foucault Welles. 2019. Women tweet on violence: from #YesAllWomen to #MeToo. *Ada: A Journal of Gender, New Media and Technology*, 15: https://adanewmedia.org/2019/02/issue15-bailey-jackson-welles/. Accessed 12 April 2019.
Jackson, Sarah J., Moya Bailey and Brooke Foucault Welles. 2020. *#Hashtag Activism: Networks of Race and Gender Justice*. Cambridge: MIT Press.
Jane, Emma A. 2017. *Online Misogyny: A Short (and Brutish) History*. London: Sage.

Jane, Emma A. 2018. Gendered cyberhate as workplace harassment and economic vandalism. *Feminist Media Studies* 18 (4): 575–591.
Jordan, Jan. 2023. *Tackling Rape Culture: Ending Patriarchy*. Abingdon: Routledge.
Kantor, Jodi and Megan Twohey. 2017. Harvey Weinstein paid off sexual harassment accusers for decades. *New York Times*, 5 October.
Kantor, Jodi and Megan Twohey. 2019. *She Said: Breaking the Sexual Harassment Story That Helped Ignite a Movement*. London: Bloomsbury.
Kay, Jilly Boyce. 2020. *Gender, Media and Voice: Communicative Injustice and Public Speech*. Cham: Palgrave Macmillan.
Kay, Jilly Boyce. 2024. The politics of the traumatized voice: Communicative injustice and structural silencing in contemporary media culture. In *The Routledge Companion to Gender, Media and Violence*, ed. Karen Boyle and Susan Berridge, 194–203. London: Routledge.
Kilkenny, Katie. 2020. Rose McGowan slams Natalie Portman's "deeply offensive" pro-female director Oscars ensemble. *Hollywood Reporter*, 11 February.
Lazard, Lisa. 2020. *Sexual Harassment, Psychology and Feminism: #Metoo, Victim Politics and Predators in Neoliberal Times*. Cham: Palgrave Macmillan.
Levy, Ro'ee and Martin Mattsson. 2023. The effects of social movements: Evidence from #MeToo. *SSRN Electronic Journal* 12 July. https://ssrn.com/abstract=3496903. Accessed 28 February 2023.
Liu, Jiacheng. 2023. Empathy as exoneration or resistance? The politics of male empathy in the Chinese #MeToo movement. *Feminist Media Studies* 23 (2): 588–605.
Loney-Howes, Rachel. 2018. Shifting the rape script: "Coming out" online as a rape victim. *Frontiers* 39 (2): 26–57.
Loney-Howes, Rachel. 2020. *Online Anti-Rape Activism: Exploring the Politics of the Personal in the Age of Digital Media*. Bingley: Emerald Publishing.
Loza, Susana. 2015. Hashtag feminism, #SolidarityIsForWhiteWomen, and other #FemFuture. *Ada: A Journal of Gender New Media, and Technology* 5: 1–29.
Lumsden, Karen and Emily Harmer. 2019. *Online Othering: Exploring Digital Violence and Discrimination on the Web*. Cham: Palgrave Macmillan.
M, Kaye. 2015. On #YesAllWomen, one year later. *The Toast*, 26 May. http://the-toast.net/2015/05/26/yesallwomen-one-year-later/. Accessed 3 April 2019.
Madden, Stephanie, Melissa Janoske, Rowena Briones Winkler and Amanda Nell Edgar. 2018. Mediated misogynoir: Intersecting race and gender in online harassment. In *Mediating Misogyny: Gender, Technology & Harassment*, ed. Vickery, Jacqueline Ryan and Tracy Everbach, 71–90. Cham: Palgrave Macmillan.

Maier, Shana L. 2023. Rape victim advocates' perceptions of the #MeToo movement: Opportunities, challenges, and sustainability. *Journal of Interpersonal Violence* 38 (1–2): 336–335.
Maitland, Eileen. 2009. *Woman to Woman: An Oral History of Rape Crisis in Scotland, 1976–1991.* Glasgow: Rape Crisis Scotland.
Mantilla, Karla. 2015. *Gendertrolling: How Misogyny Went Viral.* Santa Barbara: Praeger.
Mayer, Catherine. 2018. Diary: my sexual fantasies about equality. *New Statesman*, 25 January.
McGlynn, Clare, Erica Rackley, and Ruth Houghton. 2017. Beyond revenge porn: The continuum of image-based abuse. *Feminist Legal Studies* 25 (1): 25–46.
McKay, Ronald. 2018. The screen goddess at war with feminism…or is she? *Sunday Herald*, 14 January.
McKinney, Cait. 2015. Newsletter networks in the feminist history and archives movement. *Feminist Theory* 16 (3): 309–328.
McRobbie, Angela. 2009. *The Aftermath of Feminism.* London: Sage.
Megarry, Jessica. 2014. Online incivility or sexual harassment: Conceptualising women's experiences in the digital age. *Women's Studies International Forum* 47: 46–55.
Megarry, Jessica. 2018a. Under the watchful eyes of men: Theorising the implications of male surveillance practices for feminist activism on social media. *Feminist Media Studies* 18 (6): 1070–1085.
Megarry, Jessica. 2018b. *"Female Performers on a Male Stage": Can Social Media Reignite the Women's Liberation Movement.* Unpublished PhD thesis, School of Social and Political Sciences, University of Melbourne.
Mendes, Kaitlynn, Jessica Ringrose and Jessalynn Keller. 2019. *Digital Feminist Activism: Girls and Women Fight Back Against Rape Culture.* Oxford: Oxford University Press.
Merkin, Daphne. 2018. Publicly, we say #MeToo. Privately, we have misgivings. *New York Times*, 5 January.
Me Too (n.d.) History and Vision. *Me Too.* https://metoomvmt.org/about/#history. Accessed April 2nd 2019.
Moss, Rachel. 2018. If you found #MeToo triggering, this new mental health advice may help. *HuffPost (UK)*, 6 March. https://www.huffingtonpost.co.uk/entry/mental-health-charity-issues-advice-to-sexual-abuse-survivors-finding-media-coverage-difficult_uk_5a9d5a71e4b0479c02555b0f. Accessed 10 June 2019.
Muller, Justyna. 2018. Self-care techniques for women impacted by exposure to sexual violence media coverage. (Guidelines.) Mental Health Foundation/ Rape Crisis England and Wales/ Support After Rape and Sexual Violence Leeds. 5 March. https://www.mentalhealth.org.uk/publications/self-care-tec

hniques-women-impacted-exposure-sexual-violence-media-coverage. Accessed 10 June 2019.
Mumford, Alys. 2017. Why there aren't always two sides to every story. *Engender Blog*, 24 October. https://www.engender.org.uk/news/blog/why-there-arent-always-two-sides-to-every-story/. Accessed 20 May 2019.
National Union of Journalists. 2013. *NUJ Guidelines for Journalists Reporting on Violence Against Women.* 23 September. https://www.nuj.org.uk/docume nts/nuj-guidelines-on-violence-against-women/. Accessed 1 April 2019.
Newland, Christina. 2022. Harvey Weinstein has got it all wrong—Yet again. *i*, 26 November.
Olson, Candi Carter and Victoria LaPoe. 2018. Combating the digital spiral of silence: academic activists versus social media trolls. In *Mediating Misogyny: Gender, Technology & Harassment*, ed. Jacqueline Ryan Vickery and Tracy Everbach, 271–291. Cham: Palgrave Macmillan.
O'Neill, Tully. 2018. "Today I speak": Exploring how victim-survivors use Reddit. *International Journal for Crime, Justice and Social Democracy* 7 (1): 44–59.
Orgad, Shani and Rosalind Gill. 2019. Safety valves for mediated female rage in the #MeToo era. *Feminist Media Studies* 19 (4): 596–603.
Phipps, Alison. 2020. *Me Not You: The Trouble With Mainstream Feminism.* Manchester: Manchester University Press.
Powell, Anastasia, and Nicola Henry. 2017. *Sexual Violence in a Digital Age.* London: Palgrave Macmillan.
Powell, Anastasia, Adrian J. Scott, and Nicola Henry. 2020. Digital harassment and abuse: Experiences of sexuality and gender minority adults. *European Journal of Criminology* 17 (2): 199–223.
Rentschler, Carrie A., and Samantha C. Thrift. 2015. Doing feminism in the network: Networked laughter and the "binders full of women" meme. *Feminist Theory* 16 (3): 329–359.
Richie, Beth E. 2012. *Arrested Justice: Black Women, Violence, and America's Prison Nation.* New York: New York University Press.
Rivers, Nicola. 2017. *Postfeminism(s) and the Arrival of the Fourth Wave: Turning Tides.* Cham: Palgrave Macmillan.
Robinson, Jennifer and Keina Yoshida. 2023. *How Many More Women? The Silencing of Women by the Law and How to Stop It.* London: Endeavour.
Rosenberg, Rebecca. 2019. Harvey Weinstein: I deserve pat on back when it comes to women. *New York Post* (Page Six), 15 December.
Savigny, Heather. 2020. The violence of impact: Unpacking relations between gender, media and politics. *Political Studies Review* 18 (2): 277–293.
Scottish Women's Aid. 2017. *Speaking Out: Recalling Women's Aid in Scotland. 40 Years of Women's Aid in Scotland.* Edinburgh: Scottish Women's Aid.

Seales, Rebecca. 2018. What has #meToo actually changed? *BBC News*. 12 May. https://www.bbc.co.uk/news/world-44045291. Accessed 10 June 2019.

Serafini, Paula. 2024. Collective action, performance and the body-territory in Latin American feminisms. In *The Routledge Companion to Gender, Media and Violence*, ed. Karen Boyle and Susan Berridge, 582–591. London and New York: Routledge.

Skalli, Loubna Hanna. 2014. Young women and social media against sexual harassment in North Africa. *The Journal of North African Studies* 19 (2): 244–258.

Serisier, Tanya. 2018. *Speaking Out: Feminism, Rape and Narrative Politics*. Cham: Palgrave Macmillan.

Serisier, Tanya. 2020. Speaking out, public judgments, and narrative politics: Researching survivor stories and (not) telling my own. In *Me Too, Feminist Theory, and Surviving Sexual Violence in the Academy*, ed. Laura A. Gray-Rosendale, 167–180. Lanham: Lexington Books.

Serisier, Tanya. 2024. Public survivors: The burdens and possibilities of speaking as a survivor. In *The Routledge Companion to Gender, Media and Violence*, ed. Karen Boyle and Susan Berridge, 204–212. London: Routledge.

Sreedharan, Chindu, Einer Thorsen, and Ananya Gouthi. 2020. Times' up. Or is it? Journalists' perceptions of sexual violence and newsroom changes after #MeTooIndia. *Journalism Practice* 14 (2): 132–149.

Strauss Swanson, Charlotte, and Dawn N. Szymanski. 2020. From pain to power: An exploration of activism, the #MeToo movement, and healing from sexual assault trauma. *Journal of Counseling Psychology* 67 (6): 653–668.

Su, Chiaoning, Rebecca Mercado Jones, and Valerie Palmer-Mehta. 2022. The hall of shame: reconstituting dominant masculinities in the New York Times' representation of U.S. #MeToo offenders' apologias. *The Communication Review* 25 (1): 1–29.

TimesUp! (n.d.) History. https://www.timesupnow.com/history. Accessed 20 May 2019.

Towers, Angela. 2024. After the affect: The tenuous leadership of viral feminists. In *The Routledge Companion to Gender, Media and Violence*, ed. Karen Boyle and Susan Berridge, 511–521. London: Routledge.

Tuerkheimer, Deborah. 2021. *Credible: Why We Doubt Accusers and Protect Abusers*. New York: Harper Collins.

Vera-Gray, Fiona. 2017. "Talk about a cunt with too much idle time": Trolling feminist research. *Feminist Review* 115: 61–78.

Vera-Gray, Fiona. 2020. The whole place self: Reflecting on the original working practices of rape crisis. *Journal of Gender-Based Violence* 4 (1): 59–72.

Vickery, Jacqueline Ryan and Tracy Everbach, eds. 2018. *Mediating Misogyny: Gender, Technology & Harassment*. Cham: Palgrave Macmillan.

Waddell, Laura. 2020. 1035 reasons what MeToo movement has not gone too far. *The Scotsman*, 9 January.
Way, Katie. 2018. I went on a date with Aziz Ansari. It turned into the worst night of my life. *Babe*, 13 January. https://babe.net/2018/01/13/aziz-ansari-28355. Accessed 15 March 2019.
Weinstein, Harvey. 2017. Statement. *New York Times*, 5 October.
Williams, Sherri. 2015. Digital defense: Black feminists resist violence with hashtag activism. *Feminist Media Studies* 15 (2): 341–358.
Williams, Sherri. 2016. #SayHerName: Using digital activism to document violence against Black women. *Feminist Media Studies* 6 (5): 922–925.
Williams, Sherri. 2021. Revisiting digital defense and Black feminism on social media. *Feminist Media Studies* 21 (8): 1373–1377.
Women's Liberation Workshop. (1971/2). *An Introduction to the Women's Liberation Workshop*. Consulted at Glasgow Women's Library.
Xiong, Ying, Moohee Cho, and Brandon Boatwright. 2019. Hashtag activism and message frames among social movement organizations: Semantic network analysis and thematic analysis of Twitter during the #MeToo movement. *Public Relations Review* 45 (1): 10–23.
Zacharek, Stephanie, Eliana Dockterman and Haley Sweetland Edwards. 2017. The silence breakers. *Time*, December.
Zero Tolerance. 2018. *Handle With Care: A Guide to Responsible Reporting of Violence Against Women*. https://www.zerotolerance.org.uk/resources/Full-version-of-Handle-With-Care.pdf. Accessed 21 May 2019.

CHAPTER 3

Theorising the Relationships of Gender and Violence Through #MeToo: Continuum Thinking

INTRODUCTION

The previous chapter focused on the relationship between survivor speech and feminist theory and activism. It was concerned with the process of feminist theory-building, and the contradictory ways media figure in this process. It stressed the importance of a structural analysis of what women share in patriarchy, as well as the ways in which these experiences are stratified by other structural inequalities, including race. Of course, as I will discuss in more detail in later chapters, it is not only women who are victim/survivors of sexual harassment and assault, nor is it the case that these kinds of abuse are exclusive to heterosexual contexts, although this will be my primary focus in this chapter. Measuring sexual violence incidence and prevalence is notoriously fraught—and measuring routinised forms of sexual harassment even more so—but a consistent pattern emerging across time and place is that sexual violence is disproportionately experienced by women and perpetrated by men (Walby et al. 2017). Feminist analysis is first and foremost about seeing these as *gendered* patterns. As R.W. Connell argues:

> Most men do not attack or harass women; but those who do are unlikely to think themselves deviant. On the contrary they usually feel they are entirely justified, that they are exercising a right. They are authorized by an ideology of supremacy. (1995: 83)

© The Author(s), under exclusive license to Springer Nature Switzerland AG 2024
K. Boyle, *#MeToo and Feminism*,
https://doi.org/10.1007/978-3-031-67314-6_3

Violence against women has historically been compatible with how masculinity, and heterosexual masculinity specifically, is personally, politically, culturally and socially enacted. Whilst there is some evidence of changing norms in this respect, this is by no means uniform and many men globally and in diverse interpersonal and institutional contexts continue to be rewarded for violent and violating expressions of masculinity. That non-abusing men are typically "passive or implicated bystanders", failing to speak up against this behaviour, allows abusive men to continue to feel authorised in their actions (Herman 2023: 194). Susan Brownmiller's famous assertion that rape is "nothing more or less than a conscious process of intimidation by which *all* men keep *all* women in a state of fear" (1975/1986: 15) is still a potent one. In this formulation it is not only the material reality of rape but its *threat*—expressed both discursively and materially in routinised forms of sexual harassment and abuse—as well as its normalisation that keep women in a state of fear.

This chapter uses, and develops, Liz Kelly's (1988) influential notion of the continuum of sexual violence, a concept I introduce in the next section. I have argued (Boyle 2019a) that the development of feminist theory and a changing policy context necessitate a rethinking of the continuum: this is even more acute given the explosion of discourse on men's sexual harassment and assault of women with which this book is concerned. Instead of thinking of the continuum in the singular, I advocate "continuum thinking" which retains the importance of building from connections whilst understanding that the range of connections made does not always sit easily together and requires different continuums (in the plural). Having set out these debates, I then discuss a widely referenced interview given by Hollywood actor Matt Damon to explore the ways in which discourse around #MeToo has both exemplified continuum thinking in practice and, simultaneously, generated a backlash against the challenges this poses. This leads me to an exploration of how the sex of sexual violence can be thought of in relation to continuums both of sex (a continuum of choice and coercion) and violence (a continuum of non-consensual experiences). The sex of sexual violence has been a much-contested issue within feminist theory and activism and the Harvey Weinstein case provides a useful exemplar of what is at stake in this discussion.

From "the" Continuum to Continuum Thinking

Feminists have long argued that there are conceptual intersections between the different kinds of sexual harassment and assault which have been gathered under the umbrella of #MeToo. Liz Kelly's work on women's experiences of sexual violence is my touchstone here. In *Surviving Sexual Violence* (1988), Kelly argues that the pervasive nature of men's sexual violence means that women make sense of individual actions in relation to a continuum of related experiences across a lifetime. For Kelly, the continuum can allow us to identify a "basic common character that underlies many different events" and/or "a continuous series of elements or events that pass into one another and cannot be readily distinguished" (1988: 76). Seeing individual acts on a continuum means seeing how they work *together*—in the context of a gender-unequal society—to produce particular effects on women's lives.

This holistic understanding of women's experiences in a patriarchal culture is arguably what Alyssa Milano's #MeToo tweet called for, placing experiences of different *types* of sexual violation ("sexual harassment and assault") together as well as using the affordances of social media to place the experiences of different *women* alongside one another in order to get "a sense of the magnitude of the problem". In many ways, #MeToo has been phenomenally successful in making these connections an integral component of the wider public discourse on sexual assault. But if this demonstrates the popularity of some aspects of feminist thinking in contemporary culture, the simultaneous backlash is symptomatic of the entwining of popular feminism and popular misogyny which Banet-Weiser (2018) identifies. The element of the backlash I will focus on most in this chapter is the claim that #MeToo flattens distinctions between very different types of violence, thus disadvantaging "real" victims of sexual assault by trivialising their experiences whilst simultaneously creating an environment in which *all* men are tarred with the Harvey Weinstein brush. Although this is, in important ways, a misrepresentation of feminist thinking and activism, there are also seeds of truth in these complaints which demonstrate some of the challenges of translating complex ideas into tweets and other soundbites. In this section I want to give a flavour of some of the points of contention in feminist theory, but also the ways in which social media—and mainstream media commentary—creates a series of false equivalences antithetical to a feminist analysis.

Kelly's notion of the continuum has two key elements: it allows us to establish a common character between different experiences and to understand the continuous nature of women's experiences of sexual violation in patriarchal culture, which can make it difficult for women to articulate where individual acts against them begin and end. It is this latter point that is perhaps most challenging, particularly in a social media context. It is important to stress that Kelly is not suggesting that women cannot tell the difference between being patted on the butt by a co-worker and being raped as a child (examples I will return to in relation to Matt Damon's commentary). Rather, the continuum allows us to see how individual acts of sexual aggression are embedded within existing relationships and power structures. In this context, apparently consensual sex with a partner who has previously been abusive may be difficult for a woman to disentangle from a prior experience of being raped by this man. The rape creates the context for these later interactions, it shapes the woman's ability to give consent because she knows where refusal may lead. Listening to survivors' narratives (as Kelly does) can allow us to gain a fuller understanding of what sexual assault means in the lives of women. It is *not* to say that these events are the same, nor is it to say that they should have the same consequences for perpetrators. These are distinctions I will return to.

However, in the context of #MeToo, these two rather different understandings of the continuum are arguably blurred as the platforms on which the disclosures take place de- and re-contextualise individual experiences. On the one hand, this allows the common character of different experiences of sexual violation—and, indeed, their ubiquity—to be revealed. On the other, it removes these experiences from women's life stories and creates a continuous stream where different acts segue into one another, highlighting commonalities but also creating dissonances. Scrolling #MeToo posts in 2017 it was possible to encounter a #MeToo pat on the butt story next to testimony of rape. Kelly—and Milano's—point is that these experiences *are* linked, because of the ways in which they are gendered and sexualised. Both actions are an assertion of male sexual entitlement, both are about power and depend on inequality, and both work to remind women of their subordinate status. One is part of the context in which the other is made sense of. Social media allows us to see these connections, but its continuous and de/re/contextualised flow flattens their differences.

To focus, first, on the question of connection, in her account of her Everyday Sexism campaign, Laura Bates (2014: 19) notes that she was taken aback when women began sharing experiences of rape as everyday sexism. After all, rape is popularly constructed as always and only devastating and, so, rare—the very opposite of the "everyday". Except it isn't. At a societal level rape *is* depressingly routine. The threat of rape is the context in which women routinely make decisions about everyday life whether or not they have experienced rape (Vera-Gray 2016)—as Brownmiller's provocative statement, quoted in the introduction to this chapter, was intended to highlight. For those who have experienced rape, the consequences of that experience can be lived everyday in more and less conscious, more and less obviously traumatic ways (Brison 2002; Gay 2018; Alcoff 2018). That for some women experiences of rape can be articulated underneath the everyday sexism banner is not, then, to deny that rape can also be experienced as a violation of the everyday in very profound and life-altering ways.

Like #MeToo, Everyday Sexism also attests to more routine experiences which *in isolation* do not, typically, produce these kinds of effects. Whilst we might accept, conceptually, that they are linked, there is a legitimate question to be asked about whether these links can work—culturally and politically—to trivialise trauma. In October 2017 as #MeToo proliferated over my social media feeds, I encountered and participated in many online discussions about the boundaries and ownership of this discourse. My hesitation in sharing #MeToo was not born from the kind of trauma and silencing discussed in Kaitlynn Mendes, Jessica Ringrose and Jessalyn Keller's (2019: 125–144) work on victim/survivors' experiences of other hashtags of disclosure, nor from anxieties about how my speech could be mobilised against members of my own community (Cheema 2023). Instead, it was rooted in a hesitation to claim a space within a discourse in which I was not sure I belonged, a hesitation perhaps best encapsulated (albeit retrospectively) by the different appeals of Burke's and Milano's statements of solidarity discussed in previous chapters. Milano's statement addressed me, Burke's didn't, and there was a hesitation in contributing to a discourse which might distort or minimise the kinds of experience of child sexual abuse and rape which Burke articulated and I know some of my friends (the immediate audience for my social media posts) share. In this hesitation was a recognition of shared experience *and* difference, a concern with how these expressions would be understood both by victim/survivors and a wider public, and a worry that disclosure was becoming culturally mandated. However, within this hesitation was also a minimisation of sexual harassment in the face of its ubiquity, a sense that it was "not that bad" which speaks to a certain resigned acceptance of rape culture (Gay 2018). I am not claiming this as a universal experience, or even a universal feminist experience, of #MeToo, rather my point is to stress that the boundaries and purpose of #MeToo and other hashtags of disclosure have been the objects of both personal (e.g. Mendes et al. 2019, 125–144; Serisier 2020; Cheema 2023) and public (e.g. Serisier 2018: 93–116) debate from the outset. This has become even more marked in subsequent years as hashtag activism against femicide—such as the Argentinian #NiUnaMenos which *preceded* #MeToo by some years—has been discussed alongside it (e.g. Belotti et al. 2024; Carlson 2021). Again, I see the value in this. #NiUnaMenos, for instance, made the point that femicides are not isolated incidents, but have to be understood in the broader context of gender in/equality and men's routinised violence against women. However, strategies of this kind can also backfire. For instance, in the UK in 2021, #SheWasJustWalkingHome briefly trended following the abduction and murder of Sarah Everard in London. The testimonies under this hashtag worked to demonstrate the very *everydayness* of Everard's actions—walking home—and the pervasive sense of threat which women routinely experience in public spaces (Vera-Gray 2016). But as I wrote on Twitter at the time, this outpouring of testimony and grief also meant focusing on what *Everard* was doing (a classic strategy of victim blaming) and played into stereotypes about un/deserving victims. If a murdered woman was *not* "just walking home", but was doing something less morally acceptable—buying drugs, selling sex—would a man's decision to murder her be any less horrific, her death any less finite?

Importantly, though Kelly insists that the continuum of sexual violence should *not* be understood as a hierarchy of seriousness, she notes that sexual murder is the exception to this. Susan Berridge and I argue:

> In adopting gendered terms to more accurately name the murder of women *because they are women*, feminists have sought to preserve the distinction Kelly makes about the severity of sexual murder whilst retaining the value of the continuum as a means of understanding these crimes *as* violence against women.
>
> (Boyle and Berridge 2024: 17)

This seems to me to be precisely the kind of work these hashtags set out to do. But in decontextualised, mediated spaces these feminist arguments can be mobilised to anti-feminist ends, as I have suggested.

Moreover, in women's experiences, rape isn't just made meaningful in relation to other forms of (sexual) violence. Kelly's *Surviving Sexual Violence* (1988), alongside other important survivor-centred studies (e.g. Gavey 2005; Alcoff 2018), points to the ways women make sense of sexual violence in relation to their experiences and expectations of gender and (hetero)sexuality. This can mean understanding rape on a continuum with other *sexual* experiences: a continuum of choice and coercion in which women might understand experiences as occupying something of a "grey" area legally and/or discursively (Anitha and Gill 2009: 165; Hindes and Fileborn 2019; Angel 2021). For instance, in their work on forced marriage, Sundari Anitha and Aisha Gill (2009: 165) refer to consent and coercion in marriage as "two ends of a continuum, between which lie degrees of socio-cultural expectation, control, persuasion, pressure, threat and force". As with the research which led Kelly (1988) to propose the continuum of sexual violence, Anitha and Gill are able to highlight important connections between women's everyday experiences of constraints on marital consent and criminal, violent acts against them. Importantly, this allows them to see parallels in women's experiences across cultures. Anitha and Gill are interested in two ways of conceptualising forced marriage, then: as part of a "continuum of choice and coercion" (2009: 165) linked to limitations imposed by culturally specific, heterosexualised gender roles; and as "a specific manifestation of a wider problem of violence against women" (Anitha and Gill 2009: 166). They are concerned with dismantling binary ways of thinking which have disadvantaged women (not least in the legal system) when their experiences have occupied a "grey area" in-between coercion and consent, or violence and non-violence. Of course, these two conceptualisations are linked: compulsory heterosexuality is enforced by violence; violence is underpinned by constructions of heterosexually appropriate gender roles (Gavey 2005; Hindes and Fileborn 2020). But they are not the same: women can and do make positive choices about heterosexuality and marriage—which is not to say all women can or do.

This returns us to the tension between seeing these experiences as potentially (though not necessarily) continuous in a lifestory, and understanding the importance of the differences between them in other contexts. The context which is perhaps most relevant here is criminal justice. In a 2012 review of feminist scholarship on men's violence against women, Kelly notes an overwhelming focus on *crime* in the years since her foundational text had been published. This means, she argues (2012, p. xix), that the "everyday, routine intimate intrusions" which had been foundational to her conceptualisation of the continuum had not, at that point, received sustained feminist attention (also Adur and Jha 2018). At the same time, the emphasis on crime had some side-effects antithetical to feminist concerns, including a racialised emphasis on crime control (Alcoff 2018: 225–235; Bumiller 2008; Richie 2012) and the mobilisation of rape discourse by Western governments to justify culturally, politically and economically imperialist projects (Phipps 2014: 41). The return to the continuum—and to "grey areas"—in feminist scholarship therefore takes place in a context where crime has become a dominant framework for understanding (and responding to) sexual assault. The emphasis on crime can sit uneasily with an approach which centres women's experiences across a lifetime and can unsettle the very language we use to link these experiences together and so bring them into feminist consciousness and, beyond that, to the public domain.

For instance, in *Just Sex: The Cultural Scaffolding of Rape*, Nicola Gavey (2005) notes that the legalistic discourse of rape does not do justice to women's understandings of their experiences, even when their experiences might sit within a legal definition of rape. Instead, the women in her research make use of a range of different terms including forced sex, unwanted sex, coerced sex, unjust sex, obligatory sex and sort-of-rape. Linda Martín Alcoff's *Rape and Resistance* uses the term "sexual violation" which she explains as follows:

> To violate is to infringe upon someone, to transgress, and it can also mean to rupture or break. Violations can happen with stealth, with manipulation, with soft words and a gentle touch to a child, or an employee, or anyone who is significantly vulnerable to the offices of others. Sometimes the phrase "sexual violence" is used as a metaphor to stretch its meaning to encompass such events, but this is misleading. Violence is not determinative of what we are after. What we are concerned with is a violation of sexual agency, of subjectivity, of our will. We should also be concerned with the ways in which our will has been formed. (2018: 12)

A foundational element in Alcoff's thinking is her own experiences of violation. In the opening pages of her book, she describes waking, aged

16, to find a boyfriend having sex with her (2018: 6). For Alcoff, describing this incident as rape is not helpful or true to how she experienced it, but she does recognise it as violation. She later reveals earlier experiences of being raped aged nine (2018: 21–22), which she understands very differently. These differences are marked not only in the nature of the acts but in the nature of the relationships in which they were embedded, how they were understood by the perpetrators and how they impacted on her life. This is the continuum as Kelly initially envisaged it: women making sense of experiences cumulatively, relationally and culturally.

However, this also points to one of the more challenging elements of Kelly's original conceptualisation: namely, her insistence that placing women's experiences on a continuum is *not* intended to establish a hierarchy of seriousness or injury (with the exception of sexual murder). Alcoff presents her own experiences within a hierarchy of sorts, although she is clear that these kinds of hierarchies are by no means absolute, but rather context-dependent. That Alcoff resists labelling her experience at 16 as rape does not mean that other women can or should, nor does it tell us anything about the effects of such an experience on other victim/survivors, or how perpetrators or criminal justice systems perceive them. One of the most striking things in Roxanne Gay's collection of victim/survivor writing *Not That Bad* (2018) is the cultural and social ubiquity of the hierarchy of seriousness and the damage this does to victim/survivors. Account after account demonstrates victim/survivors of any gender forced into a narrative of comparison which frustrates their attempts to seek support or justice: it wasn't that bad; at least he didn't kill me; I'm lucky because I survived. If we genuinely listen to survivors, we will always hear a *diversity* of experiences and interpretations: this, as Kelly (1988) argues, undermines the possibility of a straightforward hierarchy of seriousness or injury.

Fiona Vera-Gray's work on street harassment (2016) is helpful here. Like Kelly, Gavey and Alcoff, Vera-Gray is also trying to make sense of experiences of violation which are not always recognised as such by women, yet have concrete impacts on the way we live our lives. For instance, in a context where women learn to see ourselves as sexual objects, intrusions such as catcalling may at times be experienced as wanted or desired (Vera-Gray 2016: 7). Yet women make routine adjustments to our own behaviour to manage, ameliorate and, at times avoid, these kinds of behaviours. Vera-Gray also demonstrates the value of using women's experiences to understand men's behaviours, noting the sense of (sexual) entitlement underpinning men's behaviour *in contexts where consent is never sought*: "in practicing intrusion [men] are unaware of whether particular practices are wanted by individual women" (*ibid*). Whether an individual woman experiences a specific act of catcalling as desirable, amusing, annoying, threatening or triggering is, therefore, at least in some respects, immaterial to how the act of catcalling functions as an expression of male entitlement to, and domination over, women in public space. Catcalling is clearly in no way equivalent to the child rape Alcoff discusses, but both are linked on a continuum not only of women's experiences (where the threat or experience of one is the context in which the other is made meaningful), but also on a continuum of men's sexual entitlement and gendered power.

Indeed, Kelly always envisaged the continuum model as applicable to men's behaviour as well as female experience, to allow us to explore and expose the interrelationships between what is constructed as "normal" and "aberrant" for men (1988: 75). I explore men's behaviour more fully in Chapters 5 and 6, but here I want to note that this in itself demonstrates the limitations of thinking of the continuum in the singular (Boyle 2019a). Thinking about men's and women's experiences can produce very different understandings of the same behaviours. Echoing Vera-Gray's work, popular discussions around #MeToo have demonstrated that sexual harassment does not need to involve physical violence or sexual assault (behaviour that is more easily marked as "aberrant") for it to have both material and psychological impacts on women. Speaking on the BBC panel show *Have I Got News For You*, comedian Jo Brand captured this point beautifully in her response to a male panellist's dismissive comment that emerging reports of sexual harassment in the Westminster Parliament were not "high level crimes":

> I know it's not high level, but it doesn't have to be high level for women to feel under siege in somewhere like the House of Commons. And actually, for women, if you're constantly being harassed, even in a small way, that builds up. And that wears you down.
> (BBC1 3 November 2017)

#MeToo has been highly effective in bringing to the fore these kinds of experiences and the ongoing work this requires from women to continually make judgements about safety and risk in public and private interactions. In her comments, Brand reorients what, following Kate Manne (2018), we can call a himpathetic discourse which centres men's behaviour (these aren't high level crimes but normal behaviour), to insist on understanding these actions on a continuum of women's experiences across a lifetime. These experiences trouble easy categorisations: in themselves they may not be violence (Alcoff's "violation" or Vera-Gray's "intrusion" are perhaps more accurate), but cumulatively they produce effects which limit women's capacity for action in the public, political sphere.

Part of the reason this has been troubling for contemporary commentators trying to make sense of #MeToo is that sexual violation has become so embedded in a discourse of crime—not only in scholarship, as Kelly (2012) argues, but also in popular culture—that linking normal and aberrant behaviours in this way is too easily assumed to be re-positioning "normal" male behaviour (and, so, "normal" men) as criminal. The concern here is *what this means for men* and Harvey Weinstein is the standard against which other men are judged. Variations of the phrase "he's no Harvey Weinstein" permeate popular discussions of the reach of #MeToo as though being investigated—and subsequently tried and convicted—for rape and sexual assault in multiple jurisdictions is the benchmark against which men's behaviour should be judged. This kind of commentary also depends upon an assumption that perpetrators are easily recognisable types and—as I explore in Chapter 5—Weinstein is deployed here as an aesthetic as much as a behavioural benchmark, making it easier to know where to draw the line at a glance. There is a conflation of consequences in much of this commentary where reputational damage (however temporary) is itself described in a language of violation so that men-behaving-badly are recast as the victims of indiscriminate moral righteousness.

Take, for example, David Sexton's article in *The Evening Standard* where he claims that:

> allowing no differentiation, refusing any appeal, #MeToo is developing into a general disparagement of all men - although women may deny it.
> (Sexton 2019)

Note that here #MeToo is positioned as the active agent, aligned with a process of justice (cast in the role of judge and jury) in which men are victims and women are the ones offering denials, echoing Catharine

MacKinnon's (2018) concerns about the roles assigned men and women in sexual harassment narratives which I cited in Chapter 1. One of the more bizarre, but telling, aspects of this article is the way it conflates men's very different experiences of being "shamed" in the #MeToo era, picturing Aziz Ansari and Matt Damon as exemplars who have been "called out online". Comedian Ansari, as discussed in the last chapter, was the focus of the "bad date" article (Way 2018) which led to a very public debate about whether his behaviour constituted violation or bad manners. Damon—who I will return to in a moment—is referenced here because of his widely criticised comments on #MeToo, not because of any accusations of abuse or sexual misconduct against him. With Ansari and Damon as the fall guys, Sexton suggests that #MeToo has created a hostile, threatening climate for *all* men. It is notable how often an amorphous #MeToo is recast in the role of perpetrator, with the victims in its sights ranging from the perpetrators themselves to anyone, male or female, who expresses any kind of reservations about "the movement". For instance, when actor Sharon Stone gave an interview in which she suggested a need for proportionality in punishments for perpetrators, the *Mail on Sunday* claimed the actor's words "put her *at risk* of a #MeToo backlash" (Zoellner 2018, emphasis added). One of the effects of this is that #MeToo is constructed as devoid of—and incapable of—nuance: something which was also central to the letter signed by Catherine Deneuve and others discussed in Chapter 2. Interestingly whilst #MeToo is constructed in this way, fictions *inspired by* #MeToo have been critically lauded for allowing for the nuance #MeToo itself does not (Flynn 2024). What is lost in this is any recognition that #MeToo is itself shaped by the affordances of the platforms on which it circulates: nuance is not something it is easy to achieve in 280 characters.

Some of the highest-profile backlashes against #MeToo have been comments like Damon's or Stone's about the potential *consequences* of victim/survivor speech for perpetrators accused of vastly different behaviours, not all of which are recognisably criminal. This cedes a huge amount of power to victim/survivor speech and hinges on an assumption that the purpose of that speech is retribution against named perpetrators. The possibility of holding perpetrators to account is not mentioned in either Burke's Me Too origin story or in Milano's call for speaking out under the hashtag of disclosure. In both, the central concern is with how women sharing their experiences can allow for a fuller understanding of those experiences, which is also the foundation of Kelly's work. As

Alcoff argues: "Accounts of responsibility should flow *from* a more fully accurate description, rather than constraining our ability to develop that description (2018: 161).

Moreover, the claims about #MeToo's indiscriminate over-reach ignore the role of legacy media in amplifying, and often distorting, survivor speech and activist speech such that a public allegation is equated with a criminal, and career-destroying, sanction. To then recast the hashtag associated with victim/survivor speech as a potential threat—putting Sharon Stone "*at risk*"—brings this full circle, neutralising #MeToo by making it an agent of violation. As discussed in Chapter 1, it is not at all clear who or what #MeToo *is* in stories such as these, but it seems to be a stand-in for a caricature of feminist activism and theory: a straw woman, to be knocked down. At the same time, insights from feminism—including the importance of continuum thinking—are often presented as common sense. Take, for instance, these two quotations from the *Los Angeles Times*:

> [...] we need to be clear about the difference between sexual assault and horny dudes who move too fast on dates. Both may exist on a continuum of disrespect for women, but one is not the same as the other. (Abcarian 2018)

> [...] we need to accept that misbehaviour is not black or white, but falls along a continuum. At one end is the rapist/ sexual predator, and at the other end is the obnoxious filth. As of yet, the MeToo movement has not grappled with this reality (Davidson 2018).

Importantly, both of these articles are focused on men: the first is a response to the "bad date with Aziz Ansari" article, the second is a first-person account from a woman whose ex-partner has had #MeToo allegations made against him. These himpathetic (Manne 2018) responses encourage us to refocus women's experiences around speculations about men's motivations in order to reinforce a line between "good" and "bad" men. At the same time, these writers position that line by drawing on the continuum metaphor in order to establish a hierarchy, precisely what Kelly (1988) resisted.

Kelly's resistance to the hierarchy was not driven by a resistance to a hierarchy *of consequences*. It was a resistance to hierarchising women's experiences. Thinking about women's experiences means thinking about the ways in which our sexual subjectivity is shaped by encounters such as the one with Ansari in a broader context where we routinely make calculations about our safety in the knowledge of sexual violence, whether we have personally experienced it or not (Alcoff 2018; Vera-Gray 2016). This is *not* to assert that women experience behaviours on the continuum—from the pat on the butt to child molestation—as equivalent or identical but rather to note that meaning is not always self-evident from a simple description of the behaviour: experiences cannot be understood independent of context.

But terminology matters. In updating this chapter for the second edition, I made a number of changes to the introductory section, replacing "sexual violence"—which I had originally used in Kelly's expansive way—with Milano's language of "sexual harassment and assault". This is partly because in the intervening years I have become concerned that the emphasis on "sexual violence" in critical discourse around #MeToo has not entirely served feminist ends, but rather has run the risk of obscuring and trivialising some of the more routinised forms of sexual harassment and assault with which Kelly and Milano were—in their different ways—concerned. This process seems to have mirrored that observed by Kelly in her 2012 article as the public discourse has moved on from disclosure to centre consequences and—specifically—*criminal* consequences. This is concerning as it suggests that the wider lessons of #MeToo in relation to the continuum are at risk of being lost as criminal conviction becomes the measure of believability.

In the next section, I provide a more detailed example of the ways in which continuum thinking is distorted in media debates about #MeToo.

Damonsplaining

In December 2017, actor Matt Damon gave a television interview with Peter Travers in which he was asked to comment on "the age of people charged with sexual misconduct". It is worth quoting Damon at some length as his comments bring together a number of the issues which have concerned me in this chapter so far:

> Matt Damon: I think we're in this watershed moment. I think it's great. I think it's wonderful that women are feeling empowered to tell their stories, and it's totally necessary ... I do believe that there's a spectrum of behavior, right? And we're going to have to figure — you know, there's a difference between, you know, patting someone on the butt and rape or

child molestation, right? Both of those behaviors need to be confronted and eradicated without question, but they shouldn't be conflated, right? You know, we see somebody like Al Franken, right? — I personally would have preferred if they had an Ethics Committee investigation, you know what I mean? It's like at what point — you know, we're so energized to kind of get retribution, I think.

And we live in this culture of outrage and injury [...]... The Louis C.K. thing, I don't know all the details. I don't do deep dives on this, but I did see his statement, which kind of, which [was] arresting to me. When he came out and said, "I did this. I did these things. These women are all telling the truth." And I just remember thinking, "Well, that's the sign of somebody who — well, we can work with that" ... [...]

And the fear for me is that right now, we're in this moment where [...] the clearer signal to men and to younger people is, deny it. Because if you take responsibility for what you did, your life's going to get ruined ...

I mean, look, as I said, all of that behavior needs to be confronted, but there is a continuum. And on this end of the continuum where you have rape and child molestation or whatever, you know, that's prison. Right? And that's what needs to happen. OK? And then we can talk about rehabilitation and everything else. That's criminal behavior, and it needs to be dealt with that way. The other stuff is just kind of shameful and gross, and I just think ... I don't know Louis C.K. I've never met him. I'm a fan of his, but I don't imagine he's going to do those things again. You know what I mean? I imagine the price that he's paid at this point is so beyond anything that he — I just think that we have to kind of start delineating between what these behaviors are.[1]

Although Damon asserts here that there is a singular spectrum or continuum—with "child molestation" at its outer reaches—he is actually discussing a number of intersecting, but non-continuous, continuums: a continuum of experience (the women empowered to tell their stories); a continuum of behaviour (the pat on the butt to child molestation); and a continuum of sanction (paying the price doesn't have to involve

---

[1] The interview was on *Popcorn with Peter Travers* (ABC, 12 December 2017). Video and a partial transcript of the interview can be found here: https://abcnews.go.com/Entertainment/matt-damon-opens-harvey-weinstein-sexual-harassment-confidentiality/story?id=51792548. Accessed 24 April 2019.

prison). More significantly for my argument, Damon's use of the spectrum or continuum is to insist on *distinction* as though the #MeToo version of connection precludes this possibility. Indeed, in coverage of #MeToo more broadly, to *compare* behaviours like the pat on the butt and child molestation, is widely asserted to be a *conflation* of those behaviours (e.g. Loughrey 2018).

Part of the reason Damon insists on the distinction is to enable a clear categorisation of good and bad men. Thus he insists that Democratic Senator Al Franken (who resigned in the light of stories of groping and non-consensual kissing) and comedian Louis C.K. (who admitted masturbating in front of non-consenting women) are not to be understood as belonging to the "same category" as Harvey Weinstein or Kevin Spacey. Although Spacey is not named, as the highest-profile figure accused of child molestation in this period he is an implicit presence. That the reports about Spacey focused on behaviour towards boys is also significant in allowing Damon to maintain a sense of the boundaries of heterosexual masculinity. Moreover, the very visibility of Franken and Louis C.K.'s behaviour is an alibi in itself. Later in the interview, for instance, Damon references a widely discussed photograph of Franken groping a woman, whilst Louis C.K.—who Damon says he is a fan of—made self-deprecating "jokes" about public masturbation in his successful stand-up routines. There is a tautological sense here that it couldn't have been that bad because we "all" saw it, but didn't accord it any significance: because we didn't think it was bad, it can't be bad, and the accused certainly could not be expected to *know* it was bad. This was essentially Weinstein's response to Kantor and Twohey's initial story (Weinstein 2017). This is also suggestive of the cultural and political value Damon accords to Franken's and Louis C.K.'s continued visibility, in comparison both with the women they groped or exposed themselves to, and also with Weinstein. One of the interesting factors about Weinstein is that whilst he was instrumental in many of the most critically celebrated films of the 1990s—including Damon's own breakthrough, *Good Will Hunting* (dir. Gus Van Sant 1997)—as a behind-the-scenes player, the films associated with him do not necessarily visibly bear his imprint. As such, their cultural standing and viewers' enjoyment of them are not imperilled by his demise. Compare this with the way in which Damon's own enjoyment of Louis C.K. as a performer is brought to bear on his judgement of his behaviour.

Damon's argument seems to be that all of these things have been conflated in the #MeToo moment: a regular, but rarely evidenced, claim against #MeToo. Damon was roundly criticised for his comments, not least for assuming interpretative authority over the meaning of women's experiences and using this to determine appropriate consequences for accused men, based on his affective affinities with them (e.g. as a fan of Louis C.K., or political ally of Franken). Among those criticising Damon on social media were Alyssa Milano and Minnie Driver. Their criticisms assert a feminist understanding of continuum thinking, noting both that women's experiences of intrusion and violation are routine, and that this means that individual acts cannot be understood in isolation as Damon's hierarchy of seriousness asserts. As Milano put it "It's the micro that makes the macro":

> We are not outraged because someone grabbed our asses in a picture. We are outraged because we were made to feel this was normal. We are outraged because we have been gaslighted. We are outraged because we were silenced for so long.
> (@Alyssa_Milano, 15 December 2017).

However, tracking mainstream coverage of Damon's comments and the responses to them, it is striking that it is the abstracted acts—the pat on the butt and the child molestation—which are remembered, *not* his misplaced defence of Franken and Louis C.K. This means that Damon can be (re)constructed as an imperilled speaker of truth, "under fire from feminists" (Schuster 2018) for daring to assert the self-evident differences between these acts. Notably, the ways in which the responses to Damon's comments are reported, often many months after the fact, position Damon as a victim of (feminist) violence. Perhaps the most extreme, though by no means isolated, example of this is director Terry Gilliam's widely quoted comment that Damon "came out and said that all men are not rapists, and he got *beaten to death*" (quoted in Kilkenny 2018, emphasis added). More than 16 months on from Damon's interview, an interview with actor Mads Mikkelsen was published using similarly hyperbolic language: "one wrong word and you're a dead person" Mikkelsen is reported as saying, before suggesting of Damon:

> He said something quite common sense and he got fucking slaughtered, so this is not a healthy discussion anymore. (Mumford 2019)

The Damon story is a cautionary one on which to end this part of my discussion of continuum thinking for a number of reasons. Firstly, and most importantly, it demonstrates the extent to which continuum thinking remains a radical feminist project precisely because it is so unsettling to binary, himpathetic ways of thinking which dominate in contemporary Western cultures. Milano's #MeToo was—and is—threatening precisely because it sought to establish connections between diverse experiences of "sexual harassment and assault", not all of which can or should be understood as criminal. As a result, for commentators like Damon, Gilliam and Mikkelsen, #MeToo is discursively excessive and indiscriminate. For this to make sense a number of simultaneous manoeuvres need to occur: women's understanding of the connections between their experiences needs to be reconstructed as an inability to distinguish between otherwise very distinct actions; this needs to put men, all men, in jeopardy as the distinction between an alleged serial abuser like Harvey Weinstein and the rest no longer holds; and "sexual harassment and assault" needs to be (re)constructed in very narrow terms, with criminality implicitly the barometer of believability and significance. This means a story of consensus-building—women *sharing* their experiences in order to build an analysis based on their common elements—can be recast as a more media-friendly story of conflict in which there are two opposing, and gendered, "sides" (Mumford 2017). That the Damon story has the additional frisson of pitting ex-lovers Damon and Driver on opposing sides makes it clear that this is in itself a sexualised story about sexual behaviour and morality, rather than violence and power.

Secondly, the Damon story exemplifies Angela McRobbie's (2009) arguments about the "double entanglement" in which feminism is taken into account in popular culture only to be disavowed. Thus, Damon (and his supporters) can be cast as the decent, upstanding inheritors of feminism and their "insights" are adopted as common sense: yes, these things are connected; no they're not the same. At the same time, contemporary feminism—encapsulated by #MeToo—is that which threatens the legacy of feminism by exceeding common sense. In this mediated reconstruction, men doing feminism are reasonable, and yet are unfairly pilloried; whilst women doing feminism are hysterical, yet unfairly given discursive prominence—an argument which resonates with previous feminist analyses of media representations of rape (Moorti 2002: 113–148). Moreover, because this is essentially a story about speech, the response to Damon can be presented as a story about censorship: #MeToo is the agent of oppression; silence breaking becomes silencing. This then sets up men's (defensive) speech as, in turn, breaking the newly imposed silence *even* in cases where the men have themselves been accused of abuse. This is now itself a well-worn formula in media interviews with, and profiles of, celebrity men accused of abusive behaviour: as I explore in more detail in Chapter 7.

Damonsplaining thus offers a way of talking about sexual assault and harassment through a himpathetic lens (Manne 2018) which centres questions of morality and sexual behaviour. However, in feminist hands continuum thinking *can* be about seeing the connections between "normal" sex and sexual violence, and it is to this fraught understanding that I now turn.

VIOLENCE *or* SEX, VIOLENCE *and* SEX[2]

A view still commonly and supportively attributed to feminists in popular discourse around rape is that rape is about violence-not-sex (Bevacqua 2000: 58–60). Such binary thinking is at odds with continuum thinking but fits more easily into mass media narratives which demand simplicity and moral clarity.

The violence-not-sex formulation seems to have its origins in Susan Brownmiller's *Against Our Will: Men, Women and Rape* (first published in 1975), or, perhaps more accurately, in the way the arguments of the book were taken up both in feminist campaigning and in popular discourse. Tellingly, in the personal statement which prefaces *Against Our Will*, Brownmiller positions herself as "a woman who changed her mind about rape" (1975/1986: 9). Brownmiller's journey, as sketched in these few pages, is from being a journalist "who viewed a rape case with suspicion", before her "moment of revelation" at a public speak out on rape (1975/1986: 7–9).

This context is important as it highlights the extent to which the violence-not-sex analysis is a *reactive* one, emerging from a mediated context in which rape is not taken seriously, and women's stories are not heard or believed (Bevacqua 2000: 58–60). It is not accidental that Brownmiller was a journalist before she became an activist: in both roles, she was involved in making meaning of rape. Similarly, Germaine Greer's

---

[2] For a longer discussion of the sex of sexual violence in feminist theory see Boyle (2019b).

pamphlet *On Rape*—itself an expansion of her controversial comments about #MeToo discussed in the previous chapter—makes the quotable distinction, "Rape is not a sex crime, but a hate crime" (2018: 69). However, unlike Brownmiller, Greer's intent in making this distinction seems to be to *restrict* the category of rape to what Susan Estrich (1987) influentially (and critically) called "real rape": that is violent rape, outside of the contexts of existing sexual or romantic relationships. This she distinguishes from "banal rape" (Greer 2018: 70). Whilst I do not have space to expand on Greer's at times contradictory arguments, their significance for my purposes here is their reiteration of a violence/sex binary and participation in a still fraught debate about the sex of sexual violence.

Although it has been argued feminists moved on from the violence-not-sex position fairly quickly as limitations became clear (Whisnant 2017), as the Greer example suggests, the violence-not-sex (or, relatedly, power-not-sex) position has become something of a media shorthand for feminist understandings of sexual violence, typically linked to the second wave, or more accurately to its media (mis)representatives. It is, for instance, in evidence in some responses to the sexual assault reports naming Weinstein and others (e.g. Mayer 2017; Threadgould 2017; de Leon 2018). Here, the claim this is *not* about sex is a means of insisting on the seriousness of his actions against a cultural context that had for decades condoned his abuse as *just* sex. It is also an understandable response to Weinstein's initial statement in relation to the story in which he presented himself as a man out-of-touch with changing, implicitly *sexual*, mores, attempting to reframe the story as one about morality and culture, *not* violence and the abuse of power:

> I came of age in the 60's and 70's [sic], when all the rules about behaviour and workplaces were different. That was the culture then.
> I have since learned it's not an excuse, in the office – or out of it. To anyone.
> (Weinstein 2017).

My concern is that these possibilities are constructed as mutually exclusive: if it's violence or power it can't also be sex; if it's sex it can't also be violence or power. Whilst this is a false dichotomy which continuum thinking seeks to disrupt, it is nevertheless understandable that this lingers as a means of challenging rape myths, both in frontline services and media reports sympathetic to feminist positions.

However, as Catharine MacKinnon (1981/1987) influentially argued, the violence-not-sex position downplays the interconnectedness of violence and (hetero)sex in a patriarchal context. MacKinnon argued that by seeing rape as violence-not-sex "we fail to criticize what has been made of *sex*, what has been done to us *through* sex, because we leave the line between rape and intercourse, sexual harassment and sex roles, pornography and eroticism right where it is" (1981/1987: 86–87). For MacKinnon, it is important for feminists to understand the sex of sexual violence because sexual violence is a large part of what (hetero)sex *means*, to women as well as to men, in a patriarchal context. This means understanding certain commonalities between "what has been made of" consensual heterosex and sexual violence, as well as considering the ways in which socio-cultural understandings of heterosex and gender roles more broadly provide the ground on which sexual violence occurs (Angel 2021).

As feminist research in this area continually emphasises, there is no one way, and certainly no right way, to survive rape or sexual assault, and a universalising narrative can make it more difficult for some victim/survivors to name their own experiences and so to seek appropriate support and redress (Estrich 1987; Gavey 2005; Powell and Henry 2017; Alcoff 2018; Jordan 2022). Here it is worth returning to the Me Too and #MeToo origin stories as the range of experiences they include within their address point to different contexts for understanding rape and sexual assault. For Tarana Burke (n.d.), the experience she implicitly shares with Heaven is one of rape. Even as both Heaven and Burke herself struggle to name their experiences, in contemporary popular accounts of Me Too there is little ambivalence about the (criminal) nature of these assaults. For Alyssa Milano, #MeToo documents the broader continuum of sexual harassment and assault in women's lives. Many of the experiences documented under the hashtag #MeToo are more clearly structured by ambivalence, by the lingering doubt about the category to which experiences belong. This is at least in part because #MeToo includes experiences that are *not* typically defined as criminal acts, even if they transgress workplace codes of conduct, but it is also because they may also be understood as sex, flirting, unrequited passion or—as I will discuss more fully in Chapter 6—as the "cost" of artistic or professional success.

The quintessential example of this is unwanted touching: the "pat on the butt" in Damon's comments, or the hand on the knee which came to dominate discussion of the downfall of British Conservative politician

Sir Michael Fallon. Fallon quit his role as Defence Secretary in Theresa May's government in November 2017 after a slew of stories pointed to his unwanted touching and kissing of female journalists. Like Weinstein before him, part of his response to this was to suggest that he had fallen short of (new) standards of behaviour to which he wanted to aspire (Stewart and Mason 2017). What concerns me is the way that this behaviour can be understood as an ungentlemanly mistake, a breach of etiquette. Whilst Weinstein's attempt at a similar reframing largely failed because of the seriousness and multiplicity of the allegations against him, Fallon's was partially successful, not least because the acts themselves could not easily be defined as "violence" (even if they could be understood through a lens of power). As a result, Jane Merrick—one of the women who came forward about her experiences of Fallon's unwanted touching—notes that the story was instead widely reported as a trivialised, sexualised farce: "kneegate" (Merrick 2017). This pattern was even more marked in online responses to the 2020 trial of former Scottish First Minister Alex Salmond on a range of charges: in much of the commentary, the concern was not whether Salmond was guilty of the acts of which he was accused but whether they could or should be understood as criminal at all.[3]

Fallon's and Salmond's behaviour could not easily be understood as violence, but the focus on acts in isolation allowed broader questions about power to be dodged. Reflecting on coverage of the Westminster harassment story in the British press, feminist linguist Deborah Cameron (2017) points to the recurrent use of the word "inappropriate" in these reports. This works, she argues, to obscure who is doing what to whom. Specifically, it renders men's actions as breaches of etiquette or exemplars of bad (ungentlemanly) manners, rather than as acts experienced by another (female) person. Moreover, it evacuates context as though it is the behaviour itself which is inappropriate, not the context in which it is enacted, and makes it a purely interpersonal problem. The language of "appropriateness" thus functions as a defence against criminality—a claim made (inappropriately!) by Salmond's lawyer, among others (Sim 2022). Cameron's critique finds echoes in an article by Melissa Gira Grant (2017) which addresses "sexual misconduct", another well-worn euphemism for sexual harassment. This obfuscation—also encapsulated in

---

[3] I am drawing here on findings from Melody House's ongoing PhD work at the University of Strathclyde.

the "Deneuve letter" discussed in Chapter 2—allows women speaking out to be constructed as a threat to male *sexual* freedom, at the same time as casting women's presence in the workplace as a risk to men who no longer know how to behave.

It is not accidental that Weinstein used non-disclosure agreements so widely and so determinedly tried to quash journalistic investigations (Kantor and Twohey 2019; Farrow 2019; Auletta 2022). Arguably, the danger to Weinstein was not that the behaviour itself became public but rather that these women's *resistance* and the mode of reporting (investigation rather than entertainment) changed the context in which it could be understood: no longer evidence of bullish but successful moviemaking in a highly sexualised and glamorised context, the investigation of their grievances placed his behaviour on a continuum of sexual abuse. Likewise, it is not that Fallon tried to kiss a female journalist which is threatening, but rather that she decided to speak out about the fact, transforming an experience about which she had felt shame and guilt, into one where the shame and guilt lay not with her but with Fallon (Merrick 2017). This is the kind of transformation which leads to the accusations that #MeToo has become a "witch hunt" against men. Men are made newly vulnerable when behaviour which has historically been rewarded or joked about is denaturalised and problematised by refocusing the narrative on how these behaviours were/are experienced by women. To return to Weinstein's non-apology, men no longer know "the rules" (Weinstein 2017).

On this point, there is a certain agreement between feminists and sexual violence apologists. What Weinstein and feminist theorists arguably share is an understanding that his behaviour was *not* inappropriate according to patriarchal logic, but rather an expression of what men are promised, what they are continually told about their position in the sexual order. Of course, where Weinstein and feminist theorists differ is in what responsibility we think individual men should bear for this. That rape is a system which benefits *all* men, as Brownmiller argues, does not mean that *individual* men are not responsible for their own behaviours within the system: as the quote from Connell with which I opened this chapter reminds us, most men are capable of making different, better, choices. A himpathetic (Manne 2018) response accepts Weinstein's terms of reference and makes this a question of sexual morality *not* power or violence. A feminist response understands that sexuality, morality, power and violence are inextricably linked. This approach allows us to see the contexts in which (hetero)sex and violence are interrelated, without conflating one with the other. Thus we don't have to replace violence-not-sex with sex-is-violence. Instead, we can understand the continuum of choice and coercion in relation to heterosexual sex and so offer a critique of heterosex in patriarchy without insisting that heterosex is always and only violence.

Conclusion

Feminist theorisations of sexual violence have been centrally about connections: connections between different acts, between victim/survivors, and among "normal" and "aberrant" men. In this sense, the public gathering of diverse experiences under the hashtag #MeToo is clearly doing feminist work. However, the #MeToo moment also points to the dangers of media decontextualisations (or recontextualisations) of women's experiences and the flattening of differences that can occur in a disembodied social media feed. Whilst I have demonstrated the continuing importance of continuum thinking in this chapter, I have also highlighted the necessity of retaining distinctions and noted a worrying tendency in mainstream media commentary to suggest that this is precisely what feminists are unable to do. In this sense, media commentary on #MeToo often echoes McRobbie's (2009) double entanglement: the theoretical innovations of feminism and the decades of scholarship and activism tackling men's violence and supporting women are represented as a kind of "common sense" which good white men have adopted, and which #MeToo has hysterically exceeded. #MeToo also reminds us what is at stake in these discussions. For victim/survivors, this is about mis/recognition of their experiences and so the ability to seek support, advocate for change and/or justice, and see oneself as belonging to a collective, a movement. For (alleged) perpetrators, this is about consequences, but also about the discursive context in which their behaviour is situated: is it criminal, immoral, unprofessional and/or old-fashioned?

The next chapter takes up questions of context more centrally, exploring different manifestations of #MeToo and related protests and the temporalities at stake in both media and academic discussions of the hashtag and "movement".

REFERENCES

Abcarian, Robin. 2018. She wanted to go slow: He wanted to go fast. She told the world. Is Aziz Ansari a victim or a perpetrator? *Los Angeles Times*, January 17.

Adur, Shweta M. and Shreyasi Jha. 2018. (Re)centering street harassment—An appraisal of safe cities global initiative in Delhi, India. *Journal of Gender Studies* 27 (1): 114–124.

Alcoff, Linda Martín. 2018. *Rape and Resistance: Understanding the Complexities of Sexual Violation*. Cambridge & Medford: Polity.

Angel, Katherine. 2021. *Tomorrow Sex Will Be Good Again*. London: Verso.

Anitha, Sundari, and Aisha Gill. 2009. Coercion, consent and the forced marriage debate in the UK. *Feminist Legal Studies* 17 (2): 165–184.

Banet-Weiser, Sarah. 2018. *Empowered: Popular Feminism and Popular Misogyny*. Durham, NC: Duke University Press.

Bates, Laura. 2014. *Everyday sexism*. London: Simon and Schuster.

Belotti, Francesca, Vittoria Bernardini and Francesca Comunello. 2024. Hashtag feminism straddling the Americas: A comparison between #NiUnaMenos and #MeToo. In *The Routledge Companion to Gender, Media & Violence*, ed. Karen Boyle and Susan Berridge, 531–542. London: Routledge.

Bevacqua, Maria. 2000. *Rape on the Public Agenda: Feminism and the Politics of Sexual Assault*. Richmond: Northeastern University Press.

Boyle, Karen. 2019a. What's in a name? Theorising the inter-relationships of gender and violence. *Feminist Theory* 20 (1): 19–68.

Boyle, Karen. 2019b. The sex of sexual violence. In *Handbook of Gender and Violence*, ed. Laura Shepherd, 101–114. Cheltenham: Edward Elgar.

Boyle, Karen and Susan Berridge. 2024. News: Introduction to Part 1. In *The Routledge Companion to Gender, Media & Violence*, ed. Karen Boyle and Susan Berridge, 15–22. London and New York: Routledge.

Brison, Susan. 2002. *Aftermath: Violence and the Remaking of the Self*. Princeton: Princeton University Press.

Brownmiller, Susan. 1975/1986. *Against Our Will: Men, Women, and Rape*. London: Pelican Books.

Bumiller, Kristin. 2008. *In an Abusive State: How Neoliberalism Appropriated the Feminist Movement Against Sexual Violence*. Durham, NC: Duke University Press.

Burke, Tarana. n.d. The Inception. *Me Too*. https://metoomvmt.org/the-inception/. Accessed 2 April 2019.

Cameron, Deborah. 2017. Men behaving inappropriately. *Language: A Feminist Guide* (Blog). 4 November. https://debuk.wordpress.com/2017/11/04/men-behaving-inappropriately/. Accessed 20 May 2019.

Carlson, Marifan. 2021. #MeToo Argentina: A protest movement in progress. In *The Routledge Handbook of the Politics of the #MeToo Movement*, ed. Giti Chandra and Irma Erlingsdóttir. 410–422. London & New York: Routledge.
Cheema, Iqra Shagufta. 2023. Preface. In *The Other #MeToos*, ed. Iqra Shagufta Cheema. Xiiv–xxxiii. Oxford: Oxford University Press.
Connell, R.W. 1995. *Masculinities*. Cambridge: Polity.
Davidson, Sara. 2018. My ex was just #MeTooed. He had it coming. But it's complicated. *Los Angeles Times*, 21 January.
De Leon, Aya. 2018. In defense of Aziz Ansari's mama: how toxic masculinity undermines mothers in rape culture. *Mutha Magazine*, 23 February. http://muthamagazine.com/2018/02/defense-aziz-ansaris-mama-toxic-masculinity-undermines-mothers-rape-culture/. Accessed 25 April 2019.
Estrich, Susan. 1987. *Real Rape*. Cambridge: Harvard University Press.
Farrow, Ronan. 2019. *Catch and Kill: Lies, Spies and a Conspiracy to Protect Predators*. London: Fleet.
Flynn, Emma. 2024. *Complexity, Complicity and Consent: Representations of Sexual Violence in English and French Literature and Film*. Unpublished PhD thesis. University of Strathclyde.
Gavey, Nicola. 2005. *Just Sex? The Cultural Scaffolding of Rape*. London: Routledge.
Gay, Roxanne, ed. 2018. *Not That Bad: Dispatches from Rape Culture*. New York: Harper Perennial.
Grant, Melissa Gira. 2017. The unsexy truth about harassment, reprinted in *Where Freedom Starts: Sex, Power, Violence, #MeToo, A Verso Report*, 145–150. New York: Verso.
Greer, Germaine. 2018. *On Rape*. London: Bloomsbury.
Herman, Judith L. 2023. *Truth and Repair: How Trauma Survivors Envision Justice*. London: Basic.
Hindes, Sophie and Bianca Fileborn. 2020. "Girl power gone wrong" #MeToo, Aziz Ansari, and media reporting of (grey area) sexual violence. *Feminist Media Studies* 20 (5): 639–656.
Kantor, Jodi and Megan Twohey. 2019. *She Said: Breaking the Sexual Harassment Story That Helped Ignite a Movement*. London: Bloomsbury.
Kelly, Liz. 1988. *Surviving Sexual Violence*. Cambridge: Polity.
Kelly, Liz. 2012. Standing the test of time? reflections on the concept of the continuum of sexual violence. In: *Handbook on Sexual Violence*, eds. Jennifer M. Brown and Sandra L. Walklate, xvii–xxvi. London: Routledge.
Kilkenny, Katie. 2018. Ellen Barkin tweets "Never get into an elevator alone" with Terry Gilliam. *Hollywood Reporter* March 17.
Loughrey, Clarisse. 2018. David Schwimmer says comparing Al Franken with Harvey Weinstein was "terrible and horrifying mistake"; "we should not conflate all claims into one column of bad behaviour". *Independent*, 11 April.

MacKinnon, Catharine. 1981/1987. Sex and violence: A perspective. In *Feminism Unmodified: Discourses on Life and Law*, ed. Catharine MacKinnon, 85–92. Cambridge MA: Harvard University Press.
MacKinnon, Catharine. 2018. #MeToo has done what the law could not. *New York Times*, 4 February.
Manne, Kate. 2018. *Down Girl: The Logic of Misogyny*. New York: Oxford University Press.
Mayer, Jane. 2017. Anita Hill on Weinstein, Trump, and a watershed moment for sexual harassment allegations. *New Yorker*, 1 November.
McRobbie, Angela. 2009. *The Aftermath of Feminism*. London: Sage.
Mendes, Kaitlynn, Jessica Ringrose, and Jessalynn Keller. 2019. *Digital feminist activism: Girls and women fight back against rape culture*. Oxford: Oxford University Press.
Merrick, Jane. 2017. I won't keep my silence: Michael Fallon lunged at me after our lunch, *Guardian*, 4 November.
Moorti, Sujata. 2002. *Color of Rape: Gender and Race in Television's Public Spheres*. Albany: State University Press.
Mumford, Alys. 2017. Why there aren't always two sides to every story. *Engender Blog*, 24 October. https://www.engender.org.uk/news/blog/why-there-arent-always-two-sides-to-every-story/. Accessed 20 May 2019.
Mumford, Gwilym. 2019. Mads Mikkelsen: "One word wrong and you're a dead person". *Guardian*, 25 April.
Phipps, Alison. 2014. *The Politics of the Body: Gender in a Neoliberal and Neoconservative Age*. Cambridge: Polity.
Powell, Anastasia and Nicola Henry. 2017. *Sexual Violence in a Digital Age*. London: Palgrave MacMillan.
Richie, Beth E. 2012. *Arrested Justice: Black Women, Violence, and America's Prison Nation*. New York: New York University Press.
Schuster, Dana. 2018. Oscars 2018: Will anyone talk to this man? *New York Post*, 4 March.
Serisier, Tanya. 2018. *Speaking Out: Feminism, Rape and Narrative Politics*. Cham: Palgrave Macmillan.
Sexton, David. 2019. #MenToo. *The Evening Standard*, 26 January.
Sim, Philip. 2022. Alex Salmond lawyer guilty of professional misconduct. *BBC News*, 25 April. https://www.bbc.co.uk/news/uk-scotland-61216821. Accessed 1 November 2023.
Stewart, Heather and Rowena Mason. 2017. Michael Fallon quits as defence secretary saying his behaviour has "fallen short". *Guardian*, 1 November.
Threadgould, Michelle. 2017. Harvey Weinstein allegations: it's all about power, not sex. *CNN*, 6 October. https://edition.cnn.com/2017/10/06/opinions/harvey-weinstein-threadgould/index.html. Accessed 25 April 2019.

Vera-Gray, Fiona. 2016. *Men's Intrusion, Women's Embodiment: A Critical Analysis of Street Harassment*. London: Routledge.

Walby, Sylvia, Jude Towers, Susie Balderston, Consuelo Corradi, Brian Francis, Markku Heiskanen, Karin Helweg-Larsen, Lut Mergaert, Philippa Olive, Emma Palmer, Heidi Stöckl and Sofia Strid. 2017. *The Concept and Measurement of Violence Against Women and Men*. Bristol: Policy Press.

Way, Katie. 2018. I went on a date with Aziz Ansari. It turned into the worst night of my life. *Babe*, 13 January. https://babe.net/2018/01/13/aziz-ansari-28355

Weinstein, Harvey. 2017. Statement. *New York Times*, 5 October.

Whisnant, Rebecca. 2017. Feminist perspectives on rape. *The Stanford Encyclopedia of Philosophy* (Fall 2017 Edition), ed. Edward N. Zalta. https://plato.stanford.edu/archives/fall2017/entries/feminism-rape/. Accessed 1 August 2018.

Zoellner, Danielle. 2018. "You can't charge a person with murder when they've only got a parking ticket": Sharon Stone slams Harvey Weinstein—But risks #MeToo backlash as she warns against punishing all sexual predator the same way. *Mail on Sunday*, 27 January.

CHAPTER 4

The Long #MeToo Moment

INTRODUCTION

One of the central arguments of *#MeToo, Weinstein and Feminism* was that #MeToo had to be understood historically, in relation to a long tradition of feminist activism and scholarship which had been elided by the mediated emphasis on #MeToo's uniqueness. This chapter revisits these arguments. It recognises that there *is* something distinctive about the virality of the hashtag that explains the attention it has received in popular culture and in academic responses. However, whilst that distinctiveness has resulted in a certain discursive centring of #MeToo (including in my own work), here I highlight some of the events and protests which created the conditions for #MeToo's virality. This includes, but is not restricted to, Tarana Burke's Me Too movement. In focusing on what I will refer to as the long #MeToo moment, I thus seek to unsettle the linear narrative of progress and failure which has coalesced around #MeToo since the publication of *#MeToo, Weinstein and Feminism* in 2019 to instead situate #MeToo as part of a wider mediated concern with gender-based violence emerging out of feminisms' "popularity" and the backlash against them in the 2010s.

However, the aim of this chapter is not, primarily, corrective. I do not seek to provide a definitive account of #MeToo which would, in any case, be impossible as its ramifications are ongoing at the time of writing even this second edition. Rather I am interested in the different ways

© The Author(s), under exclusive license to Springer Nature
Switzerland AG 2024
K. Boyle, *#MeToo and Feminism*,
https://doi.org/10.1007/978-3-031-67314-6_4

temporality are at stake in the stories of #MeToo within Western media and academia.

I begin this chapter by returning to the "origin" stories of #MeToo and Me Too to argue that these stories in themselves trouble the notion of origins and linearity in productive ways that allow us to see the varying temporalities of trauma, of virality and of work. I then map some of the contours of the *long* #MeToo moment, identifying examples of the mediations of violence and protest which created the conditions for #MeToo's virality in different communities, countries and contexts. The conditions for #MeToo are thus *both* misogynist (the violence) *and* activist (the protest), and they cannot be understood independently from questions of representation and visibility. Equally #MeToo's achievements and limitations must be understood against the context of simultaneous and continuous backlash. In disrupting linear storytelling about sexual assault, I finally consider the limitations of looking to legal judgements as offering a verdict or end point for #MeToo, drawing on Clare McGlynn and Nicole Westmarland's (2019) concept of kaleidoscopic justice to consider justice as an evolving process. Having established the general argument, I conclude the chapter with a discussion of Johnny Depp's civil cases against the *Sun* newspaper in the UK and Amber Heard in the US to illustrate the issues at stake.

Origins, Invisible Work and Permanence

Me Too.
Suggested by a friend: If all the women who have been sexually harassed or assaulted wrote "Me Too" as a status, we might give people a sense of the magnitude of the problem.
(@AlyssaMilano, 15 October 2017)

In my discussions of Alyssa Milano's #MeToo tweet thus far in this book, I have neglected a key figure: the "friend" whose suggestion prompted the tweet. The friend is important for my purposes here in positioning Milano's tweet as part of an *ongoing* conversation. The friend not only unsettles the "origin" myth now associated with the tweet, her presence reminds us that this is a story which was shared between women—as testimonies, as whispers, as warnings—in private, long before the explosion of public speech.[1] Her anonymity also highlights that speaking out publicly is not an option open to, or desired by, everyone.

Tarana Burke's account of the origins of the Me Too movement also begins with a conversation, between Burke and a young woman—Heaven—attempting to disclose her experience of sexual abuse (Burke, n.d.). As both Heaven's story *and* Burke's response demonstrate, if we place the experiences of victim/survivors at the centre of our analysis then it is obvious that sexual violence does not occupy a clearly bounded historical moment. The abuse Heaven told Burke about was not an isolated incident. Trying to make sense of what was being done to her was not the work of a moment. And speaking out about it, seeking understanding and support, was also a process, not least because Burke rebuffed that initial attempt. For Burke as a listener, the reason she "wanted no part of" Heaven's disclosure was that it was too close to her own experiences of sexual violence, detailed more fully in her book about her life and the founding of the Me Too movement (Burke 2021). Whilst those experiences were past, their ramifications clearly were not. This is a vital context for more abstract questions about the when and where of #MeToo because it is a reminder that the temporality of trauma and of survival is far from momentary and is not always linear.[2]

The hashtagged conversations around #MeToo which followed Milano's sharing of her friend's words replicated this complex temporality. Disclosures were often about experiences across a lifetime, echoing Liz Kelly's (1988) understanding of the continuum of sexual violence in women's lived experiences. Many people using the hashtag reported not having spoken about experiences before (e.g. Burke 2021: 10). The temporal lag between the *moment*(s) of sexual harassment and assault and these speech acts did not—however—mean that those speaking out had not, in varied ways, been living with the impact of those moments in the intervening periods. Whilst they may have been motivated to speak out because the promise of the hashtag was that women would be believed, speaking out in such highly mediated spaces—spaces where

---

[1] Milano's tweet does not provide any identifying information about the "friend", however, their suggested address to "all the women" and use of *Me* Too implies that this is a female friend.

[2] There are many victim/survivor accounts—both in first-person and mediated through research—which make this point. See, for instance, Brison (2002, 2008, 2014) and Miller (2019).

empathy could *not* be assumed—also carried a significant risk of future harm. As Burke describes her initial reaction to the hashtag:

> My heart dropped at the thought of inviting people to open up and share their experience with sexual violence online without a way to help them process it. I know it could lead to emotional crisis in the absence of caring, empathetic environments. There was a knot growing in my stomach. This would be a disaster if it went viral.
>
> (Burke 2021: 4)

Whilst Burke's anxiety was—to an extent—lessened by some of the practices of recognition and mutual support she saw online (*ibid*.10), that the mass explosion of testimony created huge pressure on already overstretched services is undeniable. Moreover, what happened *after* those speech acts opened some of those speaking out up to new forms of scrutiny and disbelief: as Sara Ahmed (2023) puts it, by naming the problem you become the problem. That problem then needs to be managed, controlled, contained. For the small proportion of people whose speech about sexual harassment and assault led to criminal prosecutions, that "#MeToo moment" may still be ongoing as I write this given the very significant backlogs in the processing of sexual assault cases, in the UK as elsewhere, and the protracted process of appeal which some convicted men engage in. For others, their speech was itself met by the threat—or actuality—of sanction, with powerful, wealthy men able to shut down victim/survivor speech in the courts as well as, less formally, through their influence and connections in the media (Li 2024; Robinson and Yoshida 2023; Ito 2017/2021; Farrow 2019). Speech acts both are, and are not, momentary: they happen at a particular moment in time, but they reverberate beyond it. Speaking out about sexual harassment and assault is characterised by both repetition and delay.

In Chapter 2, I use Burke's reference to "the work" as a means of distinguishing between a speech act and activist engagement over time; but as the preceding paragraphs suggest, both speech and survival are also something to be worked at over time, albeit with differing degrees of intensity (Brison 2008). In that sense, whilst, at the time of writing in early 2024, the moment of #MeToo's virality has—largely—passed, the implications of those millions of social media posts are still being felt and worked through: personally, politically, institutionally. Those implications are also, however, impacted by the differing degrees of permanence accorded to speech acts through their mediation. This is one central way in which the digital speak outs of the #MeToo era are differentiated from the consciousness-raising of the 1970s. Where speaking out depends on media platforms, the ownership and control of that speech may no longer be in survivors' and activists' hands.

In the prologue to *Unbound*, Burke describes her fear—as the hashtag went viral—that the celebrity-led coverage would eclipse her years of work: an entirely realistic fear given the recurring erasure of Black women's work (Bailey and Trudy 2018) and the inherent individualism of celebrity. Her account of those first days following Milano's tweet, though, reveals that this was not just a fear of erasure, but also a fear that individualised speech would negate both the collective work that enabled it and the work that it, in turn, demanded. I have expanded upon these points in previous chapters, so here I just want to emphasise the different scale, scope and temporality of Me Too and #MeToo. Me Too *takes time* and it *continues*. #MeToo—with the astonishing scale and speed of its uptake—12 million Facebook posts *within 24 hours*, nearly a million uses on Twitter *within 48 hours* (Lawton 2017)—flares and fades. It constructs a collective story without—necessarily—constructing a collective. The excessiveness of #MeToo is the answer to the question posed by Jan Jordan "Why is that which is not new now news?" (2022: 12) but the conditions of its newsworthiness—particularly in its relationship to white celebrity—negate its historical antecedents and threaten to foreshorten its legacies.

What has been lost in too much of the discourse about #MeToo—whether popular or academic—is the continuous present both of men's violence against women and of feminist work to challenge and end it. Since at least the earliest days of the Women's Liberation Movement, feminist and feminist-informed work to support women and challenge men's violence has been a continuous force. As Gill Hague puts it in her account of the movement against domestic abuse in the UK, "It was never the case that feminism was over" (2021: 51). Of course, that work has had greater or lesser prominence in different historical moments and cultural settings and has changed considerably during that time. But if we think of this as a continuous *movement* then we can keep in view both continuity and change, without falling into the trap Clare Hemmings (2011) identifies in the stories Western feminism tells about itself which either romanticise or reject the past. What varies most markedly over time is the degree of visibility afforded to both the work and the violence which necessitates it. In the years prior to #MeToo, men's violence against women had been a central issue within feminism's increased popularity. At the same time, the visibility of the *issue* did not necessarily result in the visibility of the *work*, a central tension which I consider throughout this chapter.

The Long #MeToo Moment

In Chapter 1, I introduced the long #MeToo moment as a way of correcting the focus on #MeToo as a unique or originary force and, instead, acknowledging the events, protests, work and representations which created the conditions for its virality. One of the key lessons from the explosion of #MeToo-adjacent[3] scholarship has been the sheer variety in the ways that #MeToo has been taken up among different communities.

Before I consider some of the cases which laid the ground for #MeToo, it is worth stressing that high-profile cases involving sexual assault are hardly confined to this moment. As Jan Jordan argues, "[s]candalous rape cases attracting nationwide attention and media coverage are relatively common occurrences" (2022: 60–61), an argument which is supported empirically by Alessia Tranchese's work on rape reporting in the British press between 2008 and 2019. In the years prior to #MeToo, Tranchese (2022: 73–75) identifies a number of peaks in coverage of rape around high-profile criminal trials whose newsworthiness was linked, in different ways, to their atypicality. Tranchese demonstrates a strong and persistent linking of rape with other physically violent crimes, up to and including murder (173–176), and with men "who could be characterised as 'Other'" (159). At the same time, 21% of (alleged) perpetrators in Tranchese's corpus were celebrities and members of the elite—including athletes, politicians and media personalities—and these stories were much more likely to be told from the perspective of the perpetrator (163–168) and privilege doubt about the veracity of the "allegations" (199–200).

---

[3] The phrase "#MeToo adjacent" is from Emma Flynn's (2024) work on fictions of the long #MeToo moment. She uses this phrase to acknowledge the importance of #MeToo as a reference point for interpreting sexual violence fictions in the contemporary period, placing text and context in conversation.

As the celebritisation of the news intensified over the period of Tranchese's study—partly, but by no means exclusively, following the Weinstein reporting—"mistrust towards women became more accentuated" (254). Notably, Tranchese points to a sharp differentiation between these celebrity-led stories and those involving "Other" cultures where mistrust towards women was far less evident and concerns about rape-supportive and misogynistic culture were more embedded (255).

News coverage is an important part of the context for understanding #MeToo, not least given the extent to which the mainstream news stories about #MeToo have become synonymous with #MeToo, even—as I argued in Chapter 1—in some academic accounts. With that in mind, the clustering of high-profile cases which achieved international notoriety in the years before #MeToo is significant. But what the discussion of news downplays is the mediated *protest* these cases also generated. Here the responses to the gang rape and murder of Jyoti Singh Pandey in Delhi can be understood as an important forerunner of #MeToo.

On 16 December 2012, Pandey—a 23-year-old student—and a male friend, Avnindra Pratap Pandey, were returning from a trip to the cinema when they were attacked by a gang of men on a bus. Pandey's male friend was beaten unconscious. The men then subjected Pandey to a brutal gang rape. The victims were abandoned by the side of the road. Pandey was taken to hospital in Delhi and later transferred to Singapore for treatment. She died from her injuries on 29 December.

Tupur Chatterjee (2019: 134) describes the attack on Pandey as the "trigger event" for a reckoning with sexual violence which bridged offline and online modes in India. The media attention this case generated—and the victim blaming some of this coverage perpetuated—made it a flashpoint for protest. As such, this case is an exemplar of the intertwining of popular misogyny (the culture which enabled the gang assault; the victim-blaming explanations) and popular feminism (the highly-visible protests responding to the attack, offline and on) which Sarah Banet-Weiser (2018) theorises in the US context. The popular feminist protests were themselves dependent on—but in an uneasy relationship with—a longer, continuing history of (unpopular) feminist protest and activism against men's violence against women in India (Shandilya 2015).

The ambivalent implications of popularity which Banet-Weiser (2018) unpicks in the US context are equally evident in Krupa Shandilya's (2015) account of the Delhi case. In the initial reporting, Pandey was anonymous. As she fought for her life, the limited information in the public domain—that she was a student, that she went to the cinema, that she took the bus—allowed the media to construct her as an "everywoman" figure. As Shandilya notes, for her to function in this way meant that her identity was discursively and politically constructed along religious, caste and class lines. This was solidified through Pandey's symbolic (re)naming by *The Times* of India (Guha 2015) as "Nirbhaya", meaning fearless in Hindi. "Nirbhaya" kept in focus Pandey's agency: her resistance during the attack and her fight for life. But, arguably, this risked downplaying the horrific materiality of the assault and the ultimately fatal injuries her attackers inflicted. In the aftermath of her death, Pandey's parents asked for her name to be used, arguing that the shame associated with sexual assault should not belong to Pandey or her family, but to those who assaulted and killed her (Bardoloi 2015). Part of what the case triggered, therefore, was a reckoning with how sexual assault, its victims and perpetrators, should be represented.

In an international context, Pandey/"Nirbhaya" was less obviously a figure for identification. Whilst certain aspects of the context of the attack made the victim's life recognisable beyond her immediate environs, the international outrage the case generated was often problematically paternalistic (e.g. Poulami 2013; Shandilya 2015: 474–475; Thapar-Björkert and Tlostanova 2018). Similar arguments can be made about other Western responses to events in the Global South, such as #BringBackOurGirls (e.g. Khoja-Moolji 2015). In this sense, many of the debates about both the possibilities *and* limitations of "global" hashtag activism which emerged in relation to #MeToo had already been rehearsed in the years prior.

The murder of Jyoti Singh Pandey thus brought together a number of the elements which would be key to the #MeToo story: men's sexual assault of women; how that is understood and represented both locally and internationally; and activism as a response to *both* material violence and its representational significance. #MeTooIndia's later focus on workplace harassment in the media, academia and politics (Sreedharan et al. 2020; Sambaraju 2020; Lakkimsetti 2021) may have mirrored the US-originating hashtag in some ways, but the conditions for speaking out had been set by the popular, local protests against spectacular acts of male violence which preceded it. The Indian context was by no means unique in that respect. Ashwini Tambe (2021: 352) suggests that the near-immediate receptivity to #MeToo in different parts of the world could be attributed to "prior activism in those locations", arguing that #MeToo "did not inaugurate activism abroad so much as provide an inflection point in ongoing activism" (2021: 353). Iqra Shagufta Cheema's recent collection *The Other #MeToos* (2023) exemplifies this, with each chapter beginning with a timeline of events leading up to the particular instances of protest authors describe.

In North America too, a number of high-profile crimes of sexualised, gendered violence had generated powerful responses in the decade prior to #MeToo. The trial and sentencing of Brock Turner for sexual assault[4] on an unconscious woman was one among a number of flashpoints. In that case, it was the publication of the victim's powerful impact statement—originally attributed to "Emily Doe" and later to Chanel Miller—that generated international attention and protest. Here too, we see the media's dual role as part of the problem and part of the solution. Doe/Miller powerfully articulates the impact of initial media coverage in her victim impact statement:

> And then, at the bottom of the article, after I learned about the graphic details of my own sexual assault, the article listed his swimming times. She was found breathing, unresponsive with her underwear six inches away from her bare stomach curled in a fetal position. By the way, he's really good at swimming. (Doe 2016/2019: 338)

Yet, the publication of this statement by *Buzzfeed* and the immediate viral response to it demonstrated the *possibilities* of media in amplifying the voices of victim/survivors and providing a platform and audience for feminist protest. Indeed, Banet-Weiser (2018: 54) argues that rape culture was "one of the most volatile cultural arenas for the dynamic relationship of popular feminism and popular misogyny" in the 2010s. Popular mobilisations which achieved some international traction in the period— including Slutwalk and the Women's March—were centrally concerned

---

[4] How to define Turner's actions—digitally penetrating an unconscious woman—is an issue Miller tackles head on in the introduction to her book, highlighting the variation in, and limitations of, legal definitions. She writes: "The FBI defines rape as any kind of penetration. But in California, rape is narrowly defined as the act of sexual intercourse. For a long time I refrained from calling him a rapist, afraid of being corrected. Legal definitions are important. So is mine. He filled a cavity in my body with his hands. I believe he is not absolved of the title simply because he ran out of time" (Miller 2019: viii). In referring to the trial specifically I have used the term "sexual assault" but elsewhere I will describe the assault as a rape and Turner as a rapist.

with responding to misogynist *expression:* a Canadian police officer's statement that "women should avoid dressing like sluts in order not to be victimised" in the first instance, Trump's "grab them by the pussy" locker-room talk in the second. Although Slutwalk and the Women's March took place on the streets rather than solely online, they arguably share with hashtag activism an emphasis on the discursive, on how sexual assault is talked about and understood. As with #MeToo later in the decade, the very visibility of these mobilisations and their engagement with exclusionary and sexualised media logics was recognised by feminists as both a strength and weakness.

The responses to Pandey's murder laid the ground for #MeToo in another way. Pallavi Guha (2015) suggests that in "an emerging digital environment such as India" feminist hashtag campaigns—such as #Nirbhaya—can only succeed if they *converge* with mainstream media. But far from being unique to "emerging" environments, this convergence is also integral to the #MeToo story, as I argued in Chapter 1. It is notable that whilst Pandey's (re)construction as "everywoman" was one of the key factors that made this case such a flashpoint, Pandey's experience of gendered violation was, by definition, not shared by those protesting her murder. This was also true for a number of other mediated protests centring femicide– including the Argentinian #NiUnaMenos—which generated widespread, and sometimes international, engagement in the years before #MeToo. These protests were organised around spectacular and, comparatively, *un*usual acts, but sought to situate them within wider contexts of gender inequality and men's violence against women. Other forerunners, such as the Brazilian #PrimeiroAssédio (#FirstHarassment) or South Korean #00_ kye_ nae_ sŏngp'oklyŏk (#my_sexual_abuse_in_00) more squarely elicited shared testimonials of everyday forms of men's violence against women. Gabriela Loureiro (2024: 501) argues that #PrimeiroAssédio—a hashtag initiated by the organisation Think Olga—was "part of a broader political context marked by the amplification of feminist visibility in Brazil" in 2014–15. Its virality may have been shortlived and local, but that was precisely its strength, responding to a media story and creating a moment of highly-visible resistance for a longer-running campaign that makes use of diverse activist strategies.

In some ways, Loureiro's account is at odds with reports of what we might think of as "digital first" hashtags of protest and/or disclosure—like #YesAllWomen, #WhyIStayed and #MeToo—which were (initially at least) exclusively discursive in their intent (Jackson et al. 2020: xxix).

Like #PrimeiroAssédio, these hashtags of protest or disclosure aimed to (re)frame and moderate how men's violence against women was talked about and understood; but, unlike Loureiro's example, their originators were not, necessarily, linked to wider feminist debates, networks and organisations. Where hashtags, or other forms of digital intervention, can be linked to individuals their newsworthiness may be enhanced, but unanticipated virality—and the almost inevitable backlash this provokes—can be difficult for individuals to manage, practically and emotionally (Serisier 2018: 99–102; Towers 2024). Hashtags provide possibilities for telling a collective story, but they do not—in themselves—provide the architecture or support structure for a movement, not least as they function within media spaces created for, and driven by, the interests of white capital (Young 2022: 45).

The examples I have given so far have primarily involved ordinary people. However, as Tranchese (2022) finds in her study of the British press, the years leading up to #MeToo were also characterised by an increased celebrification of sexual assault. One of the first internationally-reported cases of this kind was the 2011 arrest of Dominique Strauss-Kahn—the French head of the International Monetary Fund—for the rape of Nafissatou Diallo, a Black woman from Guinea who was working as a hotel housekeeper in New York when she reported being assaulted by Strauss-Kahn. Tranchese finds that the British press treated the complaint against Strauss-Kahn with considerable caution (Tranchese 2023: 231), resulting in a linguistic hedging which later became the norm in news reports about rape (237). Tranchese and other scholars (e.g. Tuerkheimer 2021: 229–234; Biressi 2019) demonstrate how the gendered, racialised, sexualised and classed attacks on Diallo's credibility by Strauss-Kahn's team were replicated in some of the press coverage. Yet, demonstrating the ambivalence that characterises feminist responses to the reporting of such high-profile cases, Tranchese also suggests that it temporarily "brought to public attention the issue of sexual assault and its relationship to power" (2022: 232).

In France, Strauss-Kahn's status and media access allowed for a different narrative to emerge alongside this, one which positioned him as a "victim of a monstrously distorted *American* justice system" (Biressi 2019: 596, emphasis added) and an American puritanism around sexual matters (Rouyer 2013). In this context, DSK's reputation and professional future were imperilled not by his own behaviour but by a feminised, racialised Americanism threatened by his virile French masculinity (e.g.

Lévy 2011). He was assumed innocent precisely because he had so much to lose, whilst Diallo's subordinate status rendered her motivations for going public immediately suspect. Whilst that was contested by some feminists in France (Rouyer 2013), this "clash of cultures" narrative was echoed in responses to Frenchwomen speaking out in the wake of the Weinstein case. For instance, two days before Milano's tweet, French journalist Sandra Muller encouraged followers to #BalanceTonPorc (or "out your pig") and outed her own "pig"—a TV executive who later sued Muller for defamation (AFP 2021).[5] #BalanceTonPorc is often presented as the "French #MeToo", something that arguably served Muller's detractors well in allowing #BalanceTonPorc to be seen as un-French, echoing some French media responses to the DSK case and pre-empting arguments that would surface in the "Deneuve letter" I discussed in Chapter 2 (Flynn 2024).

Muller's case suggests how the discursive prominence of #MeToo can be mobilised against local activists to construct their protests—and indeed the problem of sexual harassment and assault—as "imports", alien to local culture. Analyses of #MeToo in Russia (Sedysheva 2021), Poland (Grabowska and Rawluszko 2021) and China (Wu 2024) point to similar tensions. Less ambivalently, in an Icelandic context, Irma Erlingsdóttir (2021) suggests that #MeToo gave local organisations a renewed invigoration by connecting them to a larger, global resistance. In Japan, Shiori Ito's public testimony about sexual violence predated #MeToo but becoming "a symbol of Japan's #MeToo movement" (Robinson and Yoshida 2023: 94) created possibilities for international solidarity in the face of ongoing backlash in Japan (Ito 2017/2021). Mwikya et al. (2021: 386) suggest that a range of factors relating to access to technology as well as censorship have shaped #MeToo's relatively small digital footprint in Africa but argue "the #MeToo movement had a different—rather than a lesser—impact on the African continent". These analyses all demonstrate that—for good and for ill—#MeToo has become an unavoidable reference point for activist and scholarly work around sexual harassment and assault in diverse contexts in the 2010s and beyond. As Anat Schwartz (2023: 4), writing about the South Korean context, puts it, #MeToo has become a "citational tool", a means of situating discussions about sexual harassment and assault in specific local contexts in relation to wider patterns

---

[5] Muller was sued by TV executive Éric Brion with the court finding in his favour in 2019. This ruling was subsequently overturned in 2021 (AFP 2021).

and debates, thus expanding audiences for activism. As Tambe (2021) argues, it is important to see this as *inflecting* rather than *inaugurating* activism in these locations. These examples provide further evidence of the political ambivalence of media visibility from a feminist perspective and of the ways in which internationally high-profile cases are inflected by local norms around gender and sexuality.

The Strauss-Kahn story was followed, in the UK, by the Jimmy Savile case which exploded after an ITV documentary, *Exposure: The Other Side of Jimmy Savile* (3 October 2012), presented evidence of an abusive career that spanned decades. The extensive coverage of the Savile case across multiple media forms provided considerable opportunities for survivor testimony but the case was not linked to activist protest—on or offline—in the way Nirbhaya's or even DSK's was. Clearly Savile was not an individual bad apple. Criminal and journalistic investigations of a number of other prominent men in the UK followed the Savile investigation, and there were independent reviews focused on the organisational failures within the BBC, NHS and police which had enabled Savile to abuse with impunity in his lifetime. Yet the very scale of his abuses, and the fact that Savile abused children (male and female) as well as adult women, also made it easier for him to be cast as an individual aberration, a paedophile. It was striking, for instance, that the Savile case was *not* widely referenced in UK-reporting of the Weinstein case (Boyle 2018). In this way, the Savile case ironically brought into focus the contradictions which would later characterise #MeToo as a response to the reporting on Weinstein. On one hand, it facilitated an explosion of testimony that made gendered patterns of abuse legible; on the other, it depended on the visibility of one serially-abusive, atypical man, obscuring those same patterns. Add celebrity into the mix and this tension between the structural and the individual is heightened further.

The proliferation of media content on Savile—which has continued post-#MeToo with Netflix's 2022 documentary series *Jimmy Savile: A British Horror Story* and BBC's dramatisation *The Reckoning* (2023)—is also significant for my purposes here. The years before #MeToo saw an explosion of documentary and drama programming about sexual abuse (Boyle 2018: 391) which was part of a wider Anglo-American fascination with true crime associated with the rise of streaming cultures through the 2010s (Horeck 2019). This period made clear media's complex role in relation to both enabling abuse *and* enabling the exposure of that abuse, establishing some of the conventions of what Tanya Horeck (2024) would later call the "#MeToo documentary". The proliferation of content on sexual abuse through the 2010s helped to establish a lineage, and popular demand, for survivor speech with some of these survivors themselves becoming public figures with significant media profiles (Gilmore 2017; Serisier 2018; Boyle 2018). The crusading journalists enabling that public speech also came to prominence in pseudo-activist roles, an issue I return to in Chapter 7. Some of these tensions are evident in other high-profile cases which span the long #MeToo moment. In the US context, the sexual harassment story involving the chairman and CEO of *Fox News*, Roger Ailes, the rape and sexual assault story centred on comedian Bill Cosby and the *Access Hollywood* tape featuring Donald Trump boasting about sexually assaulting women mentioned above are all relevant here. The attention and, particularly in the case of Trump, protest these cases generated also helped create the conditions for #MeToo's virality. Whilst these cases predated #MeToo, like the Savile case in the UK, they have remained prominent in the long #MeToo moment in interestingly divergent ways which speak to my concerns in this chapter.

Although Ailes died before #MeToo went viral, the story of his downfall was revisited for television (*The Loudest Voice*, Showtime 2019) and film (*Bombshell*, dir. Jay Roach 2019) in its aftermath. Indeed, the coincidence of the release of these media texts with Weinstein's criminal trial in New York allowed for the parallels between the cases to be widely drawn. The white, conservative women who spoke out about Ailes were commonly presented as the trailblazers who enabled #MeToo whilst the marketing of *Bombshell* emphasised its own status as the "first" film to take on the stories and lessons of #MeToo (Flynn 2024). Whilst I am interested in these cases as creating the conditions for #MeToo, as I hope is clear from the discussion so far I am *not* simply in search of a different origin point. Indeed, the narratives around Fox's Megyn Kelly and Gretchen Carlsson—both represented in *Bombshell*—replicate the very problems with "origins" and crusading, exceptional individuals I have already identified. These highly mediated celebrity stories make claims to uniqueness which set them apart from the ongoing work of feminist activism to focus, in relative isolation, on these white celebrities and media figures as agents of change. At the same time, presenting Carlsson as a kind of "godmother" for #MeToo, negates her *ongoing* work in this area by fixing her to the moment of her vulnerability (Boyle 2020). In this sense, there are some parallels with the media's emphasis on

Tarana Burke as the *founder* of Me Too rather than its *leader*, discussed in Chapter 2.

In contrast, W. Kamau Bell's documentary series *We Need to Talk About Cosby* (Showtime 2022)—which I discuss in more detail in Chapter 7—largely eschews the "trailblazing" narrative in relation to sexual assault and activism, instead allowing a more nuanced historical account to emerge. Yes, Bell understands Cosby's own "trailblazing" status in popular culture and his particular importance for Black audiences. But throughout he also gives space to Black feminists' cultural commentary on race and gender. Countering the "different times" analysis which Weinstein, Cosby and others have attempted to mobilise to their own ends, one of the most significant achievements of this series is to situate the abuse and Black feminist resistance *within* those times. As such, Bell allows both versions of Cosby—America's dad *and* serial abuser of women—to sit side by side throughout and keeps in view the non-spectacular work that allowed the survivors' stories to emerge and become actionable (also Banet-Weiser and Higgins 2023: 58–59).

In conclusion, then, the ground for #MeToo as a high-profile and—crucially, transnational—mainstream media story was laid by a number of cases which had achieved widespread coverage and become lightning rods for protest and activism (both local and transnational) in the years before. Collectively, the examples in this section point to the difficulty of ever isolating *the* impact(s) of #MeToo whilst also highlighting some of its manifestations across time and place. Thinking beyond my initial formulation of the "#MeToo moment" to privilege this *long* #MeToo moment allows different stories and examples to gain prominence and troubles accounts which see discursive activism as a product of the digital era. #MeToo may have been used by activists as a means of leveraging attention for longer-running campaigns with more specific and localised demands, but the "#MeToo era" is best understood as a cultural moment which does not map onto (local or global) histories of activism in any straightforward way. It is also, as I explore more fully in the next section, a moment which is characterised by both popular feminism *and* popular misogyny.

The Entwining of Popular Feminism and Popular Misogyny

One of the benefits of using Sarah Banet-Weiser's (2018) understanding of the co-existence of popular feminism with popular misogyny as a framework for understanding #MeToo is that it disrupts a more linear backlash narrative which situates misogyny as the *cost* of such a high-profile reckoning with sexual harassment and assault. In this section, I will focus primarily on #MeToo in an Anglo-American context. It is, however, important to assert a caveat upfront: the temporalities of #MeToo look different outside of this context and even in different locales within it. For instance, Schwartz (2023) and Bae et al's (2021) mapping of #MeToo's virality in South Korea and Li's (2021) account of the #RiceBunny[6] hashtag in China indicate peaks in hashtag activity which are linked to high-profile local stories. It is important not to see this as a delay or late start—which implies playing catch-up with an American original— but rather as demonstrating the moment when #MeToo could be *useful* to South Korean and Chinese victim/survivors and activists. There are many more examples of these timely local adaptations which complicate any attempt to map a chronology of #MeToo as a whole. Even so, many accounts of #MeToo in specific locales or sectors note—as I will do in this section—that the backlash against #MeToo was evident from its inception and identify moments of stress or failure (as well as, sometimes, success) in the localised narrative. In that sense, whilst the argument I pursue in this section relates to the Anglo-American context, it may resonate beyond it.

In thinking of #MeToo as a cultural moment, I am drawing on Anglo-American feminist theorisations of post-feminism from the 1990s onwards (e.g. Boyle 2005; Gill 2007; Tasker and Negra 2007; McRobbie 2009) as well as on Banet-Weiser's work (2018) on popular feminism from the 2010s. This work helps us understand what is at stake in the attempts to periodise feminism. For these critics, post-feminism and popular feminism are not coherent movements but rather are moments characterised by a heightened media visibility of struggles around gender (in)equalities. These moments are therefore ambivalent ones for feminist politics. On the one hand, there are moments when key feminist issues—such as men's

---

[6] #RiceBunny is a homonym of #MeToo and was adopted by Chinese social media users as a means of evading the local censorship of the English-language hashtag.

violence against women—are visible and the reach of some forms of feminist analysis is extended to a wider audience. However, the conditions of that visibility are determined not by feminist priorities but by media logics. Moreover, the ongoing work of feminist movements to address these issues is effaced as the very visibility of the issue is deemed to speak to the success of feminism, thus relegating the need for the movement to the past. This is what Angela McRobbie (2009) influentially refers to as double entanglement: feminism is "taken into account" only to be resigned to history. Post-feminism and popular feminism can do feminist work, but this happens alongside disavowal that weakens its *ongoing* transformative potential.

So far, there are clear echoes with my discussion of #MeToo as a (long) moment—or more accurately, perhaps, a series of moments experienced at different times in different places. In recent years I have been regularly asked—both in media appearances and in academic contexts—what I think #MeToo has achieved. One of the reasons I find this question so difficult and frustrating to answer is that it positions #MeToo as an agent and disguises the work of survivors and activists (those often, but not always, being the same people). The invisibility of labour is entirely consistent with an economy of visibility in which feminism is conceived as a *product* not a *process* (Banet-Weiser 2018). The question, then, is whether the product works.

A more meaningful (but less snappy) question would be: what have survivors and activists achieved in and through #MeToo? How have they worked (with) the (media) product? For many survivors and activists it is meaningful to talk of a before and after #MeToo as the discourse around #MeToo *has* been transformative: whether that has been on an individual level for survivors speaking out, seeking support or becoming activists; or for organisations which have experienced unprecedented demands for, or engagements with, their services and campaigns. If we think of Milano's stated intent—"to make people aware of the extent of the problem"—then it can be argued that #MeToo and related hashtags of disclosure and protest have, at least partially, succeeded. This is not to say that "the extent of the problem" is *universally* recognised, but #MeToo has become such a well-established frame of reference for sexual assault stories that media reporting about sexual assault does now seem more attuned to looking for patterns when an individual story about sexual harassment breaks. For instance, when Luis Rubiales forcibly kissed Jenni Hermoso as she went to receive her winners medal at the 2023 FIFA Women's World

Cup, Spanish reporters who had tried to highlight Rubiales' problematic behaviour for years found a newly receptive international audience for their reporting (Ramírez 2023). Hermoso's teammates and supporters rallied around #SeAcabó (#It'sOver), generating widespread support on social media and achieving change within the Spanish FA. This example chimes with others discussed in this chapter in that the protest against Rubiales' highly-visible actions on women's football's biggest international stage did not come from nowhere but provided a new visibility to the players' longstanding battles against misogyny in Spanish football. But to see Rubiales' fate as an end point would be misleading. For instance, an ongoing criminal case means that, at the time of writing, Hermoso is unable to speak publicly about the case (Wrack 2023).

A further problem with the question about #MeToo's achievements—which is also suggested by the World Cup example—is that it implies that the successes (or failures) of the hashtag are entirely within the gift of the victim/survivors and activists using the hashtag. Missing is the powerful *resistance* to #MeToo that was there all along: violent misogyny was the condition for #MeToo's emergence *and* a newly urgent response to it. As Sara Ahmed (2023: 4) puts it, #MeToo was accused of "going too far before it got very far", with women's speech being framed as excessive, reckless and indiscriminate and accused men recast as the victims of women's words. That the discursive discrediting of #MeToo could sit alongside a stated belief in (some) survivors is another version of McRobbie's double entanglement: the stated belief in the individual serves as evidence that things *have* changed (we believe *her*) and, therefore, change is no longer needed. The solution to sexual violence is reimagined in individualistic terms (belief, perhaps even justice) which negates the importance of structural analysis and change.

This is a challenge for scholars thinking historically about the feminist movements to end male violence more broadly and is summed up in Jan Jordan's (2023) notion of "the rape conundrum". The conundrum, for Jordan, is how feminist activism can have achieved so much—such as the establishment and decades-long maintenance of support and advocacy services which have quite literally saved lives, as well as reshaping statutory services and producing legislative change (Hague 2021; Robertson 2024)—yet the need for that activism has not dissipated. Tanya Serisier (2018: 12) makes a similar point in relation to silence breaking:

Breaking the silence, despite its significant cultural impact, has not ended sexual violence, nor does it seem to have significantly reduced it, or to have eradicated the stigma associated with being a rape victim. Many of the stories women tell almost 50 years after the birth of the feminist anti-rape movement contain disturbingly similar elements to those from that first speak-out, even as the cultural context in which they are told has been undeniably altered by the effects of half a century of speaking out.

Depressingly, what has remained consistent throughout the period is that men abuse women in astonishing numbers and in ways which are often culturally legitimated. That feminisms and violent misogyny occupy the same moment(s) trouble any attempt to tell a linear story of feminisms' successes. #MeToo can be understood as a cultural moment but that cultural moment was never, only, the preserve of victim/survivors and activists: if it was, then that moment could not be hailed as "over" unless and until the cultural supports for men's violence against women had been dismantled. The "endings" for #MeToo proclaimed in popular culture—both the apparently happy endings, and the frustratingly unjust ones—think about change in a much narrower and more individualised way, as we will see.

Endings: Part 1

In Chapter 2, I quoted Ashley Judd in *Time's* "Silence Breakers" story describing how she "started talking about Harvey the minute that it happened" (Zacharek et al. 2017): what was *new* about the #MeToo moment was not that women spoke out but rather that what some of the women said was deemed consequential. This is an important distinction as one of the defences a number of accused men have attempted to deploy is to argue—as Weinstein (2017) did in his statement to the *New York Times*—that the reports of historic abuse related to a time when cultural norms were different, when he could not have been expected to know that this behaviour was wrong. These "different times" defences are bolstered by the broader discourse around #MeToo's newness, as though women in 2017 *suddenly* decided that being raped, sexually harassed and assaulted was not OK. This arguably supports the attempts of accused men to present themselves as victims whose past bad behaviour is being judged by new standards in the present. In defending themselves against reports of sexual harassment and assault, men who have been successful within their fields are also able to mobilise the passage of time to boost their own credibility, often whilst diminishing the credibility of victim/survivors (Tuerkheimer 2021). His success dents her credibility.

Key to all of this is that accused men ask that claims of abuse are judged against the totality of their lives *and* the promise of their futures, whilst fixing women to the moment of abuse. It is telling, for instance, that Weinstein's statement (2017) not only refers back to the "different times" when he did not know what he knows now, but also projects to the future when he will invest his energies in giving the National Rifle Association his "full attention", produce a movie critical of the President, and invest in scholarships for women directors. In Weinstein's accounting, both his past and future matter and he tries to mobilise both to defend against consequences in the present.

Weinstein is not alone in this, though the discursive formations of history—and future—which accused men draw on vary widely, not least in relation to wealth, class and race. For instance, Black feminists in the US have documented the way in which prominent Black men accused of sexual abuse have mobilised the long history of the violent policing of Black sexuality to challenge the allegations against them. This is evident, for instance, in a statement released by R. Kelly's representative in response to the campaign to #MuteRKelly (which I discuss in Chapter 6), which refers to the "attempted public lynching of a black man who has made extraordinary contributions to our culture" (Blackmon 2018). The work of Black feminists does not deny the importance of that history *or* the present inequities in the criminal justice system which see Black men incarcerated at disproportionate rates. What this work does do, however, is highlight the misogynoir inherent in these appeals to history whereby the experiences of Black women and girls are dismissed in the interests of supporting an idea of community which centres Black men (Young 2022; Lindsey 2023).

It is not just celebrity men who are imperilled by the demands for accountability in the long #MeToo moment. Here I want to turn to the Brock Turner case to discuss how encouraging us to consider the implications of assault charges to a man's whole life is dependent on fixing victim/survivors to the moment of victimisation, of not seeing their lives beyond his actions. Turner is the blond-haired, blue-eyed swimmer-with-Olympic-potential who raped Chanel Miller but received minimal jail time despite a being found guilty of sexual assault. Miller fought hard to make her story, her lost potential, matter against a context where—as we have seen—Turner's swimming times were widely reported alongside accounts of the rape (Doe 2016/2019). In contrast, Turner's father argued that his son faced a "steep price" for "20 minutes of action" in an otherwise blameless life. Others, including the probation officer whose report was presented at trial and the judge who gave a lenient sentence, were equally concerned about how his promising future had been imperilled by those 20 minutes. Notably, Turner Senior's attempts to downplay the severity of the crime demanded that we kept the rapist's past, present and future in play whilst the narrative structure of the criminal trial reduced the significance of the victim/survivor to the moment of abuse, "a minor character, a mute body" in *his* life story (Miller 2019: 211).

My use of the term "rapist" in the last paragraph is quite deliberate. In the next chapter, I argue that constructing men who rape and sexually assault women as a separate category of person—rapist, perpetrator, abuser—can be at odds with a feminist analysis of men's violence against women and its focus on the continuum of the "normal" and "aberrant" behaviour. Yet, faced with the failure of men like Turner to accept responsibility for their actions—a failure which has prolonged their victim/survivors' suffering (Miller 2019)—the permanence of the label offers a certain form of justice. As Miller noted in her powerful victim impact statement:

> [Turner] is a lifetime sex registrant. That doesn't expire. Just like what he did to me doesn't expire, doesn't go away after a set number of years. It stays with me, it's part of my identity, it has forever changed the way I carry myself, the way I live the rest of my life. (Doe 2016/2019: 356)

The importance of representation, of naming, is raised here. Whilst, as we have seen, virality may flare and fade, it can also stick.

This might be understood using Clare McGlynn and Nicole Westmarland's (2019) concept of kaleidoscopic justice. Through empirical work with victim/survivors, McGlynn and Westmarland argue that justice is a "constantly shifting pattern" in their lives, identifying six justice themes: consequences, recognition, dignity, voice, prevention and connectedness. Whilst Miller's account of the criminal justice process demonstrates how *un*justly the system treats victim/survivors, it also demonstrates other routes to justice. Through her victim impact statement—and crucially its publication by *Buzzfeed*—Miller's voice was heard in a way that allowed her to make connections with other survivors. The response to her statement was a means of restoring the dignity the assault—and trial—took from her. Miller's words – heard and amplified by other victim/survivors (Miller 2019: 211)—have had consequences, one of which is that "rapist" now sticks to Turner, it follows him around.

Just as there was backlash against Turner Senior's statement, more recently actors Ashton Kutcher and Mila Kunis faced online backlash when character references they had written to the judge ahead of the sentencing of their friend, actor and convicted-rapist Danny Masterton, were leaked. Like Turner Senior, Kutcher's and Kunis's letters (Anglesey 2023) sought clemency on the grounds of their knowledge of the convicted perpetrator *over time*, both stressing how long they had known the actor and the consistency of his good qualities, drawing on examples from different moments in their 25 years of friendship. What is interesting about these letters for my purposes here is that the apparent consistency of Masterton's good qualities depended upon him *not* being held accountable for the rapes at the time they happened and on Kutcher and Kunis not being confronted with those minor characters, those mute bodies, in his life story. The complex temporalities of speaking out and of justice therefore activate a range of narratives of loss: that Kutcher and Kunis were able to identify these qualities in their friend because he was not held accountable does not lessen the intensity of their emotional investment in their friendship and its importance to their own life histories. Nor does it mean that Masterton, in addition to being a rapist, was not *also* a good and supportive friend or a loving and protective father. I say this not to suggest that these factors should be taken into account in sentencing, but rather as a means of insisting that one of the difficulties with linear storytelling around sexual assault is that it attempts to negate these kinds of complexities and to fix identities in and through moments of assault.

This may seem to run counter to my willingness to label Turner a rapist above. But to commit to continuum thinking means seeing the continuum of "normal" and "aberrant" behaviour across individual life histories *as well as* between men recognised as "normal" and those deemed "aberrant". This is not to accept Turner Senior's minimisation of the "20 minutes of action" but rather to ask how his son's life of privilege until that point may have helped to set the scene for his assault of Miller. This is difficult work—for families, friends, communities and, in the cases of public figures, also for audiences and fans—and it is also almost universally unpopular work. It demands an ongoing reckoning, not, or not only, the surety and apparent finality of a criminal conviction.

Criminal convictions have, arguably, played an outsize role in the mainstream narrative around #MeToo, being used as a measure of its success or failure. For instance, the initial verdict in Weinstein's New York trial was widely hailed as a "victory" for #MeToo, demonstrating that juries are now better able to understand, and accept, the complex relationships victim/survivors may continue to have with their abusers, particularly when they are in positions of power (e.g. Twohey and Kantor 2020). Following the decision of the New York Court of Appeal to overturn the conviction and order a retrial, the story shifted—somewhat predictably—to focus on the purported failures, signalling the "end of Hollywood's #MeToo moment" (Siegel 2024). Beyond that specific case, it is important to recognise that not all of the experiences shared under #MeToo demand a criminal justice response. Indeed, an emphasis on criminal justice as the barometer of cultural change risks obscuring the continuum of women's experiences which #MeToo propelled into public consciousness. Even when the actions described under #MeToo in themselves meet standards of criminality in a given jurisdiction, that doesn't mean they will be actionable (e.g. due to statutes of limitations) or that victim/survivors will *want* to be involved in an adversarial, re-victimising criminal justice system. These concerns may be particularly acutely felt by victim/survivors in marginalised communities given both histories and present realities of racist policing and criminal justice responses (Richie 2012, Davis et al. 2022). Given these limitations, achieving convictions within a flawed system is a shaky foundation for genuine cultural change (e.g. Bumiller 2008; Richie 2012; Powell et al. 2015) and, indeed, for justice as victim/survivors understand it (Herman 2023).

For some victim/survivors, the recognition and dignity #MeToo afforded may have been forms of justice in themselves whilst—like consciousness-raising groups of an earlier period—pointing to the necessity of political action and structural change. Importantly, both Burke's Me Too and Milano's #MeToo offered recognition for victim/survivors which did *not* depend on naming perpetrators. When we recognise that justice for victim/survivors is not achieved solely by sanctions for perpetrators, the limitations of seeing a conviction as an end point are even more apparent. In the Weinstein case, there are powerful arguments against seeing his convictions as an end point, not only because of the impact of the protracted appeals process on the specific women in these cases but also because the criminal cases can only scratch the surface, leaving many women out as well as failing to hold to account the many who enabled Weinstein to abuse with impunity for so long. This is not to deny that criminal justice can be important to victim/survivors: in the R. Kelly case, for instance, the failure to hold him criminally accountable in his 2008 trial legitimated his continued abuse of Black women and girls, leading many of the victim/survivors interviewed in *Surviving R. Kelly* (Lifetime, 2019–2023) to see his incarceration both as essential to their safety and as a belated recognition that their lives *do* matter. However, victim/survivors speaking in the documentary are also very well aware of the contingent nature of criminal justice as highlighted by the release of Bill Cosby on a legal technicality. At the same time, the fact that victim/survivors can talk openly about both R. Kelly and Cosby under a presumption of belief is a form of justice.

The cultural reckonings of the long #MeToo moment have therefore offered informal routes to justice for some victim/survivors. Again, #MeToo is not an origin point here so much as it is a cultural flashpoint for debates about the possibilities and limitations of mediated speech which were already taking place (e.g. Salter 2013, Powell 2015) within the terms of what Nancy Fraser (2007) describes as a feminist politics of recognition. Social media has provided a public platform for pre-existing practices—from consciousness-raising groups to less explicitly political practices such as whisper networks or scribbled graffiti in public bathrooms—whereby women have sought to warn one another about predatory men in ways that have allowed collectively-authored stories to emerge. But the move online has also brought challenges both for a feminist politics and for individual victim/survivors. The platforms used to share these stories are constructed in the interests of capital with implications as to how "free" speech on these platforms is, and for whom. The same platforms that have enabled the building of solidarity among victim/survivors, have also facilitated coordinated attacks on them. Beyond the platforms themselves, authored, written speech creates liabilities and vulnerabilities for victim/survivors who may not "own" their story in any straightforward way (Salter 2013; Robinson and Yoshida 2023). But informal routes to justice are not only *legally* challenged by accused men and their defenders, they are also *discursively* delegitimated (Banet-Weiser and Higgins 2023). Whilst there are, of course, important questions to ask about the ways in which speech about sexual violence circulates and in whose interests, those critical of "trial by media" often seem to work on an assumption that "trial by judge or jury" is an inherently just system, something that has been resoundingly challenged in feminist scholarship, particularly that produced by Black feminists (Richie 2012). These points are brought together in the final section leading into a more detailed consideration of men, doubt and belief in the next chapter.

ENDINGS: PART 2

In concluding this chapter, I want to turn to Johnny Depp's 2022 defamation case against his former wife, Amber Heard, which was widely heralded as signalling the "end" of #MeToo, or, more violently, as representing its "death" (Banet-Weiser and Higgins 2023: 135). It is worth noting upfront that this was not the first high-profile case to be heralded in this way. Brett Kavanaugh's confirmation to the Supreme Court despite reports of sexual assault by Dr Christine Blasey Ford was similarly hailed in 2018. Nor is the Depp/Heard case the end of the end. As this book goes to press two years on from the Depp/Heard verdict, the overturning of Weinstein's conviction in New York has produced another end point. Ironically, endings seem to be serialised.

The Depp case, like others discussed in this chapter, spans the long #MeToo moment, beginning in 2016 when Heard was granted a restraining order against Depp and photographs of her bruised face—reportedly the result of Depp's violence—were released. The backlash against Heard from Depp's fans was immediate and intense (Robinson and Yoshida 2023), but the impact on Depp was, intially, less evident: for instance, he continued as the face of Dior's fragrance Sauvage and in the role of Gellert Grindlewald in the *Fantastic Beasts* franchise.

In April 2018, the UK-tabloid the *Sun* published an article taking aim at author JK Rowling—"a supporter of women's rights"—for defending the casting of "wife-beater" Depp in *Fantastic Beasts: The Crimes of Grindlewald* (dir. David Yates, 2018) (Wootton 2018). Depp sued the publisher and journalist, Dan Wootton, for libel.[7] The *Sun*/Wooton's

---

[7] The article on the *Sun*'s website originally carried the headline "GONE POTTY How Can J K Rowling be 'genuinely happy' casting wife beater Johnny Depp in the new Fantastic Beasts film?", but was changed the next day (and in the print edition) to "GONE POTTY How Can J K Rowling be 'genuinely happy' casting Johnny Depp in the new Fantastic Beasts film after assault claim?". The rest of the article remained

defence was that the reports that Depp had abused Heard were true, and this meant that—although she was not quoted or in any way involved in the original article—Heard gave evidence in the 2020 trial, generating further high-profile misogynist attacks outside the court and online (Robinson and Yoshida 2023: 297–305).

Depp's choice to sue the *Sun*—a paper unlikely to rouse the sympathies of feminists—may have been strategic (Robinson and Yoshida 2023: 307–308), but for my purposes here it is less his intent than the story this allowed the *Sun* to tell about feminism which is important. The *Sun* article at the centre of Depp's libel case is not really about him but about Rowling, who is described by Wootton as "a holier-thau Twitterati preacher" who "tries to present herself as a leading light for women in the entertainment industry". Rowling's defence of Depp is juxtaposed with statements from two Weinstein-survivors, "brave members of Me Too/Times Up" given an exclusive platform in the *Sun* to challenge Rowling." The anti-feminist journalist for a notoriously misogynist publication thus emerges as the improbable but *reasonable* defender of women abused by men, in the face of celebrity feminist failures. A version of this argument is also advanced in an editorial following the verdict in the libel case (*Sun* 2020) which takes a similarly adversarial approach. This time, however, Rowling is not named and the fake feminists pitted against the *Sun's* noble journalists are Depp's online supporters. The description of these supporters echoes the earlier Rowling article: we are told they "would instantly condemn any abuser whose politics they dislike" but their "concern for victims" is revealed to be "opportunistic and wafer-thin" by their vilification of Heard. So far, this story is familiar from my analysis of the representation of feminism as a site of suspicion and source of conflict between women in Chapter 2 and it is interesting that this narrative could be so easily deployed even in a moment which *could* have been hailed as a victory for women's believability (and, so, for #MeToo).

Depp's 2022 defamation case also started in 2018. Around six months after Wootton's opinion piece in the *Sun*, the *Washington Post* published an article attributed to Heard in which she describes how she "spoke up against sexual violence—and faced our culture's wrath" (Heard 2018).

---

the same (see https://globalfreedomofexpression.columbia.edu/cases/john-christopher-depp-ii-v-news-group-newspapers-ltd-and-dan-wootton/#Case%20Summary%20and%20Outcome). It is this version which can still be accessed on the *Sun's* website and is referred to in this chapter (Wootton 2018).

Although he is not named in the article, Depp sued Heard personally for defamation. On the basis of much the same evidence as had been presented in the UK trial, Depp won the defamation case. Confusingly, the same jury also found that Depp's agent had defamed Heard in calling her allegations a "hoax".

Returning to the *Washington Post* Op-Ed in the wake of the second trial is a disorienting experience. Whilst the trial was widely represented in individualistic and adversarial terms—Depp v. Heard—the article, ghostwritten by the Amercian Civil Liberties Union, is not about this. Nor does it include the salacious detail of the assaults and injuries which characterises Wootton's piece. Instead, it is about the continuum of men's abuse of women and the structures which enable it. Heard is careful to emphasise the aspects of her experience that may be deemed to be *representative* despite her celebrity. For instance, in one of the contested passages (which the jury determined was defamatory) Heard describes herself as "a public figure representing domestic abuse" and, throughout, she situates her experiences of domestic abuse on a continuum of related experiences in her—and all women's—lifetimes:

> I was exposed to abuse at a very young age. I knew certain things early on, without ever having to be told. I knew that men have the power— physically, socially and financially— and that a lot of institutions support that arrangement. I knew this long before I had the words to articulate it, and I bet you learned it young, too.

The assumption of shared experience here speaks to the #MeToo moment, a connection Heard makes explicit later in the article:

> Imagine a powerful man as a ship, like the Titanic. That ship is a huge enterprise. When it strikes an iceberg, there are a lot of people on board desperate to patch up holes — not because they believe in or even care about the ship, but because their own fates depend on the enterprise.
>
> In recent years, the #MeToo movement has taught us about how power like this works, not just in Hollywood but in all kinds of institutions — workplaces, places of worship or simply in particular communities. In every walk of life, women are confronting these men who are buoyed by social, economic and cultural power.

The article is not about Johnny Depp. It is about what follows on from women's shared public speech about assault, not only the cultural backlash but also the necessary *work* that speech demands. In identifying the need for legislative and institutional change, secure funding for women's services and highlighting the responsibility of elected representatives (as well as those who vote for them), Heard places considerable faith in the same systems that have historically patched up the holes in the iceberg-stricken ship. But, even so, she presents this as work that concerns "us" all: "We can work together to demand changes to laws and rules and social norms—and to right the imbalances that have shaped our lives" (Heard 2018).

By making *this* article the focus of his case against Heard, Depp and his team ensured that it was not just Heard's believability which was on trial, but the collective ethos of #MeToo itself. It was not just a case of "Depp v. Heard", then, but of Heard v. those women she claimed to speak for, of the individual versus the *possibility* of the collective. This is an easy story to tell because it fits with existing media templates in which men's violence against women is understood in necessarily adversarial terms with clearly defined roles: the accused and accuser; perpetrator and victim; enabler and defender; winner and loser; accuser and supporter. I argued in Chapter 3 that what was potentially radical about the explosion of testimony under the hashtag #MeToo was the way it problematised those "everyday, routine intimate intrusions" (2012, p. xix) which Kelly's continuum sought to highlight but which had been marginalised in subsequent decades because of the emphasis on crime. Although Depp's case was civil not criminal, its adversarial framing of #MeToo as a story of winners and losers undermines this more radical potential, emphasising individuals and framing legal judgement as the endpoint, the determinant of meaning.

The defamation trial was widely heralded as the "end" of #MeToo, not only because of the verdict but—even prior to that—because of the gleefully misogynist commentary it enabled. Whilst the *scale* of the misogyny Heard experienced post-#MeToo was unprecedented (Tsioulcas and Rascoe 2022), Depp fans and men's rights activists had been mobilising against Heard since news of the restraining order was first reported in 2016. If the 2022 verdict heralded "the end" of #MeToo then the beginning of the end predates #MeToo itself. This is indicative of the complex temporalities I referred to earlier in this chapter and a reminder of what is commonly referred to in feminist writings as the "second victimisation" victim/survivors experience in court and/or the media. Earlier I suggested that speech about sexual violence is characterised by repetition and delay: this applies even more forcefully to "justice". It is also, as Tarana Burke argues, a reminder of the limitations of looking to untransformed systems to deliver meaningful change:

> The "me too" movement isn't dead, this system is dead [...] This is the same legal system that y'all have been relying on for justice and accountability for decades to no avail. When you get the verdict you want, "the movement works"—when you don't, it's dead. [...] When Weinstein went to jail it was, "me too is winning!" When Cosby came home it was "What a blow, me too is losing!" In the meantime—millions of people who have never been able to utter the words "it happened to me" have released the shame that wasn't theirs to carry in the first place. This movement is very much ALIVE. (Burke, cited in Bekiempis 2022)

Burke raises the question: what does success—or failure—look like, and for whom? To see legal verdicts, civil or criminal, as evidence of either success or failure it to put faith in a system that decades of feminist—and in particular Black feminist—activism and research have shown typically work in the interests of the powerful (Richie 2012). Meanwhile, Burke reminds us of the change in people's daily lives, in their understandings of themselves and their experiences, which activism continues to achieve. This matters. This is not to say that things like the Depp verdict do not have an impact. Just as the outpouring of testimony under #MeToo created possibilities for millions to utter the words "it happened to me" so high-profile cases of this kind can stifle words not yet spoken, or mean that when they are uttered they may be less likely to be believed.

Against this backdrop, the stories Western feminism tells about itself—stories which centre progress, loss or return depending on the political and generational affiliations of the teller (Hemmings 2011)—are limited because they too focus on what feminism has/not achieved whilst negating the agency involved in shoring up the status quo. The simultaneity of men's violence against women and feminist protest, and of feminism and the backlash against it, will always frustrate linear narratives of cause and effect.

References

AFP. 2021. French woman overturns conviction for accusing man of sexual harassment. *Guardian*, 31 March. https://www.theguardian.com/world/2021/mar/31/french-woman-sued-by-man-she-accused-of-sexual-harassment-wins-appeal-case. Accessed 23 February 2024.

Ahmed, Sara. 2023. *The Feminist Killjoy Handbook*. London: Allen Lane.

Anglesey, Anders. 2023. Mila Kunis and Ashton Kutcher's letters on Danny Masterson in full. *Newsweek*, 10 September. https://www.newsweek.com/mila-kunis-ashton-kutchers-letters-danny-masterson-full-1825816. Accessed 16 February 2024.

Bae, Soo Young, Yu I. Taegyun Kim and Meeyoung Cha Ha. 2021. The medium and the backlash: The disparagement of the #MeToo movement in online public discourse in South Korea. *International Journal of Communication* 15: 768–791.

Bailey, Moya, and Trudy. 2018. On misogynoir: Citation, erasure, and plagiarism. *Feminist Media Studies* 18 (4): 762–768.

Banet-Weiser, Sarah. 2018. *Empowered: Popular Feminism and Popular Misogyny*. Durham: Duke.

Banet-Weiser, Sarah, and Kathryn Claire Higgins. 2023. *Believability: Sexual Violence, Media, and the Politics of Doubt*. Cambridge: Polity.

Bardoloi, Paromita. 2015. We won't call you Nirbhaya anymore, we will call you Jyoti Singh: This is why. *Women's Web*, 18 December. https://www.womensweb.in/2015/12/wont-call-nirvaya-anymore-will-call-jyoti-singh/. Accessed 2 January 2024.

Bekiempis, Victoria. 2022. What does the Heard-Depp verdict mean for the #MeToo movement? *Guardian*, 3 June.

Biressi, Anita. 2019. Following the money: News, sexual assault and the economic logic of the public sphere. *European Journal of Cultural Studies* 22 (5–6): 595–612.

Blackmon, Michael. 2018. #TimesUp has launched a campaign to boycott R. Kelly. *Buzzfeed*, 30 April. https://www.buzzfeed.com/michaelblackmon/times-up-r-kelly-boycott-mute. Accessed 4 February 2024.

Boyle, Karen. 2005. Feminism without men: Feminist media studies in a post-feminist age. In *Mass Media and Society*, 4th ed., ed. James Curran and Michael Gurevitch, 29–45. London: Arnold.

Boyle, Karen. 2018. Television and/as testimony in the Jimmy Savile case. *Critical Studies in Television* 13 (4): 387–404.

Boyle, Karen. 2020. Of monsters and bombshells: A blog in three parts. *Equal Media and Culture Centre for Scotland Blog*, 5 February. https://emcc.engender.org.uk/news/blog/of-monsters-and-bombshells-a-blog-in-three-parts/. Accessed 15 January 2024.

Brison, Susan. 2002. *Aftermath: Violence and the Remaking of a Self*. Princeton: Princeton University Press.
Brison, Susan. 2008. Everyday atrocities and ordinary miracles, or why I (still) bear witness to sexual violence (but not too often). *Women's Studies Quarterly* 36 (1/2): 188–198.
Brison, Susan. 2014. Why I spoke out about one rape but stayed silent about another. *Time*, 1 December. http://time.com/3612283/why-i-spoke-out-about-one-rape-but-stayed-silent-about-another/. Accessed 9 November 2023.
Burke, Tarana. n.d. The inception. *Me Too*. https://metoomvmt.org/the-inception/. Accessed 2 April 2019.
Burke, Tarana. 2021. *Unbound: My Story of Liberation and the Birth of the Me Too Movement*. London: Headline.
Chatterjee, Tupur. 2019. Rape culture, misogyny, and urban anxiety in *NH10* and *Pink*. *Feminist Media Studies* 19 (1): 130–146.
Cheema, Iqra Shagufta. ed. 2023. *The Other #MeToos*. Oxford: Oxford University Press.
Davis, Angela Y., Gina Dent, Erica R. Meiners and Beth E. Richie. 2022. *Abolition. Feminism. Now.* London: Penguin.
Doe, Emily. 2016/2019. Victim impact statement. In *Know My Name*, Chanel Miller, 333–357. UK & US: Viking.
Erlingsdóttir, Irma. 2021. Fighting structural inequalities: Feminist activism and the #MeToo movement in Iceland. In *The Routledge Handbook of the Politics of the #MeToo Movement*, ed. Giti Chandra and Irma Erlingsdóttir, 450–464. London: Routledge.
Farrow, Ronan. 2019. *Catch and Kill: Lies, Spies and a Conspiracy to Protect Predators*. London: Fleet.
Flynn, Emma. 2024. *Complexity, Complicity and Consent: Representations of Sexual Violence in English and French Literature and Film*. Unpublished PhD thesis. University of Strathclyde.
Fraser, Nancy. 2007. Feminist politics in the age of recognition. *Studies in Social Justice* 1 (1): 23–35.
Gill, Rosalind. 2007. Postfeminist media culture: Elements of a sensibility. *European Journal of Cultural Studies* 10 (2): 147–166.
Gilmore, Leigh. 2017. *Tainted Witness: Why We Doubt What Women Say About Their Lives*. New York: Columbia University Press.
Grabowska, Magdalena and Marta Rawluszko. 2021. Polish #MeToo: When concern for men's rights derails the women's revolution. In *The Routledge Handbook of the Politics of the #MeToo Movement*, ed. Giti Chandra and Irma Erlingsdóttir, 284–302. London: Routledge.

Guha, Pallavi. 2015. Hash tagging but not trending: The success and failure of the news media to engage with online feminist activism in India. *Feminist Media Studies* 15 (1): 155–157.

Hague, Gill. 2021. *Histories and Memories of the Domestic Violence Movement*. Bristol: Policy Press.

Heard, Amber. 2018. I spoke up against sexual violence—And faced our culture's wrath. That has to change. *The Washington Post* 18 December. https://www.washingtonpost.com/opinions/ive-seen-how-institutions-protect-men-accused-of-abuse-heres-what-we-can-do/2018/12/18/71fd876a-02ed-11e9-b5df-5d3874f1ac36_story.html. Accessed 16 February 2024.

Hemmings, Clare. 2011. *Why Stories Matter: The Political Grammar of Feminist Theory*. Durham: Duke.

Herman, Judith L. 2023. *Truth and Repair: How Trauma Survivors Envision Justice*. London: Basic.

Horeck, Tanya. 2019. *Justice on Demand: True Crime in the Digital Streaming Era*. Detroit: Wayne State University Press.

Horeck, Tanya. 2024. Sexual violence and social justice: The celebrity #MeToo documentary in the US. In *The Routledge Companion to Gender, Media and Violence*, ed. Karen Boyle and Susan Berridge, 232–241. London and New York: Routledge.

Ito, Shiori. 2017/2021. *Black Box*. Trans. Allison Markin Powell. UK: Tilted Axis Press.

Jackson, Sarah J., Moya Bailey and Brooke Foucault Welles. 2020. *#Hashtag Activism: Networks of Race and Gender Justice*. Cambridge, MA and London: MIT Press.

Jordan, Jan. 2022. *Women, Rape and Justice: Unravelling the Rape Conundrum*. Abingdon: Routledge.

Jordan, Jan. 2023. *Tackling Rape Culture: Ending Patriarchy*. Abingdon: Routledge.

Kelly, Liz. 1988. *Surviving Sexual Violence*. Cambridge: Polity.

Kelly, Liz. 2012. Standing the test of time? Reflections on the concept of the continuum of sexual violence. In: *Handbook on Sexual Violence*, ed. Jennifer M. Brown and Sandra L. Walklate, xvii–xxvi. London: Routledge.

Khoja-Moolji, Shemila. 2015. Becoming an "intimate publics": Exploring the affective intensities of hashtag feminism. *Feminist Media Studies* 15 (2): 347–350.

Lakkimsetti, Chaitanya. 2021. Stripping away at respectability: #MeToo India and the politics of dignity. *Feminist Formations* 33 (3): 303–317.

Lawton, Georgina. 2017. #MeToo is here to stay. *Guardian*, 28 October.

Lévy, Bernard-Henri. 2011. Lessons of the Dominique Strauss-Kahn affair. *The Daily Beast*, 2 July (updated 13 July 2017). https://www.thedailybeast.com/

bernard-henri-levy-lessons-of-the-dominique-strauss-kahn-affair. Accessed 23 February 2024.

Li, Jun. 2021. In the name of #RiceBunny: Legacy, strategy, and efficacy of the Chinese #MeToo movement. In *The Routledge Handbook of the Politics of the #MeToo Movement*, ed. Giti Chandra and Irma Erlingsdóttir, 343–359. London: Routledge.

Li, Jun. 2024. Media, courts and "#RiceBunny" testimonies in China. In *The Routledge Companion to Gender, Media and Violence*, ed. Karen Boyle and Susan Berridge, 163–173. London: Routledge.

Lindsey, Trevi B. 2023. *America, Goddam: Violence, Black Women, and the Struggle for Justice*. Oakland: University of California Press.

Loureiro, Gabriela. 2024. Hashtag feminism in Brazil: Making sense of gender-based violence with #PrimeiroAssédio. In *The Routledge Companion to Gender, Media and Violence*, ed. Karen Boyle and Susan Berridge, 501–510. London: Routledge.

McGlynn, Clare, and Nicole Westmarland. 2019. Kaleidoscopic justice: Sexual violence and victim-survivors' perceptions of justice. *Social and Legal Studies* 28 (2): 179–201.

McRobbie, Angela. 2009. *The Aftermath of Feminism: Gender, Culture and Social Change*. London: Sage.

Miller, Chanel. 2019. *Know My Name: A Memoir*. London: Viking.

Mwikya, K. Kanyali., Judy Gitau and Esther Waweru. 2021. #MeToo, the law, and anti-sexual violence activism in Kenya. In *The Routledge Handbook of the Politics of the #MeToo Movement*, ed. Giti Chandra and Irma Erlingsdóttir, 386–396. London: Routledge.

Poulami, Roychowdhury. 2013. The Delhi gang rape: The making of international causes. *Feminist Studies* 39 (1): 282–292.

Powell, Anastasia. 2015. Seeking informal justice online: Vigilantism, activism and resisting a rape culture in cyberspace. In *Rape Justice: Beyond the Criminal Law*, ed. Anastasia Powell, Nicola Henry and Asher Flynn, 218–237. Cham: Palgrave Macmillan.

Powell, Anastasia, Nicola Henry and Asher Flynn, eds. 2015. *Rape Justice: Beyond the Criminal Law*. Cham: Palgrave Macmillan.

Ramírez, María. 2023. #MeToo exposed the abuse of women in Spain. It took football and #SeAcabó to spark a revolution. *Guardian* 28 August.

Richie, Beth E. 2012. *Arrested Justice: Black Women, Violence, and America's Prison Nation*. New York: New York University Press.

Robertson, Charlotte James. 2024. *Working in Between: Women's Aid and Networks of Anti-Domestic Abuse Activism in the UK, 1971–1996*. Unpublished PhD thesis. University of Glasgow and University of Strathclyde.

Robinson, Jennifer, and Keina Yoshida. 2023. *How Many More Women? The Silencing of Women by the Law and How to Stop It*. London: Endeavour.

Rouyer, Muriel. 2013. The Strauss–Kahn affair and the culture of privacy: Mistreating and misrepresenting women in the French public sphere. *Women's Studies International Forum* 41 (3): 187–196.

Salter, Michael. 2013. Justice and revenge in online counter-publics: Emerging responses to sexual violence in the age of social media. *Crime, Media, Culture* 9 (3): 225–242.

Sambaraju, R. 2020. "I would have taken this to my grave, like most women": Reporting sexual harassment during the #MeToo movement in India. *Journal of Social Issues* 76 (3): 603–631.

Schwartz, Anat. 2023. Acceptable activism: the history of the anti-sexual violence movement and the contemporary #MeToo protests in South Korea. In *The Other #MeToos*, ed. Iqra Shagufta Cheema, 1–21. Oxford: Oxford University Press.

Serisier, Tanya. 2018. *Speaking Out: Feminism, Rape and Narrative Politics*. Cham: Palgrave Macmillan.

Shandilya, Krupa. 2015. Nirbhaya's body: The politics of protest in the aftermath of the 2012 Delhi gang rape. *Gender & History* 27 (2): 465–486.

Sedysheva, Anna. 2021. #IAmNotAfraidToSpeak, #MeToo, and the Russian media. In *The Routledge Handbook of the Politics of the #MeToo Movement*, ed. Giti Chandra and Irma Erlingsdóttir, 303–319. London: Routledge.

Siegel, Tatiana. 2024. Does Harvey Weinstein's overturned conviction signal the end of Hollywood's #MeToo moment? *Variety*, 1 May. https://variety.com/2024/film/news/harvey-weinstein-overturned-conviction-metoo-movement-1235987162/. Accessed 3 May 2024.

Sreedharan, Chindu, Einar Thorsen and Ananya Gouthi. 2020. Time's up. Or is it? Journalists' perceptions of sexual violence and newsroom changes after #MeTooIndia. *Journalism Practice* 14(2): 132–149.

Sun. 2020. THE SUN SAYS: Johnny Depp is a wife-beater and fool for thinking he could overturn the damning evidence against him. *Sun*, 3 November. https://www.thesun.co.uk/news/13090612/johnny-depp-wife-beater-libel-case/. Accessed 16 February 2024.

Tambe, Ashwini. 2021. Afterword. "Walking alongside many #MeToos". *Feminist Formations* 33(3): 351–359.

Tasker, Yvonne and Diane Negra. 2007. *Interrogating Postfeminism*. Durham: Duke University Press.

Thapar-Björkert, Suruchi and Madina Tlostanova. 2018. Identifying to dis-identify: Occidentalist feminism, the Delhi gang rape case and its internal others. *Gender, Place and Culture* 25 (7): 1025–1040.

Towers, Angela. 2024. After the affect: The tenuous leadership of viral feminists. In *The Routledge Companion to Gender, Media and Violence*, ed. Karen Boyle and Susan Berridge, 511–521. London: Routledge.

Tranchese, Alessia. 2022. *From Fritzl to #MeToo: Twenty Years of Rape Coverage in the British Press*. Cham: Palgrave Macmillan.

Tsicoulcas, Anastasia and Ayesha Rascoe. 2022. On social media, Johnny Depp is winning public sympathy over Amber Heard. *NPR*, 23 May. https://www.npr.org/2022/05/23/1100685712/on-social-media-johnny-depp-is-winning-public-sympathy-over-amber-heard. Accessed 13 October 2023.

Tuerkheimer, Deborah. 2021. *Credible: Why We Doubt Accusers and Protect Abusers*. New York: Harper Collins.

Twohey, Megan and Jodi Kantor. 2020. With Weinstein conviction, jury delivers a verdict on #MeToo. *New York Times*, 24 February. https://www.nytimes.com/2020/02/24us/harvey-weinstein-verdict-metoo.html Accessed 8 February 2024.

Weinstein, Harvey. 2017. Statement. *New York Times*, 5 October.

Wootton, Dan. 2018. GONE POTTY. How can JK Rowling be 'genuinely happy' casting Johnny Depp in the news *Fantastic Beasts* film after assault claim? *Sun*, 28 April. https://www.thesun.co.uk/tvandshowbiz/6159182/jk-rowling-genuinely-happy-johnny-depp-fantastic-beasts/. Accessed 16 February 2024.

Wrack, Suzanne. 2023. *Guardian* footballer of the year Jenni Hermoso: Glory, adversity and a cause that still burns. *Guardian*, 29 December.

Wu, Lily Jinxian. 2024. *Becoming Chinese Digital Feminists: Examining the Rural/Urban Divide and the Value of Kinship*. Unpublished PhD thesis. University of Lancaster.

Young, Kalima. 2022. *Mediated Misogynoir: Erasing Black Women's and Girls' Innocence in the Public Imagination*. London: Lexington Books.

Zacharek, Stephanie, Eliana Dockterman and Haley Sweetland Edwards. 2017. The silence breakers. *Time*, December.

CHAPTER 5

Men in the #MeToo Era

Introduction

Whilst #MeToo and Me Too have centred (predominately female) victim/survivors, what the discourse and movement mean *for men* has been a recurring concern in mainstream commentary. As Sarah Banet-Weiser and Kathryn Claire Higgins (2023: 121) note, there has been a perception that in the #MeToo moment "the believability of men is in particular crisis". However, access to believability has *always* been experienced differently by men who occupy different positions in social hierarchies—as it has for women. What is perhaps distinctive about the current moment is the extent to which men who had previously enjoyed both power and believability have had to answer for their behaviour. This, too, has been uneven—as we saw in the last chapter. This chapter more centrally investigates the position of men in the #MeToo era, focusing on three contexts: men as victim/survivors of sexual abuse (including of female perpetrators); alleged male perpetrators as victims of (feminist) women's speech; and, finally considering the acknowledged, or credible, male perpetrator as monstrous other. Running across all three sections is a concern with how violence and victimisation are deployed to police the boundaries of hegemonic masculinity in ways which suggest its adaptability in moments of "crisis".

Whilst feminist critics have been interested in the *connections* between "aberrant" and "normal" male behaviour and so in thinking of how abuse can be understood on a continuum of behaviour (Kelly 1988), this analysis is pitted against a cultural context which depends on different forms of distinction in order to understand male violence as *individual* aberrance. In non-celebrity contexts, the discursive construction of the exceptionalism of male perpetrators—particularly male perpetrators of serial sexual violence and murder (Cameron and Frazer 1987)—can be a means both of celebrification of abusive men *and* of distancing the "aberrant" from the "normal". But how does this work in contexts where the men are *already* marked (and valued) as exceptional in relation to their celebrity or political status? And (how) can a feminist understanding of the gendered nature of violence help us understand female perpetrators and male victimisation? These are some of the questions I explore in this chapter.

Men in #MeToo as Victim/Survivors

It should not be controversial to note that men are also victim/survivors of sexual assault. Whilst studies routinely show the majority of rape and sexual assault victims are women, nevertheless there is a sizable minority of male victims (Weiss 2010). The most recent US National Intimate Partner and Sexual Violence Survey, for instance, found that in 2016–2017 one in four women (26.8%) and one in 26 men (3.8%) reported completed or attempted rape victimisation at some point in their lifetime (Basile et al. 2022: 3). When lifetime experiences of other forms of sexual assault were considered, the gaps were narrower: one in four women and one in nine men reported sexual coercion (4); one in two women, and one in four men experienced unwanted sexual contact (5); and one in three women and one in nine men reported being sexually harassed in a public place (5). The survey also looked at men's experiences of being made to penetrate someone,[1] finding one in nine men had experienced this form of abuse (3). The 2022 Crime Survey for England and Wales found that 7.7% women and 0.2% men had experienced rape (Office for National Statistics 2023). Clearly there are very sizable populations of men who have experienced some form of sexual victimisation.

---

[1] Being forced to penetrate someone is not, typically, defined as rape, at least in law. For a discussion of the implications of this for an understanding of gender, sexuality and violence see McKeever (2019).

Focusing now on perpetration, the US National Intimate Partner and Sexual Violence Survey found that a significant majority of reported rapes involved male perpetrators, for both female (94.0%) and male (76.8%) victims (Basile et al. 2022: 10). However, 71.7% of male victims of sexual coercion and 47.5% of male victims of unwanted sexual contact identified female-only perpetrators (10–11). Thus whilst a majority of all sexual assaults are committed by men, there is also clear evidence of female perpetration.

When it comes to media representation, the picture is contradictory. There is limited evidence that male victims may be *over*-represented in newspaper reporting compared to national statistics (DiBennardo 2018) and that the press is more likely to portray male victims sympathetically, compared to their treatment of female victims (Jamel 2014). However, this is not true for *all* men. In a study of representations of sexual predators in the *Los Angeles Times*, Rebecca A. DiBennardo (2018: n.p.) writes "[t]o the extent that adult male victims fail to live up to masculine, heterosexual ideals, their victim status is devalued similarly to that of adult women". Thus, gay men, for instance, are more likely to be subject to victim-blaming discourses (Davies and Rogers 2006: 371–372). The relationship between victim and perpetrator also shapes representation and reception in gendered ways so that, for instance, female teachers sexually abusing male students can be presented as desirable and unproblematic (Bradbury and Martellozzo 2019). Looking beyond news to entertainment forms, male rape is too often treated as a throwaway comment or a punchline (Nagy 2023). Clearly, male sexual victimisation is culturally challenging to get to grips with.

How has this played out in the #MeToo era? In the early days of October 2017, when the Weinstein story dominated the news agenda, actor and former NFL star Terry Crews came forward with his experience of being groped by an initially unnamed male film executive (@terrycrews, 10 October 2017).[2] Crews shared his experience *before* Milano's #MeToo tweet, but he was subsequently embraced by/embraced the #MeToo discourse and, indeed, was one of the "silence breakers" featured in *Time*'s Person of the Year story (see Chapter 2). Importantly, Crews' testimony drew attention to the racialised dynamics of silence, noting that—as a "240lbs. Black Man"—he feared that in speaking out he would

---

[2] Crews later named his assailant as agent Adam Venit (Zacharek et al. 2017).

be recast as the perpetrator who "stomps out Hollywood Honcho". The extent to which both race and gender combine to encourage a "himpathetic" (Manne 2018a) response to perpetrators is something I explore in the next section. In contrast, Crews points to the fact that men occupying the victim/survivor position can face a "credibility conundrum" (Jordan 2004). The forms of scrutiny may be different for male victim/survivors than their female counterparts, but their credibility is still established in relation to their ability to occupy gender norms (Weiss 2010; Javaid 2016). For a "240lbs Black Man"—and, specifically, a 240lbs Black former *sportsman*—to speak from the position of victim/survivor upsets gendered and racialised norms around male invulnerability, power and strength. This makes it difficult for Crews' story to be understood as evidence of the sexualised *vulnerability* of Black men in the US (Curry 2019: 293). Thus, whilst speaking out achieved some sense of collectivity for women under the hashtag (which was, after all, Milano's stated intent), the same was not true for other groups.

In this context, it is perhaps not accidental that the male victim/survivors who have achieved a degree of media prominence *as* victim/survivors in the #MeToo moment, have been men who are marginalised in relation to race and/or sexuality. Anthony Rapp, who spoke out about Kevin Spacey, for example, is an out gay man, as is Nimrod Reitman who pursued a claim against New York University academic Avital Ronell. As sexual assault is discursively constructed as feminising (Weiss 2010; DiBennardo 2018), men who are already outside of hegemonic constructions of masculinity (Connell and Messerschmidt 2005) are arguably more legible as victims.

The extent to which men are recognised in #MeToo is debatable. Milano's original tweet was explicitly addressed to an audience of women, though prominent men engaging with the hashtag describe how women's testimonies enabled their own (Bradley 2018). At the same time, related hashtags such as #HimToo and #MenToo have tried to make men's experiences explicitly visible. Whilst some of this work has genuinely been about male victim/survivors, the extent to which these gender-specific hashtags have been taken up by people *protesting* #MeToo is important to recognise. The logic here seems to be that if men also experience abuse this can't be about gender and feminists are not only misguided in their critiques but risk victimising men as a result. This makes speaking out more fraught for male victim/survivors who want to position themselves as feminist allies as the language for expressing their experience has been co-opted as part of the backlash *against* #MeToo and feminism more broadly (Burrell and Dhir 2024). This is what happened with #HimToo, a hashtag which had been used by male victim/survivors positioning themselves alongside #MeToo (O'Neil 2018) but went viral during the Senate Judiciary Committee Hearings for Brett Kavanaugh's Supreme Court nomination; and it happened in more complex ways in relation to Depp v. Heard. I explore both of these cases in more detail later.

What space does this leave for male victim/survivors who do *not* want to participate in the reassertion of hegemonic masculinity and power *over* women as a response to victimisation (Burrell and Dhir 2024)? Whilst both #HimToo and #JusticeForJohnnyDepp sought to undermine the feminist and gendered discourse around #MeToo, the feminist analysis that violence is gendered does *not* depend on female victimisation but rather on an understanding of how violence is enacted and understood in relation to gender in a patriarchal context (Kelly 1996a; Boyle 2005: 94–122). For instance, I have argued in relation to the Jimmy Savile case (Boyle 2018a) that his abuse of boys—as well as girls and adult women—was enabled by particular idea(l)s about masculinity which he was seen to embody and which thus rendered his abusive behaviour unproblematic in that it was not widely recognised *as abuse*. Similar arguments could be made in relation to emerging accounts of R. Kelly's abuse of boys. How violence functions societally is indivisible from gender. Because we live in a patriarchal society, power is linked to certain kinds of expressions of masculinity, but the intersectional qualities of power mean that it is also possible for some women to hold power over some men, for instance, through racial privilege, class, wealth, workplace status or age. And some women are sexually abusive (towards women as well as other men). These facts do not invalidate a feminist analysis. Indeed, a number of scholars working in this area point to the ways that male victims are let down by the *same* investment in male power and female victimisation that harms female victims (e.g. McKeever 2019; Nagy 2023; Burrell and Dhir 2024).

Yet, the relatively small number of high-profile stories featuring (alleged) female perpetrators in the #MeToo era have been widely interpreted as a potential challenge to the legitimacy of #MeToo, and/or of feminist analysis and activism (e.g. Greenberg 2018; O'Connell 2018). I am thinking in particular of the reports focused on Asia Argento, the actor/director and prominent Weinstein-accuser, and NYU professor Avital Ronell. Much of this coverage reveals a double standard whereby an allegation against a woman is automatically read as a gender issue—something that can and should tell us about gender relations—which is rarely true of reports involving a male perpetrator. Patrizia Romito makes this point when she notes how infrequently the term "male violence" is used, not only in the documents of governments and international organisations but also in feminist activism and scholarship. It is, she notes, "acceptable to talk about violence, but never about male violence" (2008: 5). On the other hand, women accused of violence are typically marked *as women* using phrases that rarely have a commonly-used male equivalent (Boyle 2005: 94–122). Whilst writing this passage, for instance, I searched for "male suicide bombers" on Google: the first result I was offered was the Wikipedia entry for "female suicide bombers". This is what Caroline Criado Perez (2019) identifies as the "default male" principle: the unmarked term is *assumed to be* male (whether it is killer, scientist or footballer), but this makes masculinity invisible as a category for analysis. In relation to victimisation, however, a "default female" principle is in operation: victimisation feminises, creating additional challenges for male victim/survivors (Weiss 2010). At the same time, the term "gender" is often taken as a synonym for "women" and in international policy contexts this means that "*gender-based* violence" and "violence *against women*" can be used interchangeably (Boyle 2019). The apparently gender-neutral term "gender" can thus disguise the gendered realities of who is most often doing what to whom (*men's* violence *against women*) whilst simultaneously creating dissonances for male victim/survivors of sexual violence who do not find themselves reflected in the language used.

None of this is to deny that women can also be sexually abusive against men as well as other women. Rather, it is to highlight that the *meaning* of that abuse is differently constructed (Kelly 1996a). As Jan Jordan puts it, "A major difference, however, stems from men, unlike women, not being targeted *as* a gender class, but *within* a gender class" (2022: 19). In the remainder of this section I want to briefly address the Ronell story as a means of untangling these issues.

In June 2018, philosopher Brian Leiter published, on his blog, a letter written in response to an NYU sexual harassment investigation into Professor Avital Ronell signed by a number of prominent academics. Whilst the letter as published by Leiter (still in draft form) acknowledged that the signatories did not have access to the confidential dossier about the case, it nevertheless went on to offer an extended intellectual character reference for Ronell, noting her considerable academic achievements and claiming her accuser had waged a "malicious campaign" against her. For the letter writers, Ronell's scholarship, academic achievements and awards were apparently the grounds for special consideration: an academic version of "auteur apologism" (Marghitu 2018).

What made this story remarkable is not only that Ronell is a woman, but that the letter was signed by a number of key figures in feminist and/or queer theory, most notably Judith Butler. Not surprisingly, these comments attracted widespread criticism, including from feminists, though others continued to defend Ronell and malign Reitman (Arnold 2018). Butler offered an explanation of the Ronell defence in another letter, published in the *Chronicle of Higher Education* (Butler 2018a), and in a later public statement stated they made a "serious error" in helping to draft the letter, acknowledging the power dynamics between faculty and graduate students which were the context for this case (Butler 2018b). Yet, as far as I am aware, Butler has not apologised publicly to Reitman although they speak compellingly of making reparations through future work with and for graduate students. Does that matter? To the extent that this leaves unaddressed the *specific* victim-blaming discourses mobilised in relation to Reitman I think it does.

Leiter's publication of the letter, and the mainstream media response it generated, provided further opportunity for critics of #MeToo to expand upon the already-existing narrative of suspicion around feminism which, as I argued in Chapter 2, was evident from the earliest days of reporting on the hashtag. In publishing the (draft) letter, Leiter commented: "Blaming the victim is apparently OK when the accused in a Title IX proceeding is a feminist literary theorist" (2018). This was then taken up in the press with the *New York Times* asking "What happens to #MeToo when a feminist is the accused?" (Greenberg 2018) and the *Mail Online* identifying Ronell as a "lesbian feminist scholar" (Brantley 2018). This definition of Ronell was, however, disputed by a colleague who described Ronell as having "made no serious contribution to feminist scholarship" (Chu 2018). This was not an evaluative judgement of Ronell's personal politics but rather a statement about the focus of her scholarship. Yet, this label stuck, making the Ronell story, and the Argento story which followed quickly after, stories *about* feminism—or, perhaps more accurately, about feminism's perceived excesses and hypocrisies.

The Ronell case, like the others discussed in this book, raises legitimate questions about who is deemed credible as a perpetrator, what perpetrators are understood to represent, and how institutions should respond to reports of abuse. Lisa Duggan (2018) suggests that Ronell was marked as a marginal figure within the academy *at least in some respects* (protected by tenure, but vulnerable as a queer, Jewish, female member of faculty), which made her a more suspicious, more easily sacrificed, figure from the point of view of university authorities. The university did not act to protect Ronell's career and reputation as universities have so routinely and problematically done in relation to similarly accused men (Takla 2018). It is not inconsistent with a feminist analysis to note this, nor does it mean that Ronell *should* have been similarly protected: rather it is to (again) call out the double standards which routinely protect men whilst making a gendered spectacle of women. However, we need to be able to make these arguments without at the same time casting doubt on Reitman's veracity (which Duggan does in unnecessary parenthetical comments about Reitman's husband, for instance). Reitman should be granted the same "presumption of innocence" within feminist discourse as other victim/survivors (Waterhouse-Watson 2012).

Of course, some accused men also make more credible perpetrators than others. I will return to these themes in the final section of this chapter when I explore the "othering" of the credible perpetrator, but this discussion of Ronell, alongside my analysis of the early days of the Weinstein coverage in Chapter 2, suggests that linking the perpetrator to feminism *can* be part of the evaluation of credibility. Feminism is presented as part of the problem, not the solution.

Indeed, the pattern I have observed, where the accusations against Ronell were used to ask questions about feminism per se, can also be found in the coverage of Jimmy Bennett's claim of sexual assault by Asia Argento (O'Connell 2018). Here there was an added complication as Argento was a key figure in the case against Weinstein. Thus, it was not simply Argento's gender and that of her accuser which was presented as a challenge to #MeToo, her prior claims of victimisation (and the broader #MeToo discourse in which they are embedded) were rendered suspect by this development. Inherent in these responses is an assumption that feminist approaches to sexual violence depend on "fixing" the identity of the (female) victim (Mardorossian 2002: 1999). The assumption is that *both* Argento's and Bennett's claims of victimisation cannot be true: if Bennett is telling the truth, then Argento is no longer a credible victim; if Argento is telling the truth about Weinstein, then Bennett must be lying about Argento. Feminism has a long history of engaging with the complexity of victim/survivors who become abusers, but this is completely elided in these responses.

The accusations against women discussed here echo previous scholarship which has identified a tendency in media reporting of women's violence to present violent women as the *cost* of feminism (Boyle 2005: 97). In this analysis, feminism, and feminists, hurt men as well as other women. However, this discourse performs a disservice to male victims, casting them outside of the collective of victim/survivors and harnessing their stories to reactionary ends which ultimately privilege male perpetrators (who are also those most likely to abuse men). The next section demonstrates how alleged perpetrators can also be transformed into victims of a feminism gone too far, focusing on the Brett Kavanaugh case. In this reworking of the continuum of sexual violence, it is men's injuries—whether as a result of experiencing sexual assault, or losing a job opportunity because of allegedly perpetrating assault—which are linked, thus positioning male perpetrators alongside male victim/survivors.

#HimToo and Himpathy

In September 2018, Donald Trump's nominee to the Supreme Court, Brett Kavanaugh, faced a report (which he vehemently denied) that he attempted to rape Dr Christine Blasey Ford when they were both in high school. After the report was made public (not by Blasey Ford), both Blasey Ford and Kavanaugh gave televised testimony before the Senate Judiciary Committee, the committee charged with investigating Kavanaugh's suitability to sit on the Supreme Court. Almost a year on from the *New York Times'* Weinstein story, the hearings (which ultimately resulted in Kavanaugh's confirmation) were widely represented as an outcome of, and perhaps an endpoint for, #MeToo. Not surprisingly, the case generated huge amounts of commentary, not only in legacy media internationally but also on social media, with users declaring support for Blasey Ford (e.g. #BelieveSurvivors, #IBelieveChristineBlaseyFord) or Kavanaugh (#HimToo, #BeersforKavanaugh/#BeersforBrett). In this section, I am particularly concerned with the expressions of support for Kavanaugh and the ways in which these depend on narratives of male victimisation in the face of feminist excess. There are, as I will demonstrate, echoes here of the 1991 confirmation hearings for Clarence Thomas when Anita Hill testified of her experiences of sexual harassment by Thomas, her boss, but there are also important differences which highlight the importance of race to our understanding of sexual harassment and assault.

At this point, it is worth re-iterating what was at stake in these hearings. Kavanaugh was *not* on trial. Blasey Ford's evidence was given to help determine whether the President's nominee was a suitable candidate for the Supreme Court. A man of immense privilege, Kavanaugh was nevertheless presented, and indeed presented himself (Kavanaugh 2018), as a victim. #HimToo provides interesting examples of this. Although #HimToo has a longer history (Ellis 2018), including as a way for men to share experiences of sexual victimisation in the context of #MeToo (O'Neil 2018), it is of interest to me for the way in which it constructs a narrative of male victimisation with Kavanaugh at its centre. The hashtag began trending—and caught the attention of myself and my colleague Chamil Rathnayake—in the days before Blasey Ford and Kavanaugh testified (Boyle and Rathnayake 2020). Of course #HimToo was not the only hashtag doing himpathetic work around the hearings. For example, following Kavanaugh's confirmation, the beers hashtags (#BeersForBrett, #BeersForKavanaugh) allowed users—male and female—to express their support for the new Justice by asserting their affinity with his much-mocked testimonial declarations that he "liked beer". This in itself illustrates a double standard around gendered behaviour. Blasey Ford stated that she had only had one beer on the night of the attack, something Trump openly and aggressively mocked her for (Malloy et al. 2018). Blasey Ford was in a no-win situation: as a victim of attempted rape the consumption of alcohol could have rendered her incredible (Romero-Sánchez et al. 2018: 1054); but—unlike Kavanaugh—she could not use ritual social drinking as a defence. Indeed, although Kavanaugh made a series of statements about his use of alcohol which were convincingly disputed (e.g. Ludington et al. 2018), the beers hashtags suggest that the truthfulness of his testimony mattered less in certain contexts than the sociality of his address. Notably, similar patterns of gendered identification around alcohol were mobilised by Johnny Depp and his supporters using #MegaPint. That Depp's excessive alcohol consumption could be mobilised as sociability and affinity *despite* his well-documented alcoholism is striking and speaks to differential constructions of believability, responsibility and vulnerability with which this book is centrally concerned. In relation to Kavanaugh, the beer-drinking college-boy turned family-man allowed the extremely privileged Republican nominee to become a stand-in for American masculinity rendered newly vulnerable by the fallout from #MeToo.

The Kavanaugh-supportive hashtags—as well as the performance of the President and some of Kavanaugh's supposed Republican interlocutors on the Senate Judiciary Committee—provide a stark example of what Kate Manne (2018a) calls "himpathy". In a commentary on the Kavanaugh case, Manne defines himpathy as, "the inappropriate and disproportionate sympathy powerful men often enjoy in cases of sexual assault, homicide and other misogynistic behaviour". She continues:

> the higher a man rises in the social hierarchy, the more himpathy he tends to attract. Thus, the bulk of our collective care, consideration, respect and nurturing attention is allotted to the most privileged in our society.
> (Manne 2018b)

The most privileged demand our attention not least because they are so routinely represented as points of identification that a himpathetic perspective is utterly normalised. At the same time, this means that the most privileged can be represented as the most vulnerable, the most prone to malicious victimisation, *precisely because they have the most to lose*. This is what Deborah Tuerkheimer (2021) calls the "credibility boost". An important element of this is that men like Kavanaugh are able to present accusations as threatening not only *their own* reputation but those they are deemed to represent. Kavanaugh, for instance, repeatedly asserted that an attack on him was an attack on his *good name*, a name shared with his parents, wife and daughters (e.g. Kavanaugh 2018). Blasey Ford's accusations were not only an attack on (Brett) Kavanaugh but an attack on *the* Kavanaughs as exemplars of the white, upper-middle class, heterosexual family unit (Banet-Weiser 2021). This allowed Blasey Ford's testimony to be re-constructed in conservative media as an attack *on women* (House 2023). Whilst, in Manne's formulation, the most privileged are the most entitled to himpathy, it is important to recognise that this applies equally within communities. That is, even if a community is marginalised, it is men within that community who are deemed its most valuable representatives (Richie 2012: 40–43), a theme I will return to in relation to the responses to R. Kelly's abusive career in the next chapter.

My work with Chamil Rathnayake on the #HimToo hashtag (Boyle and Rathnayake 2020) demonstrates that conservative women were at the centre of the #HimToo network up until Kavanaugh's nomination was confirmed. These women were often speaking *as mothers* and/or as fearful of the implications of accusation for "*our*" men (fathers, brothers, husbands and particularly sons). Notably, although support for Trump has been famously low among Black women (and highest among white women), the most prominent actor in our #HimToo sample from this period was a female African American political activist. It would be a mistake to generalise from the Twitter-dominance of this highly atypical figure, nevertheless this does suggest that party-affiliation was key to himpathetic judgements of Kavanaugh, something our data supports. In terms of the overall arguments of this book, this is arguably of a piece with discussions of value in Chapter 6 and in relation to Avital Ronell, above: victim/survivors' statements about their experiences of sexual assault are weighed against the cultural, social and political value of (alleged) perpetrators. The judgement is not *did it happen?* Rather, there is an earlier judgement about the relative importance of the alleged perpetrator and victim/survivor, and the potential damage *to the alleged perpetrator* of the claim that it did. My argument here aligns with Tuerkheimer's (2021) more extensive analysis of credibility. As Tuerkheimer points out, it is possible for a survivor's speech to be deemed credible—as Blasey Ford's was in many contexts—but to *still* be discounted, "in the realm of blame (*it wasn't his fault*) and care (*he matters too much to suffer consequences for his actions*)" (2021: 12). That he "matters too much" is important here, as it makes clear that the potential damage of an allegation is not only to the accused himself but to those to whom he matters, a theme I explore more fully in the next chapter.

In relation to #HimToo, himpathetic judgements were primarily based on affective and familial connections, as well as on ideas about character, standing and morality. As Manne (2018a) notes, the structure of sympathy places the (usually white, wealthy, heterosexual) man at its centre so that the starting point in this discourse is what sexual assault allegations mean for the men accused (Sela-Shayovitz 2015; Banet-Weiser 2021). Whilst Manne (not writing about Kavanaugh specifically), suggests that in cases of violence himpathy works by "effectively making him into the victim of his own crimes" (2018a: 210), I would argue that, certainly in the #MeToo era, himpathetic responses suggest not that it is the crimes which victimise the (alleged) perpetrator, but rather the feminists and victim/survivors who name them *as* crimes. This is about "good" (and *known*) men, versus typically generic and anonymous (and, hence, suspicious) women, or unjust institutions dominated by "liberals" and dedicated to the demise of the American family (House 2023).

In our work on #HimToo,[3] Rathnayake and I have also identified that supporters sought to assert Kavanaugh's vulnerability by allying him with African American males and I want to expand on this potentially counter-intuitive point here. The obvious link is with Justice Clarence Thomas, now one of Kavanaugh's immediate colleagues on the Supreme Court, who also faced sexual harassment allegations during his confirmation hearings in 1991. Thomas is an African American whose nomination was largely opposed by African Americans *prior* to Anita Hill's testimony given his consistent self-presentation as a "colour-blind" candidate and his failure to advocate for African Americans (Morrison 1992a). However, in the wake of Hill's sexual harassment testimony, Thomas's description of the hearings as a "high-tech lynching" generated support for Thomas on the (white, male) committee as well as among many African Americans. Of course, this also meant disbelieving an African American woman (Hill) who was subject to horrendous racialised and sexualised caricature and abuse (Hill 1997). As many of the contributors to Toni Morrison's 1992 collection on the Hill/Thomas hearings argue, Black women's victimisation is so routinely ignored that when Thomas drew on a recognisable history of white violence against Black men he was able to recast himself as the victim and Hill was no longer legible *as* Black (Morrison 1992a). Rather Hill was recast as a representative of feminists "hopelessly out of touch with the real women of America" (Ross 1992: 44), a phrase that finds powerful echoes in many #HimToo responses as well as in responses to the #MuteRKelly campaign and the documentary series *Surviving R. Kelly* (Lifetime, 2019–2023), discussed in Chapters 4 and 6.

It is important to note the very different ways in which Blasey Ford and Hill were treated during their respective testimonies and in their widespread coverage. As my discussion of #HimToo suggests—and as the threats to Blasey Ford which continued for months after her testimony starkly demonstrate (Ryan 2018)—Blasey Ford was, like Hill, called a liar and explicitly re-victimised through the process of speaking out. However, it is notable that the Senate Judiciary Committee on the whole took a very different approach to Blasey Ford and refrained from direct attacks during her testimony. Blasey Ford was widely deemed credible,

---

[3] Our #HimToo dataset comprises over quarter of a million tweets, collected between September 25 and October 12 2019: see Boyle and Rathnayake (2020) for more detail.

if mistaken. Kavanaugh's own testimony did not consistently denigrate Blasey Ford and, indeed, suggested the need to extend compassion to a woman so confused as to make this accusation. In contrast, Hill's credibility was consistently in doubt: she was "out of place" in the hearings, too sexual, too aggressive, too composed, too explicit and factual in her testimony, not emotional enough. Most importantly, as a Black woman—and a conservative, educated Black woman at that—she was not *legible* in existing narratives (Crenshaw 1992). As Nell Irvin Painter argues, Hill "chose not to make herself into a symbol Americans could recognise, and as a result she seemed to disappear, a feat reserved for black women who are educated and thus doubly hard to see" (Painter 1992: 210). One effect of the Kavanaugh hearings has been that Hill's appalling treatment in front of the committee has received renewed attention, though there are justifiable concerns that the lessons of Hill's experience have still not been learned (Crenshaw 2018).

Re-reading Morrison's collection on the 1991 hearings in the wake of Kavanaugh, I was struck by her introductory claim that "an accusation of such weight as sexual misconduct would probably have disqualified a white candidate on its face". Whilst this clearly no longer holds, Morrison's argument about why these charges would have been disqualifying for a white man in 1991 are worth returning to as I try to make sense of the kinship of vulnerability between Kavanaugh and Thomas which emerged in the #HimToo data. Morrison argues:

> in a racialized and race-conscious society, standards are changed, facts marginalized, repressed, and the willingness to air such charges, actually to debate them, outweighed the seemliness of a substantive hearing because the actors were black.
> (Morrison 1992b: xvii)

Racialised and sexualised notions of Black bodies made Thomas and Hill legitimate objects of spectacle and investigation. Morrison does not ignore that white men in power have routinely committed these kinds of assaults (clearly they have). Rather she draws our attention to the way that white men's violence is invisible as such. White men could not bear the weight of this kind of investigation because, as the normative subjects of narrative, to render them object would be to compromise their power in an untenable way. The twists and turns of logic this demands are vividly demonstrated in some of the online responses to the video of Johnny

Depp's drunken, violent rage filmed by Amber Heard. In rendering him object of her camera, *she* was rendered suspect, her documentation of abuse re-constructed as a failure to care for her vulnerable, alcoholic, yet exceptional husband.

However, the Depp v. Heard case is more complicated than the Kavanaugh or Thomas cases as the victimisation reported by Depp was not solely discursive/reputational and it is worth pausing to discuss it here in relation to Morrison's statement. Obviously, Depp was not running for office but he was the one who initiated the proceedings which would result in the scrutiny of his behaviour in both UK and US courts. The potential burden of objectification which Morrison discusses was a calculated risk for Depp and it was one he was able to take partly because he was able to rely on the mass mobilisation of popular misogyny. This allowed Depp and his supporters to use claims of his physical victimisation to discursively position him as an advocate for all men against the excesses of #MeToo (Banet-Weiser and Higgins 2023, 127). Notably, though Depp reported domestic abuse, there was little attempt made by Depp or his supporters to connect with men who had experienced domestic abuse, or with male domestic abuse support and advocacy services—this would arguably be too great a compromise to his status as normative *subject*. Instead, these reports were incorporated into his star persona as evidence of his exceptionalism and *agency* in speaking out against the cultural zeitgeist.

Emma Flynn, Melody House, Chamil Rathnayake and I have explored how Heard's reports of Depp's abusive behaviour—and, indeed, the video, photographic and text-based evidence supporting her accounts—have been reworked by Depp's supporters to boost *his* credibility (Boyle, Flynn, House and Rathnayake 2024). This, in itself, is a recognised tactic of perpetrators, first described as DARVO (deny, attack, reverse victim and offender) by Jennifer J. Freyd (1997). Freyd, along with Sarah J. Harsey, has written about the way the courts can be mobilised as part of DARVO strategies, including in the Depp v. Heard case (Harsey and Freyd 2022). In my work with Flynn, House and Rathnayake, we focus on online discourses a year on from the verdict in the US defamation case, and document how Depp's own well-documented problems with drugs and alcohol are mobilised by fans to disavow his personal responsibility (even if it did happen he can't be held responsible) and to assert his vulnerability and the importance of fans' own reparative actions of care. The logic here appears to be that given Depp is, and long has been, explicit about who he is, if he did assault Heard it is evidence of *her* failure to protect and care for him: his abuse of her is evidence of *his* vulnerability (linked to his exceptionalism), and so of the credibility of his claims against her. Perplexingly, this allows fans to construct Depp's volatile behaviour as evidence of his consistency and loyalty: he is *the same* Johnny Depp and they (unlike Heard) remain loyal to him. This has also allowed Depp's case to be widely taken up within culturally-regressive men's rights groups on and offline in often explicitly abusive ways, targeting Heard, her legal team and supporters (Robinson and Yoshida 2023).

To return to the Hill/Thomas hearings, from Morrison's collection it is clear that whilst Thomas was able to call on a history of the literal lynching of African American males to defend himself against Hill's testimony, this was only credible to his white, male interlocuters precisely because—as a conservative with a long history of opposing civil rights measures—he was *not* perceived to embody "blackness" up until this point (Morrison 1992a). Supporting Thomas was thus a *posture* of anti-racism which did not require actual anti-racist work and this is arguably central to Thomas's appeal to Kavanaugh and his supporters. These discursive manoeuvres find a parallel in the assertions that to support Depp was to support victim/survivors of domestic abuse. Both in the Supreme Court hearings and in online fan culture these gestures demonstrate the distortion of progressive political discourse to support the status quo and, importantly, reduce the *work* of social justice to the affirmation of privileged men rendered newly vulnerable. Thomas establishes a powerful precedent: for the Senate Judiciary Committee to then treat Kavanaugh "differently" could open up a charge of racism, that he was not treated as fairly as his Black predecessor. Here it is white women who are the imagined perpetrators, allowing white men's role in lynching to be rewritten to create an affinity between men of different racial groups on the basis of (white) women's allegations. (That this depended, and still depends, on a denial of Anita Hill's racial identity is a recurring theme in Morrison's collection.) This also underscores the sense that in the #MeToo era no man—not even a white, God-fearing, family-loving one—is safe from feminist excess.

In the #HimToo data, it is also African American men who are mobilised as warnings of feminism gone too far. Thus, Kavanaugh and the nascent #HimToo "movement" are not only linked to Thomas but also with: Brian Banks, a footballer wrongly convicted of rape; Herman Cain, whose campaign for the 2012 Republican Presidential nomination was derailed by reports of sexual harassment; and, staggeringly, Emmett Till, the 14-year old boy brutally murdered in Mississippi in 1955 for allegedly offending a white woman. These moves establish continuities between the accused perpetrator and actual Black male victims of physical and sexual violence. This only makes sense if you accept that Emmett Till's loss of life is on the same plane as Clarence Thomas or Brett Kavanaugh's potential loss of a lucrative job opportunity. But in a himpathetic world view this *does* make sense because the question we are invited to ask is *what does it mean for him*? Kavanaugh's (and, to an extent, Thomas's) privilege is such that his greatest fear is the loss of his name and reputation (his physical safety is not at risk, nor is his material advantage). As such, this is what a himpathetic response asks us to care most about. And his loss can be presented as *our* loss, because of his cultural, or in this case social and political, value—a theme I explore in more detail in the next chapter.

Of course, the Kavanaugh hearings also generated much explicitly feminist commentary both on social and legacy media. But in crucial ways, the himpathetic response won out: Kavanaugh was, after all, confirmed to the Supreme Court, a lifetime position which gives him power over important decisions, not least those affecting the rights of marginalised Americans. At the same time, again paralleling events in 1991/1992, Kavanaugh's confirmation was also a precipitating factor—along with Trump's election and #MeToo—in the election of record numbers of women in the 2018 midterms. As I have argued throughout this book, this remains a profoundly contradictory time for feminist politics, activism and visibility, and Kavanaugh is a cautionary reminder of the resilience of white male power, even as critical responses to the hearings and his confirmation demonstrate the continued resurgence of resistance.

If Kavanaugh, along with other white men including Depp and Brock Turner (who I discussed in Chapter 4), was an incredible perpetrator who could credibly, if temporarily, adopt a victim position to re-assert his entitlement to himpathetic treatment, what is it that allows others—like Weinstein or Savile—to be (finally) seen as credible perpetrators, largely undeserving of himpathy? It is to this question that I turn my attention in the final section.

Credible Perpetrators

The celebrity men whose reputations have been most spectacularly and overwhelmingly negatively impacted by sexual abuse allegations—both in terms of criminal justice and popular opinion—are rarely men like Kavanaugh who are at the height of their fame and power. When the Jimmy Savile story finally gained traction Savile was already dead and, in the UK, celebrity figures who have been jailed for sexual abuse *and* widely demonised as a result—Gary Glitter, Rolf Harris, Stuart Hall, Max Clifford—have rarely been in their prime. More recently, it is notable that the reports about Russell Brand finally achieved mainstream visibility at a point when the actor/comedian had positioned himself outside of the mainstream, a move that could itself be read as an insurance policy to protect his career against the possibility of these allegations which had bubbled below the surface of mainstream commentary for some time. Indeed, Brand's (2023) pre-emptive response to the *Dispatches/Sunday Times* investigation was to present the reports as a mainstream conspiracy. Without buying into the conspiracy narrative, it is certainly legitimate to note that *ongoing* profitability and power undoubtedly continues to protect some abusers, in the media as in other spheres.

Indeed, these cases provide striking contrasts with others against still successful sportsmen—Benjamin Mendy, Mason Greenwood, Ched Evans, Adam Johnson, Cristiano Ronaldo and the Belfast rugby players at the centre of the 2018 rape trial, to name just a few—who tend to receive more himpathetic coverage with concerns routinely raised about *their* potential or import to club or country (Garraio et al. 2024; Waterhouse-Watson 2013). As I finalise the updates to this chapter in March 2024, the conviction of Brazilian and Barcelona footballer Dani Alves for sexual assault serves as a reminder that himpathy does not always insulate successful men against the consequences of their actions, but there are still some conditions in which it is more likely to be successfully mobilised than others. For instance, the older a perpetrator is, the less wasted potential seems to be at stake in media coverage (unless, perhaps, he is nominated to the Supreme Court or running for President). However, I want to argue that this is not just about potential, but rather the extent to which the perpetrator can be convincingly re-constructed as an outsider. A himpathetic engagement depends on a certain *fit* between the reputation or potential of the individual and the priorities and values of the institution, community or even nation.

Of course the *scale* of the alleged abuse, the number of victim/survivors coming forward, and the quality of the investigative journalism are all important in understanding why the reports of sexual abuse finally "stuck" to Weinstein in public opinion in 2017. Yet, as established elsewhere in this book, multiple rumours surrounded Weinstein for years to no significant effect, so this isn't the whole story. Weinstein's own declining position of power, artistic and financial, within the film industry was also an important context for the eventual credibility of his accusers. By the time of Kantor and Twohey's story, Weinstein's declining significance had been documented for some time and he was no longer able to control media coverage in the way he had done during his heyday (Auletta 2022; Perren 2012).

However, it is also notable that Weinstein was always constructed, and indeed often sought to construct himself, as a partial outsider to the industry that made him, and that he made. Weinstein's self-construction as an outsider could, at times, be a way of insisting on his exceptionalism. For instance, in a lengthy 2002 profile in the *New Yorker*, Weinstein claimed outsider status as a means of asserting his cinephilic tastes and knowledge in an industry where commerce rules (Auletta 2002). In an interview with CNN early in 2017, his self-identification as an underdog was equally integral to his construction of discerning taste, creating affinities with the leading characters of some of his most successful films of recent years: *The King's Speech* (dir. Tom Hooper 2010), *The Imitation Game* (dir. Morten Tyldum 2014) and *Lion* (dir. Garth Davis 2016).[4] As with Kavanaugh or Thomas, his strategic self-identification with victimised and/or marginalised characters is a means of disavowing or re-interpreting his own problematic behaviour. In both these pieces, Weinstein-the-cineaste and Weinstein-the-underdog are placed alongside Weinstein-the-bully, but this allows his bullying behaviour to be rewritten as evidence of passion *on behalf of the marginalised* (whether that is marginalised characters, or artists whose vision is subordinated to commerce). Of course, this is a very expansive understanding of marginalisation, where even the British King can heroically overcome the odds.

At the same time, this chimes with the story that is told of Weinstein's own history, a version of the American dream whereby a Jewish boy can

[4] Weinstein CNN interview: https://www.youtube.com/watch?v=yVUMeLsvzjw. Accessed 6 June 2019.

"climb out of the Queens shtetl where he grew up" (Biskind 2004: 54), learn to love foreign and independent film (*ibid*. 61), and hence make his fortune. Weinstein's Jewish identity is repeatedly—though often implicitly—marked in discussions of his critical and commercial success prior to October 2017. Renov and Brook (2017: ix) note that the term "mogul", frequently used in relation to Harvey Weinstein, is of antisemitic origin. In a discussion of the studio-bosses of classical Hollywood, Brook expands on this point:

> The term mogul itself, derived from the word "Mongol" and coined specifically for the immigrant studio bosses, referred pejoratively to their "alleged Asiatic [read: alien] provenance and appearance, perceived boorish [read: uncivilised] behaviour, and admittedly aggressive [read: unscrupulous] business practices."
> (Brook 2017: 5)

The use of "mogul" in relation to Weinstein—and, indeed, his own apparent embrace of the term—thus speaks in complex ways to the history of Jewish men in Hollywood, all at once suggesting his outsider status and control, his uncivilised and unscrupulous behaviour and his success. Nor is it just in this terminology that Weinstein's Jewishness is discursively foregrounded—reports of his use of Israeli secret service agents to deceive and intimidate potential witnesses are also relevant here (Farrow 2019). There is much more thinking to be done about how Weinstein's Jewishness is central to the ease with which he is othered, not least because it speaks to this long and complex history and the ways in which the "moguls" have come to represent power, control, success but also amorality, depravity and excess (Brook 2017).

Weinstein's outsider status is also repeatedly *aesthetically* marked in ways that align with what Ashley Joel Mack and Bryan J. McCann (2021: 109) describe as "ocular registers of anti-Semitism". For instance, the *New Yorker* story mentioned above is entitled "Beauty and the beast" and makes repeated reference to Weinstein's physical bulk, all "two hundred and fifty pounds", of it (Auletta 2002). He is "a fearsome sight—his eyes dark and glowering, his fleshy face unshaved, his belly jutting forward half a foot or so ahead of his body". His size is rendered cartoonish as we are told that in his recently-remodelled office "everything in it seems too small for the large man who occupies it". But physical bulk is not the only way in which Weinstein is marked as excessive: his temper as well as his body is seen to exceed boundaries, to "burst" out. Weinstein's aesthetic "otherness" in the groomed world of Hollywood made him easier to mark as monstrous when the *New York Times* story broke,[5] though this also has implications for victim/survivors: the implicit (and sometimes explicit) question is how could they *not* know just by *looking* at him? Whilst victim/survivors of those easily marked as "other" can find their credibility tested by the monster myth, Mack and McCann (2021: 104) suggest that for those assaulted by "normal" men, "the myth of the monstrous rapist can function to gaslight victims into believing that their experiences of rape were not 'monstrous enough'". In short, monsterisation does not work in the interests of victim/survivors (Herman 2023: 186) and, by encouraging the drawing of a clear and definitive line between the "good" and "bad" men, it leaves hegemonic constructions of masculinity largely untroubled.

As I have argued elsewhere (Boyle 2021: 193), Weinstein's 2020 trial also showed how aesthetic otherness can be mobilised as a victim-blaming strategy. The prosecution's case provided plenty of evidence of aesthetic otherness in witness descriptions of his blackhead-marked back, apparently "deformed" genitals, the quality and consistency of his semen and his body odour. This also played into well-established discourses about monstrosity which Weinstein and his defence team sought to exploit, arguing that Weinstein's physical appearance rendered him relatively powerless with beautiful women. Indeed, in a podcast interview for the *Guardian*, Zoë Brock describes this as part of Weinstein's abusive modus operandi (Asthana 2020). Echoing my description of DARVO above, Brock recalls Weinstein breaking down after he tried to assault her, claiming that she didn't like him because he was fat and recasting the scenario as one in which *she* caused harm for fat-shaming him and contesting his sexual entitlement. There are parallels here with the rhetoric of incels whose frustrated sense of entitlement to women's sexual attention plays out violently on and offline (Ging 2019; Manne 2018a). That this was deemed a viable defence strategy was evidenced not only in court but in interviews Donna Rotunno gave before and during the trial where she tried to recast her client as the victim, bringing together his age, acquired disability, fatness and appearance as evidence of his vulnerability. In an article for *Newsweek*, for instance, she describes Weinstein as

---

[5] See Mack and McCann (2021) for examples of Weinstein's labelling as "monster" in the aftermath of the *New York Times* report.

"a 67-year old man" who "can't undergo surgery without ridicule", "is attacked for his appearance and accused of faking his ailments" and "chastised in public and derided during meals" (Rotunno 2019). This "poor monster" version of himpathy did not win out (at least in the original trial), nevertheless the monster narrative persists in ways which limits our understanding of male violence (Boyle 2021: 193).

There are clear parallels between Harvey Weinstein and, in a UK context, Jimmy Savile. Although very much a figure of the establishment in terms of access and influence, Savile's heavy regional accent, working-class background and outlandish dress marked him as "other" in a BBC of received pronunciation and Oxbridge graduates. Savile cultivated a deliberately outlandish persona and, as he aged, his youthful but out-of-date costuming (tracksuits, string vests, medallion), flyaway hair and poor dentistry all made him a markedly odd and physically unattractive figure (Boyle 2018b). When the sexual assault claims against him finally stuck, he was fairly easily re-constructed as the monstrous "other", the paedophile (Kitzinger 1999; Kelly 1996b). As with Weinstein, this re-construction allowed Savile to be held at a distance, even (or especially) as questions of institutional complicity in enabling his decades of abuse were explored. As I have argued elsewhere, this also meant that the *gendered* lessons which might have been learned were largely effaced (Boyle 2018a). Savile represented no one other than himself and, like Weinstein, became a yardstick against which subsequent stories of celebrity abuse could be measured. This is beautifully captured in the Channel 4 drama *National Treasure* (2016) where the accused comedian, Paul Finchley (played by Robbie Coltrane) exclaims in horror: "They think I'm fucking Jimmy Savile". The fact that he is patently *not* Jimmy Savile (he wears suits, is married, has a daughter, lives in luxury, is "respectable") is mobilised in his defence.

These celebrity examples speak to a broader context where other men's crimes are deployed by abusive men as a kind of mitigation: they are not "as bad as" men who have committed more extreme crimes. For instance, in his work with abusive men, Jeff Hearn (1998) notes how their repeated use of the word "just" works to establish an exculpating hierarchy of seriousness. When a hierarchy, rather than a continuum, is in operation, men's violence can be more easily normalised and excused. Monsters work to (re)define the norm: instead of seeing different kinds of male violence as connected, the figure of the monstrous other allows "normal" male behaviour to go unremarked. In this sense, Weinstein and

Savile are convenient figures as they are so easily marked as "other". That this is possible even for men who have enjoyed such power, privilege and prestige *within* the establishment, highlights how much more precarious the position is for men without that power. As feminist scholars have consistently noted, allegations of sexual violence—whether in criminal justice or media contexts—are much more likely to "stick" to men who do not conform to hegemonic notions of masculinity (Boyle 2005: 68–73).

Writing in the aftermath of the Delhi rape and murder of Jyoti Singh Pandey, Benedict (2013, n.p.) additionally notes that "*why* the men do it" is only considered when the rapes take place in "other" cultures: "as soon as we look at rape among our own, whether civilian or military, this perspective is entirely neglected. Instead, we ask questions about the victim" (also Durham 2015). However, in the context of my discussion here, I would place the emphasis differently and, following Romito (2008), note that "why the *men* do it" is the more challenging question, demanding an understanding of the role of gender inequality and hegemonic masculinity in perpetuating male violence against women. If men accused of rape or other forms of sexual violence are from minority communities or "other" cultures they are much more likely to be portrayed as representatives of those communities than as *men*. For instance, writing in a US context, Mack and McCann (2021) argue that the line between "good" and "bad" *Black* men is not policed by the monster because Black masculinity is always already constructed as inherently monstrous. In contrast, when white men are the perpetrators, the work of "othering" which I have discussed in this section functions to keep them at a distance from categories of race and gender whilst focusing on questions of individual deviance. A number of studies have demonstrated this process by comparing the coverage of similar cases involving different categories of perpetrators, for instance, so-called "honour" killings within minority ethnic communities compared to family murder/suicides perpetrated by white men in Canada (Shier and Shor 2016), or "sex grooming" cases in the UK involving Asian male perpetrators compared to earlier cases in the same city involving stories of ritual child abuse within white families (Salter and Dagistanli 2015).

This demonstrates a marked reluctance to understand men's violence against women structurally and consider what men (as a group) stand to gain from violence against women. Focusing on individual perpetrators or alleged perpetrators—as I have done in this chapter and, indeed, throughout the book—can exacerbate this problem, contributing to the construction of the perpetrator as a unique and exceptional case. However, by placing this discussion of Weinstein, Savile and others in a broader context informed by feminist scholarship on representations of male perpetrators, the individual monster begins to look like a decidedly generic figure. This mirrors the impact of the cumulation of stories around #MeToo: the attribution of responsibility to the individual monster starts looks increasingly incredible when there are so many of them, in so many different sectors, whose behaviour has been legitimated, supported or covered up. In relation to celebrity perpetrators—and, indeed, to perpetrators whose crimes render them celebrities, such as serial killers (Boyle and Reburn 2015)—this can provide a way of puncturing that narrative of exceptionalism whilst also reminding us of who and what is let off the hook in the stories we tell about himpathetic victim/perpetrators and monstrous others.

Conclusion

The feminist understanding of the gendered nature of violence remains profoundly threatening in a patriarchal context where the maleness of male violence is both taken for granted and invisible. In contrast, the mainstream portrayal of female violence is routinely about gender, thus creating implicit and explicit links between female violence and feminism. The examples explored in this chapter demonstrate the persistence of these patterns in the long #MeToo moment, whilst also highlighting some of the ways in which representations of male victimisation and perpetration are shaped by race, ethnicity and class, as well as by aesthetic considerations.

Weinstein may—at the time of writing at least—[6] be behind bars, his absence in public life largely celebrated, but not all of the men who have been identified as harassers, assailants and rapists in the long #MeToo moment have faced criminal, professional or personal sanctions for their actions. There are many reasons for this of course—statutes of limitations, poor investigations, their own power and influence and a lack of care for their victims among them—but what I have suggested here is that the

---

[6] In April 2024, the New York Court of Appeal overturned Weinstein's New York conviction and ordered a retrial. The verdict in his LA case—which carries a 16-year sentence—still stands as of 1 May 2024.

monsterising discourse may have provided a further layer of insulation. At the same time, it is important to remember that Kelly's continuum is *not* about consequences for perpetrators: seeing the connections between different men is *not* to assert that their actions are equivalent or that they require the same response. Indeed, the sheer scale of the mass disclosures under #MeToo would make such a reckoning all but impossible. Situating these disclosures within the contexts in which sexual harassment and assault take place allows us to think differently about the kind of change—organisational, social, cultural and attitudinal—needed to end men's violence. In the next chapter, I return to the media and cultural industries to explore how men's violence has historically been *valued* and to ask how dismantling those value systems might contribute to the kind of kaleidoscopic justice Clare McGlynn and Nicole Westmarland (2019) imagine for victim/survivors of sexual harassment and assault.

References

Arnold, Amanda. 2018. What's going on with Avital Ronell, the prominent theorist accused of harassment? *The Cut*. 21 August. https://www.thecut.com/2018/08/avital-ronell-professor-accused-of-harassment-what-to-know.html. Accessed 3 June 2019.

Asthana, Anusuka. 2020. Zoë Brock: My case against Harvey Weinstein. *Today in Focus* [Podcast]. 22 January. Available at: https://www.theguardian.com/news/audio/2020/jan/22/zoe-brock-my-case-against-harvey-weinstein-podcast. Accessed 2 March 2024.

Auletta, Ken. 2022. *Hollywood Ending: Harvey Weinstein and the Culture of Silence*. New York: Penguin.

Banet-Weiser, Sarah. 2021. 'Ruined' lives: Mediated white male victimhood. *European Journal of Cultural Studies* 24 (1): 60–80.

Banet-Weiser, Sarah, and Kathryn Claire Higgins. 2023. *Believability: Sexual Violence, Media and the Politics of Doubt*. Cambridge: Polity.

Basile, Kathleen .C., Sharon G. Smith, Marcie-jo Kresnow, Srijana Khatiwada and Ruth W. Leemis. 2022. *The National Intimate Partner and Sexual Violence Survey: 2016/2017 Report on Sexual Violence*. Atlanta, GA: National Center for Injury Prevention and Control, Centers for Disease Control and Prevention. https://www.cdc.gov/violenceprevention/pdf/nisvs/nisvsReportonSexualViolence.pdf. Accessed 17 February 2024.

Benedict, Helen. 2013. Covering rape responsibly. *WMC: Women Under Siege* (Blog). 1 February. http://www.womensmediacenter.com/women-under-siege/covering-rape-responsibly. Accessed 20 May 2019.

Biskind, Peter. 2004. *Down and Dirty Pictures: Miramax, Sundance, and the Rise of Independent Film*. New York: Simon & Schuster.
Boyle, Karen. 2005. *Media and Violence: Gendering the Debates*. London: Sage.
Boyle, Karen. 2018a. Hiding in plain sight: Gender, sexism and press coverage of the Jimmy Savile case. *Journalism Studies* 19 (11): 1562–1578.
Boyle, Karen. 2018b. Television and/as testimony in the Jimmy Savile case. *Critical Studies in Television* 13 (4): 387–404.
Boyle, Karen. 2019. What's in a name? Theorising the inter-relationships of gender and violence. *Feminist Theory* 20 (1): 19–68.
Boyle, Karen. 2021. Of moguls, monsters and men. In *Routledge Handbook of the Politics of the #MeToo Movement*, ed. Giti Chandra and Irma Erlingsdóttir, 186–198. London: Routledge.
Boyle, Karen and Chamil Rathnayake. 2020. #HimToo and the networking of misogyny in the age of #MeToo. *Feminist Media Studies* 20 (8): 1259–1277.
Boyle, Karen, Emma Flynn, Melody House and Chamil Rathnayake. 2024. #CannesYouNot?: oppositional and asymmetrical versions of believability in the Depp/Heard case. *European Journal of Cultural Studies*. Online first: https://doi.org/10.1177/13675494241262438.
Boyle, Karen and Jenny Reburn. 2015. Portrait of a serial killer: Intertextuality and gender in the portrait film. *Feminist Media Studies* 15 (2): 192–207.
Bradbury, Paula, and Elena Martellozzo. 2019. 'Lucky boy!'; public perceptions of child sexual offending committed by women. *Journal of Victimology and Victim Justice* 4 (2): 160–178.
Bradley, Linda. 2018. "I was terrified, and I was humiliated.": #MeToo's male accusers, one year later. *Vanity Fair*, 4 October.
Brand, Russell. 2023. So, this is happening. [Video] YouTube, 15 September. https://www.youtube.com/watch?v=ZGr_PVUHn2I. Accessed 15 January 2024.
Brantley, Kayla. 2018. Lesbian feminist scholar, 66, is SUSPENDED by NYU after sending racy texts and "inappropriately touching" her 34-year-old married gay former doctoral student. *MailOnline*, 14 August. https://www.dailymail.co.uk/news/article-6057541/World-renowned-female-NYU-professor-facing-MeToo-moment.html. Accessed 10 June 2019.
Brook, Vincent. 2017. Still an empire of their own: how Jews remain atop a reinvented Hollywood. In *From Shetl to Stardom: Jews and Hollywood. (An Annual Review of the Casden Institute for the Study of the Jewish Role in American Life: Volume 14.)* Eds. Michael Renov and Vincent Brook, 3–21. West Lafayette: Purdue University Press.
Burrell, Stephen R. and Alishya Dhir. 2024. The media and male victim-survivors of abuse. In *Routledge Companion to Gender, Media and Violence*, ed. Karen Boyle and Susan Berridge, 34–43. London: Routledge.

Butler, Judith. 2018a. Judith Butler explains letter in support of Avital Ronell. *Chronicle of Higher Education*, 20 August.
Butler, Judith. 2018b. My life, your life: equality and the philosophy of nonviolence (Part 2). Public lecture. University of Glasgow. 2 October.
Cameron, Deborah and Elizabeth Frazer. 1987. *The Lust to Kill: A Feminist Investigation of Sexual Murder*. Cambridge: Polity.
Chu, Andrea Long. 2018. I worked with Avital Ronell. I believe her accuser. *Chronicle of Higher Education*, 20 August.
Connell, R.W., and James W. Messerschmidt. 2005. Hegemonic masculinity: Rethinking the concept. *Gender and Society* 19 (6): 829–259.
Crenshaw, Kimberlé. 1992. Whose story is it anyway? Feminist and antiracist appropriations of Anita Hill. In *Race-ing Justice, En-gendering Power: Essays on Anita Hill, Clarence Thomas, and the Construction of Social Reality*, ed. Toni Morrison, 402–440. New York: Pantheon.
Crenshaw, Kimberlé. 2018. We still haven't learned from Anita Hill's testimony. *New York Times*, 27 September.
Criado Perez, Caroline. 2019. *Invisible Women: Exposing Data Bias in a World Designed for Men*. London: Chatto & Windus.
Curry, Tommy. 2019. Expendables for women: Terry Crews and the erasure of Black male victims of sexual assault and rape. *Women's Studies in Communication* 42 (3): 287–307.
Davies, Michelle and Paul Rogers. 2006. Perceptions of male victims in depicted sexual assaults: A review of the literature. *Aggression and Violent Behavior* 11: 367–377.
DiBennardo, Rebecca A. 2018. Ideal victims and monstrous offenders: how the news media represent sexual predators. *Socius Sociological Research for a Dynamic World*. 4: 1.
Duggan, Lisa. 2018. The full catastrophe. *Bully Bloggers* (Blog). 18 August. https://bullybloggers.wordpress.com/2018/08/18/the-full-catastrophe/. Accessed 3 June 2019.
Durham, Meenakshi Gigi. 2015. Scene of the crime: News discourse of rape in India and the geopolitics of sexual assault. *Feminist Media Studies* 15 (2): 175–191.
Ellis, Emma Grey. 2018. How #HimToo became the anti #MeToo of the Kavanaugh hearings. *Wired*, 27 September. https://www.wired.com/story/brett-kavanaugh-hearings-himtoo-metoo-christine-blasey-ford/. Accessed 27 November 2018.
Farrow, Ronan. 2019. *Catch and Kill: Lies, Spies and a Conspiracy to Protect Predators*. London: Fleet.
Freyd, Jennifer J. 1997. Violations of power, adaptive blindness and betrayal trauma theory. *Feminism and Psychology* 7 (1): 22–32.

Garraio. Júlia, Inês Amaral, Rita Basílio Simões and Sofia José Santos. 2024. Forward and backwards: sexual violence in Portuguese news media. In *Routledge Companion to Gender, Media and Violence*. Eds. Karen Boyle and Susan Berridge. 145–154. London and New York: Routledge.
Ging, Debbie. 2019. "Alphas, betas and incels": Theorizing the masculinities of the manosphere. *Men and Masculinities* 22 (4): 638–657.
Greenberg, Zoe. 2018. What happens to #MeToo when a feminist is the accused? *New York Times*, 13 August.
Harsey, Sarah and Jennifer J. Freyd. 2022. Defamation and DARVO. *Journal of Trauma and Dissociation* 23 (5): 481–489.
Hearn, Jeff. 1998. *The Violences of Men*. London: Sage.
Herman, Judith L. 2023. *Truth and Repair: How Trauma Survivors Envision Justice*. London: Basic.
Hill, Anita. 1997. *Speaking Truth to Power*. New York: First Anchor.
House, Melody. 2023. From "borking" to getting "Kavanaughed": Language, repetition, and the importance of a (male) name. *Feminist Media Studies* 23 (8): 4285–4301.
Jamel, Joanna. 2014. Do the print-based media provide a gender-biased representation of male rape victims. *Internet Journal of Criminology* https://docs.wixstatic.com/ugd/b93dd4_9378310f905442eaa439aba1032586a5.pdf. Accessed 3 June 2019.
Javaid, Aliraza. 2016. Feminism, masculinity and male rape: Bringing male rape "out of the closet." *Journal of Gender Studies* 25 (3): 283–293.
Jordan, Jan. 2004. *The Word of a Woman? Police, Rape and Belief*. Hampshire: Palgrave Macmillan.
Jordan, Jan. 2022. *Women, Rape and Justice: Unravelling the Rape Conundrum*. Abingdon: Routledge.
Kavanaugh, Brett. 2018. I am an independent, impartial judge. *Wall Street Journal*, 4 October.
Kelly, Liz. 1988. *Surviving Sexual Violence*. Cambridge: Polity.
Kelly, Liz. 1996a. When does the speaking profit us? Reflections on the challenges of developing feminist perspectives on abuse and violence by women. In *Women, Violence and Male Power*, ed. Marianne Hester, Liz Kelly, and Jill Radford, 34–49. Buckingham: Open University Press.
Kelly, Liz. 1996b. Weasel words: Paedophiles and the cycle of abuse. *Trouble and Strife* 33: 44–49.
Kitzinger, Jenny. 1999. The ultimate neighbour from hell? Stranger danger and the media representation of "paedophilia." In *Social Policy, the Media and Misrepresentation*, ed. Bob Franklin, 207–221. London: Routledge.
Leiter, Brian. 2018. Blaming the victim is apparently OK when the accused in a Title IX proceeding is a feminist literary theorist. *Leiter Reports: A Philosophy Blog*, 10 June. https://leiterreports.typepad.com/blog/2018/06/blaming-

the-victim-is-apparently-ok-when-the-accused-is-a-feminist-literary-theorist. html. Accessed 31 May 2019.

Ludington, Charles, Lynne Brookes and Elizabeth Swisher. 2018. We were Brett Kavanaugh's drinking buddies. We don't think he should be confirmed. No one should be able to lie their way onto the Supreme Court. *Washington Post* (Blogs), 5 October.

Mack, Ashley Noel and Bryan J. McCann. 2021. "Harvey Weinstein, monster": antiblackness and the myth of the monstrous rapist. *Communication and Critical/cultural Studies* 18 (2): 103–120.

Malloy, Allie, Kate Sullivan and Jeff Zeleny. 2018. Trump mocks Christine Blasey Ford's testimony, tells people to "think of your sons". *CNN.* 3 October. https://edition.cnn.com/2018/10/02/politics/trump-mocks-christine-blasey-ford-kavanaugh-supreme-court/index.html. Accessed 5 June 2019.

Manne, Kate. 2018a. *Down Girl: The Logic of Misogyny*. New York: Oxford University Press.

Manne, Kate. 2018b. Brett Kavanaugh and America's "himpathy" reckoning. *New York Times*, 26 September.

Mardorossian, Carine M. 2002. Towards a new feminist theory of rape. *Signs: Journal of Women in Culture and Society* 27 (3): 743–775.

Marghitu, Stefania. 2018. "It's just art": Auteur apologism in the post-Weinstein era. *Feminist Media Studies* 18 (3): 491–494.

McGlynn, Clare and Nicole Westmarland. 2019. Kaleidoscopic justice: Sexual violence and victim-survivors' perceptions of justice. *Social and Legal Studies* 28 (2): 179–201.

McKeever, Natasha. 2019. Can a woman rape a man and why does it matter? *Criminal Law and Philosophy* 13 (4): 599–619.

Morrison, Toni, ed. 1992a. *Race-ing Justice, En-gendering Power: Essays on Anita Hill, Clarence Thomas, and the Construction of Social Reality*. New York: Pantheon.

Morrison, Toni. 1992b. Introduction: Friday on the Potomac. In *Race-ing Justice, En-gendering Power: Essays on Anita Hill, Clarence Thomas, and the construction of social reality*, ed. Toni Morrison, vii–xxx. New York: Pantheon.

Nagy, Victoria M. 2023. *Male Rape Victimisation on Screen*. Bingley: Emerald Publishing.

O'Connell, Jennifer. 2018. #HimToo: What happens if the aggressor is a woman? *Irish Times*, 25 August.

Office for National Statistics. 2023. *Sexual Offences in England and Wales Overview*. https://www.ons.gov.uk/peoplepopulationandcommunity/crimeandjustice/bulletins/sexualoffencesinenglandandwalesoverview/march2022. Accessed 17 February 2024.

O'Neil, Luke. 2018. #HimToo: how an attempt to criticise #MeToo went delightfully wrong. *Guardian*, 9 October.
Painter, Nell Irvin. 1992. Hill, Thomas, and the use of racial stereotype. In *Race-ing Justice, En-gendering Power: Essays on Anita Hill, Clarence Thomas, and the Construction of Social Reality*, ed. Toni Morrison, 200–214. New York: Pantheon.
Perren, Alisa. 2012. *Indie Inc: Miramax and the Transformation of Hollywood in the 1990s*. Austin: University of Texas Press.
Renov, Michael and Vincent Brook. 2017. Editorial introduction. In *From Shetl to Stardom: Jews and Hollywood. (An Annual Review of the Casden Institute for the Study of the Jewish Role in American Life: Volume 14.)* Eds. Michael Renov and Vincent Brook, ix-xvi. West Lafayette: Purdue University Press.
Richie, Beth E. 2012. *Arrested Justice: Black Women, Violence, and America's Prison Nation*. New York: New York University Press.
Robinson, Jennifer and Keina Yoshida. 2023. *How Many More Women? The Silencing of Women by the Law and How to Stop It*. London: Endeavour.
Romero-Sánchez, Mónica., Barbara Krahé, Miguel Moya and Jesús L. Megías. 2018. Alcohol-related victim behaviour and rape myth acceptance as predictors of victim blame in sexual assault cases. *Violence against Women* 24 (9): 1052–1069.
Romito, Patrizia. 2008. *A Deafening Silence—Hidden Violence Against Women and Children*. Bristol: Policy.
Ross, Andrew. 1992. The private parts of justice. In *Race-ing Justice, En-gendering Power: Essays on Anita Hill, Clarence Thomas, and the Construction of Social Reality*, ed. Toni Morrison, 40–60. New York: Pantheon.
Rotunno, Donna. 2019. How the media is keeping Harvey Weinstein from getting the fair trial he deserves. *Newsweek*. 21 December. https://www.newsweek.com/harvey-weinstein-sexual-assault-fair-trial-media-bias-1478579. Accessed 2 March 2024.
Ryan, Lisa. 2018. Christine Blasey Ford is still being put through hell. *The Cut*. 8 November. https://www.thecut.com/2018/11/kavanaugh-accuserchristine-blasey-ford-harassment.html. Accessed 27 November 2018.
Salter, Michael and Selda Dagistanli. 2015. Cultures of abuse: "sex grooming", organised abuse and race in Rochdale, UK. *International Journal for Crime, Justice and Social Democracy* 4 (2): 50–64.
Sela-Shayovitz, Revital. 2015. "They are all good boys": The role of the Israeli media in the social construction of gang rape. *Feminist Media Studies* 15 (3): 411–428.
Shier, Allie and Eran Shor. 2016. "Shades of foreign evil": "honor killings" and "family murders" in the Canadian press. *Violence Against Women* 22 (10): 1163–1188.

Takla, Nefertiti. 2018. Reitman vs. Ronell: rethinking the role of gender and patriarchy in sexual harassment cases. *Bully Bloggers* (Blog). 7 September. https://bullybloggers.wordpress.com/2018/09/07/reitman-vs-ronell-rethinking-the-role-of-gender-and-patriarchy-in-sexual-harassment-cases/. Accessed 3 June 2019.

Tuerkheimer, Deborah. 2021. *Credible: Why We Doubt Accusers and Protect Abusers*. New York: Harper Collins.

Waterhouse-Watson, Deb. 2012. Framing the victim: Sexual assault and Australian footballers on television. *Australian Feminist Studies* 27 (71): 55–70.

Waterhouse-Watson, Deb. 2013. *Athletes, Sexual Assault, and "Trials by Media."* New York and London: Routledge.

Weiss, Karen G. 2010. Male sexual victimization: Examining men's experiences of rape and sexual assault. *Men and Masculinities* 12 (3): 275–298.

Zacharek, Stephanie, Eliana Dockterman and Haley Sweetland Edwards. 2017. The silence breakers. *Time*, December.

CHAPTER 6

The Cultural Value of Abuse

Introduction

This chapter shifts focus from acts of sexual violation, and the ways in which they are (not) understood, to consider the wider culture in which these acts became both possible and excused, if not actively enabled.

My arguments here intersect with existing feminist scholarship around rape culture (Buchwald et al. 1993). Feminists coined the term rape culture in the mid-1970s to refer to "the cultural practices that reproduce and justify the perpetration of violence" (Rentschler 2014: 67), consistent with the feminist emphasis on sexual violence as a structural rather than individual problem. Feminist work tackling rape culture has had unprecedented visibility in recent years (Phillips 2017: 2–3), thanks in no small part to digital feminist activism (Rentschler 2014; Sills et al. 2016; Mendes et al. 2019). This calling out of rape culture has encompassed on and offline protests against, for instance, the glamorisation or normalisation of rape in popular media texts, such as the Robin Thicke song "Blurred Lines" (Phillips 2017), the sexually abusive behaviour of public figures, most notoriously, Donald Trump (Maas et al. 2018) and judicial, community and media responses to rape from Steubenville (Rentschler 2014) to Delhi (Adur and Jha 2018) and South African university campuses (Mitchell 2023). As these examples suggest, rape culture encompasses both an analysis of representations which are rape supportive, *and* the ways in which actual rape and other forms of sexual

© The Author(s), under exclusive license to Springer Nature Switzerland AG 2024
K. Boyle, *#MeToo and Feminism*,
https://doi.org/10.1007/978-3-031-67314-6_6

violation are celebrated or trivialised culturally and socially. Thinking about rape culture therefore means thinking about the different inter-relationships of rape and culture, behaviour and representation, act and context.

These interrelationships are at the centre of Roxanne Gay's post-#MeToo collection of victim/survivor testimony: *Not That Bad: Dispatches from Rape Culture* (2018). By placing victim/survivor writings in the context of rape culture, Gay and her contributors are able to retain a central focus on the difficulty of thinking about experiences of rape and other forms of sexual assault outside of the cultural context in which they occur. That context is one which creates hierarchies of victimisation—encapsulated in the book's title *Not That Bad*—which encourage victim/survivors to minimise what happened to them, whilst supporting perpetrators by disguising their abuse as something else (sex, a compliment, great art). Similarly, this chapter is concerned not only with the behaviour of bystanders or institutional practices which enable men's abuses, but also with the ways in which the stories emerging from Hollywood since October 2017 are themselves indivisible from wider discussions about the role of the media in constructing and supporting rape culture. This is not only about production contexts (though I discuss these in the next section), but also about representational practices.

Feminists have long highlighted the ways in which representation can engender harm and produce discrimination (MacKinnon 1993) and the online context has created new possibilities for representational violence which has material consequences (McGlynn et al. 2017; Powell and Henry 2017). But placing threatening language on a continuum of sexual violence should not mean equating speech—or, for that matter, memes, jokes or songs—with actual rape. This is consistent with my argument about the importance of continuum thinking as a means of making connections, whilst noting the importance of clarity in relation to the *nature* of these connections and the necessity of distinction within this (see Chapter 3). As I've argued, this necessitates thinking about continuums in the plural. For instance, the abusive production practices of the media and cultural industries exposed in #MeToo testimonies are entirely appropriately positioned on a continuum of sexual violence. However, the end *products* of these industries—the song, book, theatre production, film—will not necessarily present audiences with representations of sexual violence and, even if they do, the representations will likely have a complex relationship with what happened in the production. On the other hand, products with apparently non-abusive production histories might still represent sexual violence in ways which support rape culture. To deploy another concept from Liz Kelly, the representational continuum might provide a *conducive context* (Kelly 2016) for additional, material acts of sexual violence: legitimating and supporting a culture of male sexual entitlement, dominance and coercive control (Boyle 2019). That the term rape culture can encompass these different continuums does not necessarily blunt its usefulness but it does mean that it is not always clear what we are talking about when we talk about rape culture.

Partly as a result of this confusion, in this chapter I want to refocus the discussion of context to instead think about the cultural *values* which are accorded to abuse in the media and cultural industries. There are, of course, many manifestations of this, and "auteur apologism" (Marghitu 2018) is perhaps the most widely commented upon. The logic of auteur apologism is that the value of the great art produced by the abuser outweighs the importance of the abuse. This is a discourse Weinstein himself championed when he organised a petition in support of director Roman Polanski who fled the US after his conviction for statutory rape in 1977, arguing:

> Roman Polanksi is a man who cares deeply about his art and its place in the world. What happened to him on his incredible path is filled with tragedy, and most men would have collapsed. Instead, he became a great artist and continues to make great films. (Weinstein 2009)

This narrative hinges on the figure of the tortured artist, a highly gendered figure, who is able to create great art from his suffering: the suffering of those he abused is eclipsed by the beauty of his art. Although Weinstein's defenders attempted to mobilise the films with which he is associated as evidence of his continuing cultural value (Sullivan 2019), this was largely unsuccessful. There are many reasons for this, including the scale of abuses with which he is now associated, as well as the lesser cultural value accorded to the role of the producer and distributor. However, this does not mean that competing notions of cultural value have not been at stake in Weinstein's case, as I will demonstrate. Thinking about cultural value opens up questions of complicity in contradictory ways for feminist analysis, simultaneously allowing us to understand the structural support for, and legitimation of, men's violence against women *and* potentially allowing abusive men to dodge responsibility and so avoid consequences for their actions. Thinking about the cultural value of abuse necessitates a different kind of reckoning with the consequences of victim/survivor speech that takes us beyond the realm of criminal justice to think about institutions and audiences.

In the next section, I use the oft-repeated claim that abusers have hidden "in plain sight" in the media and cultural industries as my starting point. I argue that the cultural normalisation of men's violence against women offers an alibi for abusive men, not least by rendering so many others complicit. Indeed one way of understanding the (partial) historical visibility of sexual violation is to acknowledge the cultural value of these stories in the contexts in which they circulate. This allows men's violence to remain hidden *as violence* despite—as we have heard so often since October 2017—a prevailing sense that this is also common knowledge. I then turn my attention to Harvey Weinstein and this allows me to develop an argument which links Weinstein's behaviour to film industry norms. Here I argue that there is (and long has been) a cultural value to sexual violation in the film industry which is exacerbated by the complex relationships between on-screen and off-screen norms. I explore the conditions in which stories of abuse can be understood as abuse and so damaging to prominent men, and those in which abuse can be folded back into existing narratives of masculine success. Through a discussion of Kevin Spacey's *Let Me Be Frank* video, I open up questions around audience investment in texts and personae which normalise abuse. This leads me, in the final section of this chapter, to a consideration of cancellation as a response to victim/survivor testimony about public figures, particularly those in the media and cultural industries. Who or what is being cancelled here, and whose interests are served by cancellations?

Hiding in Plain Sight

It has become something of a cliché of stories about celebrity abusers to note that they hid "in plain sight", that is, that they—and those around them—publicly acknowledged aspects of their abusive behaviour, providing the conducive context in which it could flourish. Before Weinstein, the most prominent celebrity example of this in the UK was (Sir) Jimmy Savile who was posthumously revealed to have been a serial sexual predator, targeting women and children over a period of nearly 50 years. In previous work, I have explored the way in which press coverage of the abuse story unfolded in the year following Savile's death (Boyle 2018a) as well as how Savile's public image was extensively reworked in and through television documentaries about the case (Boyle 2018b). In both contexts I have been centrally concerned with the conditions in which Savile's abuse was both visible and yet disguised (not visible *as abuse*), and the contexts in which it could finally be acknowledged as abuse. I have argued that it was sexism that allowed Savile to hide "in plain sight" in his lifetime and immediately following his death, on the basis of two central points: firstly that the cultural value of sexism meant that his criminally abusive behaviour was consistent with his public persona; and secondly, that the women who tried to report Savile during his lifetime (and even immediately after his death) simply did not matter enough for this to be a risk to the reputation of a celebrity whose cultural and monetary value for the BBC extended beyond his death.

I want to briefly unpick the point about the cultural value of sexism as this is an argument I will extend to other contexts in this chapter, building on the discussion of continuum thinking. For readers for whom Savile has only become a familiar figure through the posthumous revelations, his importance for British culture is easy to underestimate, but in his heyday he was one of the BBC's biggest stars, regularly fronting *Top of the Pops* (BBC 1964–2006) as well as hosting the long-running, prime-time family entertainment show *Jim'll Fix It* (BBC1 1975–1994). His cultural ubiquity was reinforced by his persistent presence in light entertainment genres even after his death (Boyle 2018b: 393) and through his extensive charity work. On his death, he was widely described as a "national treasure" with extensive tributes in print and on television, spanning a number of months (Boyle 2018a: 1566).

Rumours circulated about Savile's sexual preferences during his lifetime but were relatively easily absorbed within a public persona which hinged on his exceptionalism. Although he abused boys as well as girls and women, the cultural value of sexism was central to Savile's ability to remain undetected as an abuser. For instance, Savile's typical greeting to women involved kissing up their arms, he routinely groped young women on camera, and made repeated "jokes" about his preference for young women under the age of consent. Watching archival footage or reading historic interviews with Savile now, his behaviour seems so obvious (Cross 2016; Davies 2014), but part of my argument is that its very visibility is part of what made this invisible *as abuse*, not least as this implicated his audience: the millions who tuned in every week, who read the profiles, who laughed at his jokes and saw nothing amiss. Indeed, when the reports that he was a serial sexual predator were initially acknowledged after his death, they too were folded back into a dominant narrative which positioned him as a (sexual) maverick whose performances of everyday sexism were not only accepted but integral to his "national treasure" persona (Boyle 2018a: 1568–1570).

For Savile to have continued to get away with it when many of the women and children he abused *did* attempt to speak out during his lifetime, their words, their experiences, and their lives had to matter less than his. Whilst this is certainly a reflection of celebrity culture and Savile's power relative to his victims, this is not the only significant factor. Many of the women and children Savile abused were marginal figures in other ways because, for instance, of perceived behavioural problems (one of his grooming grounds was an approved school for girls), mental health issues (another was a secure hospital) and physical illness and disability (mainstream hospitals). Feminists have long argued that—whether in a police station, court or the media—women reporting sexual assault face what Jan Jordan (2004) calls the credibility conundrum: it is *their* credibility which is routinely under scrutiny. Women are more likely to be believed, and for their cases to receive sympathetic media attention, if they are: either very young or very old; if they are assaulted by a stranger; if they suffer physical injury; if they are from the dominant ethnic group in the society (and if the perpetrator is not); if they are deemed sexually "respectable" (a deeply classed and racialised notion); if they haven't been drinking or taking drugs; and if they report the crime to the police immediately (e.g. Jordan 2004; Boyle 2005; Gilchrist 2010; Sela-Shayovitz 2015; Lykke 2016). These patterns have changed little since the 1980s (Soothill and Walby 1991; Benedict 1992).

In the Savile case, the highly sexualised contexts in which Savile groomed his victims—who were typically positioned as fans, either of Savile or the pop stars on his shows—damaged *their* credibility, not his. It is not incidental that fan is a derivative of fanatic and, particularly in relation to music, has long had a clearly gendered and sexualised dimension (Cline 1992; Ehrenreich et al. 1992) which has allowed male musicians' abuse of female fans to be rendered invisible as such (DeRogatis 2019). Whilst the women who publicly named Weinstein as an abuser were typically in very different positions of privilege than the marginalised women and children targeted by Savile, nevertheless, their credibility was still at stake because of the sexualised nature of the industry in which they worked or aspired to work. Yes, Weinstein was typically in a position of professional power over the women (targeting women at the beginning of their careers), but—like Savile—he was also in a position of credibility whilst the women, not least on account of their sexualised profession, were not. To be clear, to argue that film acting is a sexualised profession for women is not to pass a value judgement on women in the industry. Rather it is to illustrate the double bind in which women working in the film are caught: their success depends on their sexualisation (particularly, but not exclusively, for those in front of the camera), yet their sexualisation undermines the seriousness with which they are judged not only as professionals but also (as I argue in this chapter) as victim/survivors of sexual exploitation and abuse.

In previous work, I have explored the cultural and economic value of abuse to the US audio-visual porn industry (Boyle 2011) and there are parallels here worth exploring. In this work I argue that stories about the abuse of female performers are part of the promotional culture of contemporary pornography. That performers and commentators can disclose abuse whilst they are still tied to the industry suggests that these stories do nothing to damage the profitability of pornography but rather contribute to its commercial appeal. Accounts of rape and horrendous physical injuries can co-exist with claims that these women actually love and take sexual pleasure from appearing in pornography. This depends upon the construction of female pornography performers as a breed apart, meaning there is no necessity to approach their stories with empathy. But these stories also work because the sexual instability and duplicity of women is a recurring theme in this kind of pornography, meaning that the contradictory evidence of abuse, injury and choice can sit relatively comfortably together, without troubling the reader's pornographic investments.

Events since October 2017 have suggested that conditions for women in mainstream entertainment industries may not always be a million miles away from those of women in pornography. The "in plain sight" narrative similarly suggests that sexual and sexualised abuse has not just been tolerated but has been consistent with the stories these industries—film, music, comedy—want to tell about themselves. For instance, in film, the sexual abuse of female creatives is woven into the mythology of the "casting couch" of Hollywood's so-called Golden Era (Zimmer 2017; Hutchinson 2017) and the stories about gendered labour which have long linked women to decadence and sexual scandal (McKenna 2011: 5).

Shelley Stamp (2004), for instance, highlights the way in which celebratory discourses around cinema in its early days coexisted with cautionary tales about the excesses and false promises of careers in the industry which were typically aimed at women. There are parallels here with my study of the paratexts of contemporary heterosexual pornography where I argue that women who experience sexual abuse are frequently criticised for not properly equipping themselves with an understanding of the industry before getting involved (Boyle 2011: 596). Sexualising women's ambition—whether in porn, Hollywood, music or comedy—makes it extremely difficult for men's behaviour to be seen as abuse as the focus is on women's choices and morality in a context of always-sexualised labour (Hardie 2017).

Indeed, one of the notable things about Hollywood #MeToo stories is how many rely on material that has been in the public domain for some time, without damaging the careers of the men involved. For instance, when I read the stories about Dustin Hoffman's pattern of sexually harassing behaviour on set in 2017 (Hunter 2017; Rossetter 2017) I was reminded not only of the stories about Savile—many of these incidents were also witnessed by others who laughed—but also of an interview with Hoffman's co-star Susan George on the re-release of *Straw Dogs* (dir. Sam Peckinpah 1971). In this interview, George first described how director Sam Peckinpah coerced her into the film's infamous rape scene, and then outlined how Hoffman extended his on-screen role as "wronged husband" to his treatment of her off-screen, manipulating and emotionally abusing her (Weedle 1995: 24). George's account is clearly of a different order to those of female performers raped on porn sets and there is no suggestion from George that Hoffman's behaviour constituted sexual harassment. However, it shares with these accounts a matter-of-factness about abusive behaviour, as though it is perfectly normal for male directors and actors to behave this way. Notably, George's account is not given in an article *critiquing* the industry, but rather is part of a discussion of the film's social, cultural and aesthetic significance on its cinematic re-release. Moreover, there is a sense that this role was (and is) valuable to George herself, that Peckinpah's and Hoffman's efforts helped to produce her performance in the film, casting her in a relatively passive role whereby her performance is something that is *done to her*, rather than produced through her own labour. George's account is not unique: a biography of Meryl Streep adapted for *Vanity Fair* (Schulman 2016) tells a remarkably similar story of Streep's experience with Hoffman in *Kramer vs. Kramer* (dir. Robert Benton 1979). Again, this is not presented as a critique of the industry: it is a matter-of-fact account of the conditions on set which produced Streep's first Oscar-winning performance. Embedded in these accounts is the normalisation of abusive male behaviour in the service of "method" acting. As Rose McGowan puts it in a typically forthright fashion:

> I have never met a female method actor. To me, "I'm a method actor" is usually synonymous with "I'm going to be a fucking dick to everybody on set" [...] I've never been on a set where that bad behaviour wasn't indulged. (2018: 100–101)

These popular accounts bear investigation not (or not only) because they necessarily reveal the unvarnished truth about production cultures, but because their circulation is suggestive of the narrative of cultural value attached to them. The abuse, particularly (though not exclusively) of actresses, is part of the promotional and critical culture around film and, until #MeToo at least, could typically be admitted without negative repercussions for the way the films and the men involved in them were understood. Indeed, the abuse may even have contributed positively to movie men's public personae or to the mythology around an individual film with stories of behavioural extremes contributing to narratives of artistic exceptionalism or edgy, innovative filmmaking. Jim DeRogatis captures the cultural value of abuse perfectly when he notes of R. Kelly, "[c]onsciously or not, some people love him and his music *because of*, not *despite* his predatory behavior" (2019: 234).

In the next section, I build on the work outlined here to demonstrate how the Weinstein abuse story hid in plain sight prior to October 2017, drawing on a range of examples which have attracted renewed scrutiny since the *New York Times* story.

Weinstein and the Cultural Value of Abuse

Like Jimmy Savile, Harvey Weinstein's abusive behaviour arguably went undetected for so long partly because it was always already an open secret. In the first days of the October 2017 story, three popular culture examples were widely used to demonstrate that Weinstein's behaviour was not only *known* but that this knowledge in no way detracted from Weinstein's status within the industry. All three were intended as comedy: a joke by Seth MacFarlane at the 2013 Oscars; two mentions of Weinstein in the comedy *30 Rock* (NBC 2006–2013); and finally a barely disguised Weinstein-esque character, Harvey Weingard, in the TV series *Entourage* (HBO 2004–2011). I will focus on the first two here.

Given what we know about Weinstein's attempts to control and manipulate media coverage (Kantor and Twohey 2019; Farrow 2019), it may seem surprising that these jokes were in mainstream circulation. Yet, portraying Weinstein as a sexually powerful bully in many ways resonated with the persona he constructed for himself: the ruthless but successful producer in the mould of the misogynist moguls of Hollywood's still-celebrated Golden Era (Hutchinson 2017). According to Matt Damon, Weinstein was proud of being an "a**hole" (Damon quoted by Spargo 2017) and the mythology around the success of Miramax depended on this larger-than-life figure, whose abusive behaviour was chronicled as passion, dogged determination, aggression, belligerence, and even explicitly as bullying (e.g. Auletta 2002; Biskind 2004; Perren 2012). Although the sexual nature of his abusive behaviour was less explicitly chronicled, never taking no for an answer was frequently portrayed as central to Weinstein's success.

At the same time, Weinstein was widely portrayed as a champion of women in film. Part of the critical narrative around the American independent film scene with which Weinstein is associated is its contradictory gender politics (Badley et al. 2016). On one hand, independent film creates more opportunities for women in creative roles; on the other, there is an emphasis on male auteurs and male-driven content in which women largely appear as male fantasies. Sex—and the sexualisation of women in particular—was key to Miramax's distribution strategy from its earliest successes (Auletta 2022: 54). Miramax was known for films that seemed to promise sexual content, notably by using female nudity in marketing, yet failed to deliver (Perren 2012: 116). As Dana Stevens commented in October 2017:

> Even before he was exposed as a serial abuser and alleged rapist, Weinstein was well-known for trafficking in women. The shock is just in discovering how literal, and how violent, that traffic has been. (Stevens 2017)

Of course, the Oscars were absolutely central to the Miramax and Weinstein mythologies: films he had produced or distributed were nominated for 341 awards and won 81 (Robehmed and Berg 2017), and he had been thanked in more Oscar speeches than God, with only Steven Spielberg ratcheting up more thank yous (Ziv 2017). MacFarlane's Oscar joke is therefore particularly worthy of comment. When MacFarlane and Emma Stone presented the nominees for the Academy Awards on 10 January 2013, MacFarlane addressed the nominees in the Supporting Actress category: "Congratulations, you five ladies no longer have to pretend to be attracted to Harvey Weinstein".[1] That MacFarlane was able to make these comments publicly without apparent repercussions is itself a striking contrast to the cost to women of speaking out discussed in Chapter 2. The same was not true, for instance, for Courtney Love, who warned other women not to accept invitations to Weinstein's hotel room in a red-carpet interview in 2005. Referring to this interview after the October 2017 stories broke, Love wrote on Twitter:

> Although I wasn't one of his victims, I was eternally banned by CAA for speaking out against #HarveyWeinstein (@Courtney, 14 October 2017).

There was no such backlash against MacFarlane, though when his comment resurfaced in October 2017 MacFarlane issued a statement claiming that his joke "came from a place of loathing and anger" after his friend and colleague Jessica Barth had confided in him about "her encounter with Harvey Weinstein and his attempted advances" (@SethMacFarlane, 11 October). What is it that allowed MacFarlane's joke—whatever his intent—to be absorbed into Weinstein's mythology, whilst Love's comment threatened it?

The mode of delivery is obviously significant here as the joke provides a built-in alibi, but more than that I want to suggest that the context of MacFarlane's joke focused attention on *women's* complicity. As Hutchinson (2017) argues, you didn't have to have heard specific allegations about Weinstein for the joke to work because it refers to a much-older story about women trading sexual favours for film fame: a story Weinstein's defence team attempted to mobilise in his criminal trial, suggesting that his disputed encounters with women were not abusive but transactional. MacFarlane's joke acknowledges Weinstein's power, but in doing so he reinforces it, upholding Weinstein's logic in reducing the women's Oscar nominations to a question of sexual contract. Numerous

---

[1] The 2013 Oscar nominations can be viewed on You Tube: https://www.youtube.com/watch?v=SzNoT3Zcw2A&feature=youtu.be&t=3m9s. Accessed 6 May 2019.

accounts from women coerced and abused by Weinstein attest that he would use the success of actors like Gwyneth Paltrow or Renée Zellweger as evidence of what he could do for women's careers if they acquiesced to his sexual demands. This is not to say that Paltrow or Zellweger *did* acquiesce to his sexual demands, but rather that Weinstein could credibly claim that they did precisely because of the gendered power differentials and sexualisation of women's labour in the film industry. What "everyone knew" was not just that Weinstein was abusive, but that his abuse worked:

> "Everyone knew if you were in a Harvey movie, chances are you were going to win or be nominated for an Oscar," said Sasha Stone, founder and publisher of AwardsDaily.com, an industry awards tracker since 1999. "It's a sick thing to be in a business where that was the collateral used to coerce women." (Robehmed and Berg 2017)

Even after the *New York Times* story, the success of actresses in Weinstein's movies was widely used against them, their acceptance-speech thanks used as evidence of their complicity: *Bustle* ran a story detailing which women had, and which had not, thanked Weinstein in their Oscar speeches (Florio 2017).

There is a similar logic at play in the *30 Rock* Weinstein-moments where a female character says she successfully resisted Weinstein's advances three times (out of five) and later jokes about Weinstein passing out on top of her (Stolworthy 2017). The female character, and not the absent Weinstein, is the one sexualised through the reporting of these encounters: neither Weinstein's "persistence", nor the grotesque image conjured of the over-weight, inebriated Weinstein is at odds with his public persona. Indeed, that a man so physically unattractive by Hollywood standards could command the apparently endless attention of beautiful movie stars reinforced his success rather than detracted from it, whilst rendering the women complicit at best, sexually duplicitous at worst.

This scrutiny of women's behaviour is something I have already observed in my discussion of the discursive construction of feminism in popular discourse around the Weinstein case in Chapter 2. The promotional cultures of the film industry add another layer to this analysis as many of the women who have publicly accused Weinstein of abuse were also pictured with him at glamorous public events afterwards. The gendered nature of red-carpet reporting, with the emphasis on women's appearance rather than their achievements, has long been criticised. But whilst #AskHerMore might be attempting to shift the red-carpet narrative to emphasise women's achievements,[2] the conventions of these events remain skewed towards the sexualised display of women. Red-carpet photographs function as something of a scarlet letter for Weinstein's accusers, sticky with shame not for Weinstein (who wouldn't want their photo taken with a beautiful woman?) but for the women. The polished, glamorous images undercut their narratives of victimisation. That they don't look or act like "real" victims has been the focus of recurring online commentary, including in numerous memes which place quotes from women's testimonies over smiling red-carpet photographs of them with Weinstein. There is something at stake in the fascination with the (apparent) juxtaposition of female glamour and male monstrosity. Weinstein does not embody the aesthetic norms of the industry and memes abound in which he is portrayed as the grotesque, slimy, slobbering *Star Wars*' villain Jabba the Hutt, among other characters (Andreasen 2020). Although these representations are clearly not flattering to Weinstein, his monstrosity is often constructed as *their* shame as the women pose with arms around him, a signal of their apparent willingness to sacrifice their sexual morality to get ahead in the industry. This is, to borrow Jan Jordan's (2023: 151) provocative formulation, evidence of how beauty can function as a rape myth.

Whilst MacFarlane's comment was widely and sometimes appreciatively reported in 2017, in 2013 it was easily folded back into pre-existing narrative about women's sexualised labour in Hollywood. As Oscar host in February 2013, MacFarlane's performance drew heavily on this narrative for humour, most notoriously in a comedic song "We Saw Your Boobs" in which he detailed the films in which "we" had seen the breasts of the female nominees and other women in the audience, including in films produced by Weinstein. The song included at least two examples where the actor's nudity was in a sexual assault scene—Jodie Foster *The Accused* (dir. Jonathan Kaplan 1988) and Hilary Swank in *Boys Don't Cry* (dir. Kimberly Peirce 1999)—as well as reference to the non-consensual circulation of nude images of Scarlett Johansson stolen from her phone. Moreover, the skit depended upon the reactions of some of the named women. Although these were pre-filmed, presumably with the actors'

---

[2] See http://therepresentationproject.org/the-movement/askhermore/.

foreknowledge and consent, that they were required to play along with being the butt of a sexualised joke at an event supposedly celebrating their professional achievements is in itself a form of sexualised harassment for which MacFarlane was criticised at the time. Yet, the relatively scant reference to the skit in the extensive 2017 coverage of MacFarlane's comments about Weinstein is striking: I found only two articles (both by women) which mentioned MacFarlane's sexist performance as Oscars host alongside his alleged "outing" of Weinstein (Hutchinson 2017; Garavelli 2017).[3] MacFarlane could, as Dani Garavelli (2017) notes, "recast himself as a feminist champion using humour to expose the film industry's sexist ways" despite his own complicity in trivialising sexual abuse in that same Oscar season.

The MacFarlane example is a useful reminder that calling out individuals without examining the structural factors which enabled their abuse can only get us so far. Sexism remains so unremarkable in many ways, so embedded in cultural norms and practices, that it continues to accrue cultural value even as individual monsters fall.

However, sexualised misogyny is only part of the story: the comingling of abuse, power and masculinity is a heady mix and does not, always, necessitate a female victim. In the next section, I turn my attention to Kevin Spacey who was accused of sexual assault by actor Anthony Rapp in October 2017. MacFarlane features in Spacey's story too. A 2005 scene in his animated comedy *Family Guy* shows baby Stewie running naked through a shopping mall screaming "Help! I've escaped from Kevin Spacey's basement". (Rapp was 14 at the time he was assaulted by Spacey.) When Rapp went public, Spacey's now infamous response was to try to reorient the news agenda by combining his apology to Rapp with a statement in which he came out as a gay man. Spacey was widely criticised for this, not least as his statement enabled a slew of homophobic online commentary (Andreasen 2024). However, here I want to focus not on Spacey's non-apology, but rather on a later attempt to incorporate the sexual assault reports into his star image in an astonishing short film, *Let Me Be Frank*, which he released via social media on Christmas Eve 2018.[4] In my analysis of the film, I argue that Spacey seeks to capitalise on the

---

[3] This is based on a Nexis search for Harvey Weinstein and Seth MacFarlane, focusing on October 2017, which returned 166 results (excluding duplicates).

[4] *Let Me Be Frank*, https://www.youtube.com/watch?v=JZveA-NAIDI. Accessed 30 April 2019.

moral duplicity of his most celebrated character to advance his own "plain sight" argument, rendering viewers complicit. This opens up a discussion of what it means to position audiences in this way with reference to a range of other celebrity cases.

"You Loved It": Complicity, Cancellation and Comebacks

Let Me Be Frank is a three-minute film in which Spacey reprises his celebrated role as Frank Underwood from *House of Cards* (Netflix, 2013–2018), a role he lost in the aftermath of Anthony Rapp's public statement accusing him of sexual assault. Spacey uses the short film—released to social media following the critically lukewarm reception of the Spacey-free final season of *House of Cards*—to obliquely address the sexual assault reports and highlight the cultural costs of these allegations *for viewers*. Spacey/Underwood reminds viewers of the pleasure they derived from his character's moral duplicity, using the direct-to-camera address frequently deployed to reveal his character's cunning and crimes in the show, making viewers complicit in his nefarious schemes. The mise-en-scène evokes the dark, expensive domestic interiors of *House of Cards*' early seasons but, with Spacey/Underwood wearing a Santa Claus kitchen apron whilst undertaking mundane domestic chores, it also offers an ironic commentary on Spacey/Underwood's removal from the *House of Cards* finale. For fans of the series, the Spacey/Underwood of *Let Me Be Frank* is thus both thrillingly familiar and uncomfortably different.

The Spacey/Underwood of *Let Me Be Frank* echoes Weinstein's non-apology in response to the *New York Times* article (Weinstein 2017), suggesting that he is being unfairly held to account for behaviour which had previously been culturally legitimated, or even celebrated. However, for my purposes here, it is Spacey's gamble that the reports of sexual assault can themselves be integrated into his star persona that is interesting. Although this was by no means uniformly successful and *Let Me Be Frank* attracted considerable criticism (Kornhaber 2018; Segalov 2018; Zhong 2018), even a quick glance at comments on Spacey's Twitter feed or below the YouTube video demonstrates a continued investment in Spacey as an actor and Underwood as a character. That Spacey released a similar video in December 2019 suggests that the gamble did, to some extent, pay off for him.[5] Whilst, for some fans, this continuing investment is based on disbelieving Rapp and the other men who have disclosed sexual abuse at Spacey's hands, the victim/survivors don't have to be disbelieved for them to be disregarded. This depends on two—related, though potentially contradictory—moves: one in which the viewers' pleasure and Spacey's talent are valued above the rights of his accusers (a version of auteur apologism: he's a great actor so it shouldn't matter); the other in which the assault reports are not incoherent with their pleasure but potentially contribute to it (we've known this about Spacey all along, it's what makes him a great actor and his characters enjoyable antiheroes).

The pervasiveness of this attitude was brought home to me, in an academic context, shortly before #MeToo when two former male colleagues concluded a presentation about securing academic grants with a slide showing Kevin Spacey as Underwood with the caption "don't take no for an answer". My colleagues—however ironically they intended it—positioned themselves within Underwood's homosocial address and recognised the cultural (and potential economic) value of a particular kind of masculine performance. This refusal to hear "no" has itself become mythologised in many competitive contexts including academia, business, sport and film. Indeed, it was explicitly referenced by Uma Thurman when she told *New York Times* about her experiences on the set of *Kill Bill* (dir. Quentin Tarantino 2003, 2004) during which she sustained serious physical injury as a result of director Quentin Tarantino's refusal to hear "no" (O'Dowd 2018).

Spacey's performance in *Let Me Be Frank* is of a piece with this, recasting reports of abuse in relation to morality in a context where immorality is associated with the positive values of risk-taking and fearlessness. It is not supposed to be comfortable: "I told you my deepest darkest secrets. I showed you exactly what people are capable of. I shocked you with my honesty, but mostly, I challenged you and made you think", Spacey/Underwood tells us. He continues:

> We weren't afraid, not of what we said and not of what we did, and we're still not afraid. Because I can promise you this: if I didn't pay the price for the things we both know I did do, I'm certainly not going to pay the price for the things I didn't do. Of course, they are going to say I'm

---

[5] *Merry Christmas from Kevin Spacey*, https://youtu.be/TEOmsz52r_8. Accessed 25 January 2024.

being disrespectful and not playing by the rules, as though I ever played by anyone's rules before. I never did, and you loved it.

Because "we" have always known what Spacey/Underwood is—like Weinstein, it's not something he has hidden—it is "our" current condemnation of him which is marked as inauthentic and misjudged. We have changed the rules. He has remained consistent.

The 2019 video offers a very similar performance. This time, lit by the flicker of an open fire and clad in an out-of-character seasonal jumper, Spacey/Underwood smirkingly extols the virtues of kindness to a soundtrack of menacing music:

> The next time someone does something you don't like you can go on the attack but you can also hold your fire and do the unexpected. You can .... kill them with kindness.

Here Spacey/Underwood seems to be speaking back to his—much debated—"cancellation" in the wake of Rapp's statement and, in doing so, builds on online fan responses which had already demonstrated both a concern with what fans stood to lose and a certain pleasure in the sexual abuse reports in and of themselves. For instance, Maja Brandt Andreasen's (2020) work on Spacey memes identifies how they address a *knowing* audience, invested in the moral duplicity of Spacey's most iconic characters from his breakthrough roles as Kayser Soze (*The Usual Suspects*, dir. Bryan Singer 1995) and John Doe (*Se7en*, dir. David Fincher 1995) to his more recent performance as Underwood. In these memes, it is naïve victim/survivors and gullible media commentators who are often the butt of the joke for failing to understand what has been in front of them all along. Indeed, following the Rapp story, it was suggested that Spacey had alluded to—and sought to excuse—his misdeeds in his acceptance speech at the 2000 Oscar ceremony, when he won Best Actor for his role as the morally duplicitous Lester Burnham in *American Beauty* (dir. Sam Mendes 1999):

> To my friends, for pointing out my worst qualities. I know you do it because you love me, and that's why I love playing Lester, because we got to see all of his worst qualities and we still grew to love him.
> This movie to me is about how any single act by any single person put out of context, is damnable. But the joy of this movie is that it is real beauty [...]. (Spacey, quoted in Vincent 2017)

For my purposes, whether this was an admission from Spacey is not the central issue. Rather, I am interested in the way Spacey collapses the distance between himself, his character and his audience, rendering all potentially complicit, anticipating his performance in *Let Me Be Frank*. The function of this speech re-emerging in November 2017 also interests me. On one hand, this is obviously consistent with the "plain sight" narrative that I have discussed in this chapter. But in its scrutiny of Spacey's past roles and statements, this story also performs a certain kind of fan-like labour which reinstates the value of the work as a source of truth. The truth was there all along if only we'd paid attention. Spacey told us who he was, and we applauded.

There is a long tradition of comedy being used by abusers as a means of deniability. For instance, Louis C.K. frequently made reference to public masturbation in his comedy performances: the shock of the *New York Times* exposé (Ryzik et al. 2017) was arguably not the actions themselves but the attempt to hold him accountable for them. As documented in the series *We Need to Talk About Cosby* (Showtime 2022), Bill Cosby made jokes about drugging and raping women—crimes for which he would be later tried and convicted—[6] not only in his stand-up but in his phenomenally successful family sitcom. Likewise, the 2023 *Dispatches* investigation into Russell Brand—tellingly entitled *Russell Brand: In Plain Sight* (Channel 4, 16 September 2023)—includes clips of his 1990s comedy performances in which he describes violent oral sex in visceral and gleeful detail. That these stories are *not* new allows the accused and their fans to feel aggrieved that they are *now* being held accountable for behaviour that they have long been rewarded for.

Prior to the release of the documentary series *Surviving R. Kelly* (Lifetime, 2019–2023) at least, similar arguments could be made about the aggressively hypersexual performances and lyrics of R. Kelly which "flouted his obsessions" with teenage girls (DeRogatis 2019: 153). As music journalist Ann Powers puts it, Kelly occupied "a position of outrageousness" which was highly profitable: "his transgressions solidified his status" (*Surviving R. Kelly*, Episode 1.5). When Black feminists began organising against R. Kelly their aim was to create space for the voices

---

[6] Cosby was convicted of aggravated indecent assault against Andrea Constand in April 2018. This retrial was widely hailed as a victory for #MeToo not least as in the original trial (pre-#MeToo), the jury had been unable to reach a unanimous verdict. The 2018 conviction was overturned in 2021 on a procedural technicality.

and experiences of Black women and girls whilst challenging the cultural and material value Kelly had accrued, at least in part, through his abuse of them. An early digital example of this was #FastTailedGirls, started by Mikki Kendall and Jamie Nesbitt Golden in 2013 in response to Lady Gaga (an outspoken advocate for sexual violence survivors) performing with R. Kelly at the American Music Awards. The hashtag was initially intended to provoke intra-community discussion on Black Twitter and provide a space for Black women to share their stories, but it was also taken up—albeit to a relatively limited extent—by mainstream media outlets (Jackson et al. 2020: 35–42; Kendall 2020: 47–49). A few years later, in July 2017, Oronike Odeleye and Kenyette Tisha Barnes started #MuteRKelly, targeting radio stations, streaming platforms, performers and industry gatekeepers and challenging them to take a stand against Kelly (Ng 2022: 55). Like so many of the cases discussed in this section, the Kelly story was not new and the work of activists—in both 2013 and 2017—was to make the women at its centre *matter* against a broader cultural and affective investment in Kelly, his music and his standing within the Black community. A central aspect of this activist work was to bring to the fore the double standard whereby a hypersexualised, aggressive Blackness can *enhance* an accused man's cultural value at the same time as it *detracts* from a Black woman's value and credibility.

These twinned processes of credibility boosting and discounting—to use Deborah Tuerkheimer's (2021) terms—are extensively explored in the series *Surviving R. Kelly* as well as in *We Need to Talk About Cosby*. Both series offer commentary from Black fans, cultural critics and activists about the cultural and affective significance of the abusers and wrestle with their abuse and legacies in that context. As activists and journalists, including Oronike Odeleye and Tarana Burke, repeatedly assert across these two series, that these men were defended by many in the Black community was not only a reflection of their cultural value but, heartbreakingly, of the *lack* of value accorded Black women and girls. As R. Kelly survivor Lizzette Martinez puts it about survivors' quest for justice, "That's why it took 30 years, because we didn't matter enough" (*Surviving R. Kelly,* Episode 3.3).

Discussing R. Kelly among others, Andrea McDonnell (2024) identifies a process of "self-cleaving" at work in celebrity responses to allegations of sexual misconduct through which the celebrity attempts to dismiss abusive behaviour as the work of a public, inauthentic persona separate from their "real" self. Whilst this may seem to be at odds with the "frank" narratives I have discussed so far, in both accused men seek to use the idea of cultural value to their own advantage whilst simultaneously rendering suspect those who have invested in their texts, performances or celebrity personae. Fans are complicit: they "loved it" or were "duped" by something that wasn't true. There are powerful echoes here of victim-blaming discourses which surround sexual assault. The investment in popular culture which provides an alibi for abusers is mobilised as evidence against victim/survivors, particularly when they are themselves fans. How could they *not* know what was so obvious to everyone else? The problem is not his behaviour but their misreading of it: assuming it was "just a joke" when it was an admission; assuming it was an admission when it was a performance.

Moreover, for non-fans, what Brenton J. Malin (2023: 161) calls the "retroactive 'toxifying'" of the celebrity abuser can be a source of performative pleasure through which to assert their superiority in ways that can themselves become implicitly, and sometimes explicitly, abusive towards culturally denigrated fans. There are parallels here with Chamil Rathnayake and I's analysis of #HimToo where we suggested that online take downs of supporters of #HimToo risked replicating some of the gendered performances users apparently wanted to critique (Boyle and Rathnayake 2020). In a variation on this, when Channel 4 announced the *Dispatches* programme about Russell Brand—without specifying it was about Brand—the social media rumour mill went into overdrive with gleeful anticipations of the downfall of any number of male celebrities. On one hand, this demonstrates the persistence of the in plain sight narrative—there is no shortage of male celebrities whose problematic behaviour has long been reported as entertainment rather than news. On the other, that responses to #MeToo have become their own genre of entertainment allows accused men to dodge the very serious—and well-sourced—reports of abuse revealed in investigations like those into Brand (Urwin et al. 2023). Spacey's "Let me be Frank", Louis C.K.'s mining of aggrieved masculinity for his comeback comedy (North 2019), or R. Kelly's track "I Admit" (released whilst he was awaiting trial) are thus not only attempts to re-activate their existing cultural value, they are alternatives to what is perceived as #MeToo's pleasure-destroying approach to popular culture, celebrity and fandom.

CANCELLATIONS?

Pleasure—*our* pleasure as audience members—is central to understanding how cultural value insulates abusers from the consequences of their actions. Campaigns like #MuteRKelly make difficult demands that audience members give up something that they love, something that is meaningful in the context of their own life stories. The consequences of believing survivors are not, therefore, just those faced by accused men but also by those who have invested in them and looked the other way despite the evidence which had long circulated about their abusive behaviour. Whilst that is true in all spheres, in this section I am concerned with what it means—for accused men and for audiences—in celebrity sexual assault cases in the long #MeToo era. Notably, whilst a number of the cases I discuss in this section were well known prior to October 2017, it is in the wake of #MeToo that the questions of consequences (not only for the accused men but also for their "art" and its audiences) began to be taken up more widely.

As a way in to this discussion, I want to turn to the response to Dylan Farrow's 2014 open letter to the *New York Times* in which she detailed her experience of childhood sexual abuse by her father, filmmaker Woody Allen. Although this story (like so many recounted in this chapter) was not *new* at this point—having been extensively reported during Allen and Mia Farrow's custody dispute—it was the first time Dylan herself had spoken publicly. Tanya Serisier (2018) provides a compelling argument about the ways in which, prior to #MeToo, Dylan was constructed as an unreliable narrator of her own life through her failures—as well as those of her mother—to tell her story dispassionately, using legalistic frameworks, language and evidence. As a lone voice, Dylan's story lacked what Serisier (2018: 108) calls "semantic thickness", where narratives with common elements can act as cultural corroboration of each other: post-#MeToo, Dylan's story could take on a different meaning.

However, I want to suggest that another part of the reason Dylan Farrow's 2014 story failed to gather traction is perhaps that it posed too direct a challenge to readers, demanding an ethical (re)action from those who work in, profit from or even watch her father's films. The open letter both begins and ends with the question: "What's your favourite Woody Allen movie?" (Farrow 2014). As such, Dylan could be cast not only as hysterical and unreliable (as Serisier argues) but also as censorious and moralising, placing "our" pleasures in an industry we turn to for entertainment under unwarranted scrutiny, killing our joy in those films and their place in our lives. As Sara Ahmed (2010) argues, being disappointed in something that is supposed to make us happy—that perhaps *used to* make us happy—is not only to experience negative affect but to place us at odds with powerful cultural norms: to fail to "get" the joke, appreciate the art, enjoy the film, remember fondly. It is easier not to know. Or not to say that/what we know. At the height of #MeToo and its mainstream media coverage, I had countless conversations where friends would share their concerns about which male celebrity would be next to be accused. Running through many of these discussions was a thinly veiled concern that hearing these testimonies would—like Dylan Farrow's open letter—make concrete demands on us as ethical viewers or consumers. They would demand we gave something (pleasurable) up.

One of the most disorienting professional experiences I had in the immediate wake of #MeToo was when I asked a feminist film scholar a question about whether/how we should reckon with Dylan's story following her paper about Allen's films which made no mention of it. Her angry and defensive response caught me off-guard as she seemed to suggest that by asking this question I was somehow impugning her *personally*. This has really stayed with me as an example of what is at stake in reckoning with Dylan's letter and the many other stories I have referred to in this book. Being asked whether something—someone—in whom we have invested our time, money, emotions and, potentially, our professional or personal identities, could be harmful, could have caused harm, *is* difficult and disorienting. As someone without that investment in Allen, my question was perhaps too easy, too flip, but it is something Clare Dederer (2023) reckons with thoughtfully in *Monsters: A Fan's Dilemma*. In particular, she describes how the "stain" now attached to men like Allen rubs off on those attached to them. The "stain" is a useful metaphor here because it reminds us that what is new is not the behaviour itself but the *meaning* attached to it. This is further complicated when the abusive behaviour has, itself, been central to the (alleged) abuser's art—the source of their success and status. For instance, Dederer describes rewatching *Annie Hall* (dir. Woody Allen 1977) and being newly alert to Allen's "artistic grooming of the audience", his normalisation of the sexualisation of youth and of power differentials (2023: 28). This disrupts, but does not completely do away with, her pleasure, not least as film is never a solo enterprise: her appreciation of the film's style, of the costuming, of Diane

Keaton's performance is undimmed. She discusses it with a friend who shares, "I don't know where to put all my feelings about Woody Allen" (Dederer 2023: 23). As Dylan's brother, the journalist Ronan Farrow, puts in the documentary series *Allen v. Farrow* (HBO 2021):

> There's an additional layer of distortion when this kind of allegation is raised against someone who is not just beloved in a traditional sense, but beloved in a way where people have an identity association with it, where it's existential to them that they grew up loving Woody Allen. (*Allen v. Farrow*, Episode 4)

But for Dylan, the continued public investment in "loving Woody Allen"—of working with him, programming and watching his films, awarding his work—was a means of denying her communicative justice (Kay 2020). In the documentary series, both Dylan and Ronan identify a shift in public attitudes between the publication of her 2014 open letter and a later article in 2017. In the wake of #MeToo, her story could be heard differently, her demands responded to: "every message of support has been a gift", she tells the filmmakers (*Allen v. Farrow*, Episode 4).

Allen is not the only one to be accused of grooming his audience. During the investigation into Jimmy Savile which followed the broadcast of the *Exposure* documentary Commander Peter Spindler of the Metropolitan Police similarly claimed that Savile "groomed the nation" (Laville et al. 2013). It is helpful to put Allen and Savile together as whilst there has been considerable hand-wringing about divorcing the art from the artist in relation to men like Allen, these are not terms which have typically been used in relation to accused men involved in television and light entertainment. This isn't accidental. Television and its audiences have long been feminised, deemed *less* culturally valued than their silver screen counterparts. Yet—as Spindler acknowledges—the cultural impact of television, radio and their stars is no less powerful. Echoing Dederer's friend, Sylvia Nicol, who worked at Stoke Mandeville Hospital (one of the charitable causes with which Savile was most aligned), told documentary filmmaker Louis Theroux that she is "a victim of losing those memories" associated with Savile (*Louis Theroux: Savile*, BBC2, 2 October 2016). One of the most affecting moments of her interview is when she shows Theroux her Savile memorabilia: once proudly displayed and now largely hidden away, these objects which are meaningful *in the context of her own life* are now stained; and, she fears she is too, by association. But whilst the object of Nicol's affection is incontrovertibly stained, Dederer has no difficulty finding Allen "on-demand" (2023:20). Even in the post-#MeToo environment, he continues to attract funding, audiences and acclaim: his 50th film premiered at the Venice Film Festival in 2023.

Though neither Allen nor Savile have ever been convicted of the abuse of which they stand accused, there are, of course, important differences between them in terms of the scale and scope of their reported abusive behaviour. I have already discussed Savile's "monsterisation" in Chapter 5, so the point I want to make here is that another factor that made Savile easier to dismiss was precisely the lesser cultural value associated with his cultural productions *and* with the people who consumed them. In contrast, Dederer suggests that monsterisation is *built-in* to the figure of the artistic genius as a positive value. Their genius is their get-out-of-jail-free card and an invitation to the audience to disregard the suffering of others:

> Part of the reason so much attention has been trained on men like Picasso and Hemingway is exactly *because* they're assholes. We are excited by their asshole-ness. [...] We want the asshole to cross the line, to break the rules. We reward that rule-breaking, and then we go a step further, and see it as endemic to art-making itself. We reward and reward this bad behaviour until it becomes synonymous with greatness.
> (Dederer 2023: 109–110)

If, as I have suggested in this chapter, the cultural value of abuse is dependent on valuing the life, art and perspective of the abuser above those of victim/survivors, it is also dependent—at least in part—on whether there is an *alignment* between the art and the (alleged) abuse. There is for Allen, Picasso and Hemingway. There is not for Savile.

Jenessa Williams' (2022) work on fans of indie and hip hop musicians accused of sexual assault provides further evidence here. Wiliams identifies three stances—cancelling, conflicted and anti-cancelling—which fans adopt in response to #MeToo accusations. Williams finds cancelling stances most strongly associated with indie fans, in part, because of the perceived *disconnect* between the musician's persona, their perceived lyrical sensitivity and the behaviour they are accused of. In contrast, where sexual assault allegations are *aligned* to fans' experiences of the musician and their music—more commonly in hip hop—Williams' finds that fans are more likely to defend the accused men, dismiss the assaults or even find them humorously consistent with the musician's enjoyably villainous characterisation. There is a racialised dimension to this: all the hip hop fans Williams interviewed were fans of Black men accused of assaulting Black women. Williams does not suggest that this is an entirely clear-cut opposition between indie and hip hop music, and she identifies fans of both genres who are conflicted in their responses, condemning the behaviour in public (particularly where that aligns to their political self-presentation) whilst remaining affectively invested in the musician and their music in private. In other words, responses are not solely determined by the values in the creative work but also by the political positioning of the fans themselves.

So, to take up the terms used by Williams, what are the implications of cancellation (or the failure to cancel) in the post-#MeToo era? In the case of public figures, could cancellation be part of McGlynn and Westmarland's (2019) kaleidoscopic approach to justice? McGlynn and Westmarland crucially note that justice for victim/survivors is neither absolute nor fixed. This may seem to sit somewhat awkwardly with the popular discourse around cancellation, which suggests a very fixed and final position. However, as Eve Ng (2022) notes in her account of the development of cancel culture, the intentions and effects of cancel practices can be very variable. Certainly, as my discussion of Spacey's cancel video above demonstrates, calls for cancellation are rarely uncontested, as Ng (2022: 54–60) also demonstrates in her discussion of responses to sexual misconduct reports relating to comedian Louis C.K. and actor James Franco. The relative positions of power of those involved in cancelling and being cancelled are key to any evaluation of the practice (Ng 2022: 4).

To return to #MuteRKelly, then, it is important to recognise that this campaign was a response to the way the women abused by Kelly were failed, not only by criminal justice but also by the mainstream media's selective and racialised attention to victim/survivors in the long #MeToo moment. The purpose of muting R. Kelly was not only to impact Kelly's status and profitability but, crucially, to quieten him so that the women he abused could be heard and seek (communicative) justice. Through the *Surviving R. Kelly* series (which was in part inspired by the #MuteRKelly activism as well as by the investigative reporting of Jim DeRogatis)—and the cultural and criminal reckoning which followed—the victim/survivors of Kelly *have* been heard and, at least in some contexts, believed. In 2021, Kelly was found of sex trafficking and racketeering in a New York trial; in

2022 he was convicted in Chicago of charges relating to child abuse. Of course, there are still many fans who blame the victim/survivors and assert Kelly's innocence. But even so, it is now much more difficult to engage with Kelly's music without some knowledge of his abusive behaviour.

In this new context, must we still mute the music? Journalist Jim DeRogatis, one of the first mainstream journalists to try to tell the stories of the women and girls abused by Kelly, offers a usefully nuanced answer to this question:

> Nobody's saying burn his records, right, they're saying be aware of the context. Be aware of what he's really saying in that canon of music. Be aware of the pain he caused to people. And then I think there's no right or wrong in art. If you can still listen to "Ignition Remix" or "Step in the Name of Love" or "I Believe I Can Fly" and take pleasure from it, I understand that. Because it played at your kid's kindergarten graduation. It played at every backyard barbeque you ever went to. It was your wedding song. It is your song as much as it's his. But know the pain he caused and condemn it. You can condemn the man and still appreciate the art. Personally I can. And I don't think there's one answer. I think every single individual is going to have a different answer to that question of when she can separate art from artist.
> (DeRogatis, speaking in *Surviving R. Kelly*, Episode 2.5)

As DeRogatis suggests, the question is not only can we separate the art from the artist but can we separate the art from our own life histories. But DeRogatis also points to the need to acknowledge what we might have previously ignored in the art itself ("what he's really saying in that canon of music") as well as in the biography of the artist ("the pain he caused"). In short, he is suggesting that we need to be willing to undo the cultural value of abuse and dis-invest in the abuser before we can recover the personal value of the art. A condition of unmuting R. Kelly should be a willingness to listen to the women and girls he abused (also DeRogatis 2019).

DeRogatis' concern here is with our personal investments but there is a further question as to what that adds up to culturally. Should radio stations and streaming platforms continue to #MuteRKelly, for instance? Should other cultural productions which have made use of his music be muted too?

These are tricky questions to answer for a number of reasons and, in what follows, I am not concerned with debating the relative merits of cancellation per se (for that, see Ng 2022) but with thinking through their complex implications in celebrity sexual assault cases. Here we have to start with the fact that, despite the outpouring of victim/survivor testimony relating to the media and cultural industries in recent years, what is publicly known is, inevitably, still only the tip of the iceberg. Cancelling the art or artists we *know* about might be understood as an endorsement of those that remain on our playlists, in our festivals or on our curricula. It can have the effect of marking *some* production cultures as exceptional rather than seeing the gendered inequality that is endemic to the media and cultural industries as a conducive context for male violence against women. This is one reason why the website Rotten Apples[7] makes me slightly uneasy. Rotten Apples was created in 2017 in the wake of the explosion of survivor testimony relating to the media and cultural industries. Initially its aim was consumer awareness: to let users search for information about whether anyone involved in the production of a film or television show had allegations of sexual misconduct against them. However, the term "sexual misconduct" is not defined and given the site's more explicitly activist turn—it now links sexual misconduct in the film and television industries to gender inequality per se, advocates for the ratification of the Equal Rights Amendment and links to support and advocacy organisations—the exclusion of other forms of gender-based violation requires interrogation. For instance, the film *She Said* (dir. Maria Schrader 2022) has a "fresh apples" rating though Brad Pitt, who has an executive producing credit, has been accused of physical and emotional abuse of Angelina Jolie and two of their children (Horton 2022). This example is interesting for me here not just because of the question of definition, but also because it raises questions about authorship. Films typically involve huge numbers of cast and crew: do all of them have the potential to "stain" the text? If so, then pretty much all art and culture is stained. If not, then in isolating particular figures there is a danger we end up reinforcing the very systems of cultural value that got us to this point. And then there is a further question about what—or whose—interests are served by cancellation?

The Brad Pitt/*She Said* example also raises a question about how to "balance" contradictory evidence. Here I am thinking not of the

[7] Rotten Apples: https://rottenappl.es. Accessed 1 February 2024. For an interesting use of Rotten Apples to disrupt a canon of work, see Ian Garwood's *Indy Vinyl, Interrupted* (2020).

contested nature of the domestic abuse report—as with all the other cases I refer to in this book, I am interested in the representation of the reports and how they function in wider debates, not in judging their truth—but rather what these mean in the context of this film. *She Said* is based on Jodi Kantor and Megan Twohey's 2019 book of the same name which chronicles their experiences researching and breaking the Weinstein story. In that story, Pitt plays a different role, corroborating Gwyneth Paltrow's account of assault and confronting Weinstein about it (Kantor and Twohey 2019, 39–40, 45–46). What would cancelling the film (and Pitt's role in it) mean in the context of *that* story? I don't have an easy answer. At the very least, it is a reminder that people can credibly occupy different roles in narratives around abuse. Weinstein's "forgotten man" interview with the *New York Post* on the eve of his first criminal trial (Rosenberg 2019) where he sought to balance his good and bad deeds, takes me into similar territory. Should his support for female (and feminist) artists be forgotten? I'd say no, not just because that could mean further marginalising *their* work, but also because this was always part of Weinstein's alibi, it's how he got away with it for so long and if we lose that from our understanding of who Weinstein was then we are missing an important part of the story.

Perhaps it is because Weinstein has faced clear consequences for his actions—reputational, financial, legal—that cancellation seems less urgent in his case. To return to McGlynn and Westmarland's (2019) metaphor, kaleidoscopic justice does not always comprise the same elements. But where other forms of justice have *not* been open to victim/survivors—as initially in the R. Kelly case, for instance—then cancellation may come into play more forcefully. At the same time, I am not comparing like with like here: that the cultural products associated with Weinstein less obviously bear his imprint means that the question of what to do with, for example, Miramax's back catalogue is less fraught than the questions relating to Kelly's music, or the Woody Allen example with which I opened this section. In these examples—as also in Jimmy Savile's on-camera groping or Louis C.K.'s or Russell Brand's stand-up—the cultural product itself is a form of evidence. Whilst DeRogatis argues that R. Kelly's songs belong to the listener as much as to Kelly, creative interpretative practices do not change the qualities of the lyrics, performance or music videos themselves. And creative—even resistive—interpretative practices can still keep these cultural productions in circulation, doing little to challenge the profitability of abuse for the media and cultural industries. Moreover, as Spacey's videos suggest, the cultural value of abuse has not been entirely overturned by the challenges of #MeToo and amoral, dangerous and violent masculinity remains appealing to both audiences and media companies. Johnny Depp's "wild at heart" ads for Dior's Sauvage maintained the alignment of Depp with risky, violent masculinity throughout the fallout from his marriage to Amber Heard. The profitability of this association for the brand is demonstrated by the recent $20 million extension to Depp's contract, described as one of the most lucrative celebrity fragrance deals ever (Gardner 2023). This version of masculinity remains culturally (and economically) valued.

The questions about cancellation raised in this section are not, however, just questions for consumers. I also find myself coming up against these questions as a media academic, and I am not alone in this. Debates about what #MeToo has—and should—mean for the curriculum have been taking place in various disciplinary contexts. In Literary Studies, for instance, this has dovetailed with questions not only about the role of biography in understanding the text but also about the place of sexual violence and rape culture in the classroom (Holland and Hewett 2021). In her essay on the Film Studies curriculum post-#MeToo Rebecca Harrison (2018) poses the question rather differently, asking what we have *missed* by focusing on the work of abusive men? This makes me think of the very many accounts from women in the media and cultural industries I have heard since 2017 which described how the normalisation of abuse (on screen and off) led them to leave those industries. What about their lost work, their lost potential? Harrison's suggestion is not to "cancel" the abusive men—which would, in the context of collaborative industries like film, also mean losing the work of women—but rather to look for the women and people of other genders who have been missing in our approach to film. This might mean approaching questions of authorship differently—challenging auteur apologism by challenging the notion of the auteur—and/or looking at texts, genres, filmmakers whose work has been eclipsed by narrow constructions of cultural value which have had male entitlement baked in, creating the conducive context for abuse which I have detailed in this chapter.

Conclusion

In drawing this chapter to a close, I want to return to a discussion I took part in back in 2002 which foreshadowed the cultural struggles over reports of abuse against well-known men in the #MeToo moment. I was on a panel discussing screen representations of child sexual abuse organised by the Women's Support Project in Glasgow. Also on the panel was John Yorke, who was, at that time, an Executive Producer on BBC1's soap opera *EastEnders*. We were responding to an episode of *EastEnders* in which Kat Slater reveals that she was raped by her uncle as a child. In the discussion, Yorke divulged that when they were developing the child sexual abuse story, they had initially intended that it would focus on another character (Janine Butcher) being abused by her step-father (Roy Evans). Unlike Kat's Uncle Harry, who was only in the soap for the duration of this storyline, Roy was a regular and popular character. The team decided that this would alienate their viewers, who, having emotionally invested in Roy over years, would feel betrayed by such a revelation.

The #MeToo stories involving public figures parallel the one *EastEnders* felt unable to tell all those years ago. These stories involve men we think we know, doing things which prompt us to re-examine our affective investments in them. Of course, this process also takes place in families and communities in relation to non-celebrity abusers, but what has concerned me in this chapter are the wider reverberations for our understandings of media cultures. The #MeToo moment has presented a sustained challenge to rape culture, partly by revealing how pervasive its operations have been. But this also means that it has implicated an increasing number of us: as viewers, readers, fans, subscribers, consumers, critics as well as victim/survivors, bystanders or perpetrators. If this has forced us to see our own cultural practices as part of the problem, it has also offered ways in which we can become part of the solution, offering recognition to victim/survivors, for instance.

#MeToo has put the conditions of our pleasures in the media and cultural industries under the microscope. But giving those pleasures up is not entirely straightforward. Nor is it always obvious that cancellation practices serve the best interests of victim/survivors or that they help us reckon, collectively and culturally, with the value of abuse as I have defined it in this chapter. To properly and permanently upset the cultural value of abuse we not only need to listen to the stories and expertise of victim/survivors, activists and researchers on gender-based violence, we need alternative stories. That necessitates access to the means of production. In that sense, Rotten Apples is right: we do not solve the problem of sexual misconduct in film and television (or any other industry) simply by making it visible. Once visibility has been achieved—as it has been in many sectors as the result of victim/survivor testimony, activist work and media representation in the long #MeToo moment—is there a continued need to speak out? This is the question I take up in the next chapter.

References

Adur, Shweta M., and Shreyasi Jha. 2018. (Re)centering street harassment— An appraisal of safe cities global initiative in Delhi, India. *Journal of Gender Studies* 27 (1): 114–124.
Ahmed, Sara. 2010. Feminist killjoys (and other willful subjects). *Scholar and Feminist Online* 8 (3). http://sfonline.barnard.edu/polyphonic/ahmed_01.htm#text1. Accessed 20 May 2019.
Andreasen, Maja Brandt. 2020. *Not Just a Joke: Rape Culture in Internet Memes About #MeToo*. Unpublished PhD thesis. University of Strathclyde.
Andreasen, Maja Brandt. 2024. Homophobic humour in rape memes. In *The Routledge Companion to Gender, Media and Violence*, ed. Karen Boyle and Susan Berridge, 423–431. London: Routledge.
Auletta, Ken. 2002. Beauty and the beast. *New Yorker*, 8 December.
Auletta, Ken. 2022. *Hollywood Ending: Harvey Weinstein and the Culture of Silence*. New York: Penguin.
Badley, Linda, Claire Perkins and Michele Schreiber. 2016. Introduction. In *Indie Reframed: Women's Filmmaking and Contemporary American Independent Cinema*, ed. Linda Badley, Claire Perkins and Michele Schreiber, 1–14. Edinburgh: Edinburgh University Press.
Benedict, Helen. 1992. *Virgin or Vamp: How the Press Covers Sex Crimes*. Oxford: Oxford University Press.
Biskind, Peter. 2004. *Down and Dirty Pictures: Miramax, Sundance, and the Rise of Independent Film*. New York: Simon & Schuster.
Boyle, Karen. 2005. *Media and Violence: Gendering the Debates*. London: Sage.
Boyle, Karen. 2011. Producing abuse: Selling the harms of pornography. *Women's Studies International Forum* 34 (6): 593–602.
Boyle, Karen. 2018a. Hiding in plain sight: Gender, sexism and press coverage of the Jimmy Savile case. *Journalism Studies* 19 (11): 1562–1578.
Boyle, Karen. 2018b. Television and/as testimony in the Jimmy Savile case. *Critical Studies in Television* 13 (4): 387–404.
Boyle, Karen. 2019. What's in a name? Theorising the inter-relationships of gender and violence. *Feminist Theory* 20 (1): 19–36.

Boyle, Karen and Chamil Rathnayake. 2020. #HimToo and the networking of misogyny in the age of #MeToo. *Feminist Media Studies* 20 (8): 1259–1277.

Buchwald, Emilie, Pamela R. Fletcher and Martha Roth, eds. 1993. *Transforming a Rape Culture*, Minneapolis: Milkweed.

Cline, Cheryl. 1992. Essays from *Bitch: The women's rock magazine with bite*. In *The Adoring Audience: Fan Culture and Popular Media*, ed. Lisa A. Lewis, 69–83. London: Routledge.

Cross, Simon. 2016. Disclosure and enclosure: revisiting media profiles of Jimmy Savile. In *Profile Pieces: Journalism and the "Human Interest" Bias*, eds. Sue Joseph and Richard Lance Keeble, 100–115. London: Routledge.

Davies, Dan. 2014. *In Plain Sight: The Life and Lies of Jimmy Savile*. London: Quercus.

Dederer, Claire. 2023. *Monsters: A Fan's Dilemma*. London: Sceptre.

DeRogatis, Jim. 2019. *Soulless: The Case Against R. Kelly*. New York: Abrams.

Ehrenreich, Barbara, Elizabeth Hess and Gloria Jacobs. 1992. Beatlemania: Girls just want to have fun. In *The Adoring Audience: Fan Culture and Popular Media*, ed. Lisa A. Lewis, 84–106. London: Routledge.

Farrow, Dylan. 2014. An open letter from Dylan Farrow. *New York Times Blog*, https://kristof.blogs.nytimes.com/2014/02/01/an-open-letter-from-dylan-farrow/. Accessed 14 May 2019.

Farrow, Ronan. 2019. *Catch and Kill: Lies, Spies and a Conspiracy to Protect Predators*. London: Fleet.

Florio, Angelica. 2017. Here's every woman who did and didn't thank Harvey Weinstein at the Oscars. *Bustle*, 3 November https://www.bustle.com/p/heres-every-woman-who-did-didnt-thank-harvey-weinstein-at-the-oscars-295 3763. Accessed 14 May 2019.

Garavelli, Dani. 2017. Faux outrage adds to agony of Weinstein revelations. *Scotsman*, 14 October.

Gardner, Chris. 2023. Source: Johnny Depp extends Dior Sauvage partnership in new $20M-plus deal. *Hollywood Reporter*, 12 May.

Garwood, Ian. 2020. *Indy Vinyl, Interrupted*. [Video Essay]. https://indyvinyl.gla.ac.uk/indy-vinyl-interrupted/.ac.uk. Accessed 24 March 2024.

Gay, Roxanne. ed. 2018. *Not That Bad: Dispatches from Rape Culture*. New York: Harper Perennial.

Gilchrist, Kristen. 2010. "Newsworthy" victims? *Feminist Media Studies* 10 (4): 373–390.

Hardie, Kate. 2017. Time to make the link between abuse and film content. *Guardian*, 15 October.

Harrison, Rebecca. 2018. Fuck the canon (or, how do you solve a problem like Von Trier): teaching, screening and writing about cinema in the age of #MeToo. *Mai: Feminism and Visual Culture* 9 November. https://maifeminism.com/fuck-the-canon-or-how-do-you-solvea-problem-like-von-trier-tea ching-screening-and-writing-about-cinema-in-the-age-of-metoo/. Accessed 25 April 2018.

Holland, Mary K. and Heather Hewett. 2021. *#MeToo and Literary Studies: Reading, Writing, and Teaching About Sexual Violence and Rape Culture*. New York: Bloomsbury Academic.

Horton, Adrian. 2022. Angelina Jolie alleges physical abuse by Brad Pitt in countersuit. *Guardian*, 4 October.

Hunter, Anna Graham. 2017. Dustin Hoffman sexually harassed me when I was 17. *Hollywood Reporter*, 1 November.

Hutchinson, Pamela. 2017. Moguls and starlets: 100 years of Hollywood's corrosive, systemic sexism. *Guardian*, 19 October.

Jackson, Sarah J., Moya Bailey and Brooke Foucault Welles. 2020. *#Hashtag Activism: Networks of Race and Gender Justice*. Cambridge: MIT Press.

Jordan, Jan. 2004. *The Word of a Woman? Police, Rape and Belief*. Hampshire: Palgrave Macmillan.

Jordan, Jan. 2023. *Tackling Rape Culture: Ending Patriarchy*. Abingdon: Routledge.

Kantor, Jodi and Megan Twohey. 2019. *She Said: Breaking the Sexual Harassment Story that Helped Ignite a Movement*. London: Bloomsbury.

Kelly, Liz. 2016. The conducive context of violence against women and girls. *Discover Society*, 1 March. https://discoversociety.org/2016/03/01/theorising-violence-against-women-and-girls/. Accessed 20 May 2019.

Kendall, Mikki. 2020. *Hood Feminism: Notes from the Women White Feminists Forgot*. London: Bloomsbury.

Kitzinger, Jenny. 1999. The ultimate neighbour from hell? Stranger danger and the media representation of "paedophilia." In *Social Policy, the Media and Misrepresentation*, ed. Bob Franklin, 207–221. London: Routledge.

Kornhaber, Spencer. 2018. The disturbing truth about Kevin Spacey's "Let Me Be Frank" video. *The Atlantic*. 27 December.

Laville, Sandra, Esther Addley and Josh Halliday. 2013. Police errors left Jimmy Savile free to "groom the nation". *Guardian*, 11 January.

Lykke, Lucia C. 2016. Visibility and denial: Accounts of sexual violence in race- and gender-specific magazines. *Feminist Media Studies* 16 (2): 239–260.

Maas, Megan K., Heather L. McCauley, Amy E. Bonomi and S. Gisela Leija. 2018. "I was grabbed by my pussy and its #NotOkay": A twitter backlash against Donald Trump's degrading commentary. *Violence Against Women* 24 (14): 1739–1750.

MacKinnon, Catharine. 1993. *Only Words*. Cambridge, MA: Harvard University Press.

Malin, Brenton J. 2023. "I never liked him": Ryan Adams and the toxification of masculinity in the post-MeToo digital era. *Women's Studies in Communication* 46 (2): 160–178.

Marghitu, Stefania. 2018. "It's just art": Auteur apologism in the post-Weinstein era. *Feminist Media Studies* 18 (3): 491–494.
McDonnell, Andrea. 2024. *Celebrity Rhetoric and Sexual Misconduct Cases*. New York: Routledge.
McGlynn, Clare, Erica Rackley and Ruth Houghton. 2017. Beyond revenge porn: The continuum of image-based abuse. *Feminist Legal Studies* 25 (1): 25–46.
McGlynn, Clare and Nicole Westmarland. 2019. Kaleidoscopic justice: Sexual violence and victim-survivors' perceptions of justice. *Social and Legal Studies* 28 (2): 179–201.
McGowan, Rose. 2018. *Brave*. London: HQ.
McKenna, Denise. 2011. The photoplay or the pickaxe extras, gender, and labour in early Hollywood. *Film History: An International Journal* 23 (1): 5–19.
Mendes, Kaitlynn, Jessica Ringrose and Jessalynn Keller. 2019. *Digital Feminist Activism: Girls and Women Fight Back Against Rape Culture*. Oxford: Oxford University Press.
Mitchell, Lize-Mari. 2023. Hashtag activism and #MeToo in South Africa. In *The Other #MeToos*, ed. Iqra Shagufta Cheema, 140–158. Oxford: Oxford University Press.
Ng, Eve. 2022. *Cancel Culture: A Critical Analysis*. Cham: Palgrave Macmillan.
North, Anna. 2019. Louis C.K. and Aziz Ansari have an opportunity for redemption. They're squandering it. *Vox*, 9 January. https://www.vox.com/2019/1/9/18172273/louis-ck-comeback-parkland-aziz-ansari-metoo. Accessed 20 May 2019.
O'Dowd, Maureen. 2018. This is why Uma Thurman is angry. *New York Times*, 3 February.
Perren, Alisa. 2012. *Indie Inc: Miramax and the Transformation of Hollywood in the 1990s*. Austin: University of Texas Press.
Phillips, Nickie D. 2017. *Beyond Blurred Lines: Rape Culture in Popular Media*. Lanham: Rowman and Littlefield.
Powell, Anastasia, and Nicola Henry. 2017. *Sexual Violence in a Digital Age*. London: Palgrave MacMillan.
Rentschler, Carrie. 2014. Rape culture and the feminist politics of social media. *Girlhood Studies* 7 (1): 65–82.
Robehmed, Natalie and Madeline Berg. 2017. Oscar hero to zero: how Harvey Weinstein's power enabled him—And led to his decline. *Forbes*, 13 October.
Rosenberg, Rebecca. 2019. Harvey Weinstein: I deserve pat on back when it comes to women. *New York Post* (Page Six), 15 December.
Rossetter, Kathryn. 2017. New Dustin Hoffman accuser claims harassment and physical violation on Broadway. *Hollywood Reporter*, 8 December.
Ryzik, Melena, Cara Buckley and Jodi Kantor. 2017. Louis C.K. is accused by 5 women of sexual misconduct. *New York Times*, 9 November.

Schulman, Michael. 2016. How Meryl Streep battled Dustin Hoffman, retooled her role, and won her first Oscar. *Vanity Fair*, April.

Segalov, Michael. 2018. Kevin Spacey's creepy video looks like a cynical attempt at distraction. *Guardian*, 28 December.

Sela-Shayovitz, Revital. 2015. "They are all good boys": The role of the Israeli media in the social construction of gang rape. *Feminist Media Studies* 15 (3): 411–428.

Serisier, Tanya. 2018. *Speaking Out: Feminism, Rape and Narrative Politics*. Cham: Palgrave Macmillan.

Sills, Sophie, Chelsea Pickens, Karishma Beach, Lloyd Jones, Octavia Calder-Dowe, Paulette Benton-Greig and Nicola Gavey. 2016. Rape culture and social media: Young critics and a feminist counterpublic. *Feminist Media Studies* 16 (6): 935–951.

Soothill, Keith and Sylvia Walby. 1991. *Sex Crime in the News*. London: Routledge.

Spargo, Chris. 2017. Matt Damon reveals he KNEW Harvey Weinstein harassed Gwyneth Paltrow from his "buddy" Ben Affleck while George Clooney admits mogul was a bully who bragged of bedding stars—But says every industry has this issue. *Mail Online*, 23 October https://www.dailymail.co.uk/news/article-5008429/Matt-Damon-KNEW-Harvey-Weinsten-harassed-Gwyneth-Paltrow.html. Accessed 6 May 2019.

Stamp, Shelley. 2004. "It's a long way to filmland": Starlets, screen hopefuls, and extras in early Hollywood. In *American Cinema's Transitional Era: Audiences, Institutions, Practices*, ed. Charlie Keil and Shelley Stamp, 332–351. Berkeley: University of California Press.

Stevens, Dana. 2017. Stories from Slate; just as the election challenged my perception of American, the past week has transformed my whole understanding of Hollywood. *Slate Magazine*, 13 October.

Stolworthy, Jacob. 2017. 30 Rock joke referenced Harvey Weinstein allegations in 2012. *Independent*, 11 October.

Sullivan, Eric. 2019. "I'm not the morality police": Inside Benjamin Brafman's defense of Harvey Weinstein. *Esquire*, 15 January.

Tuerkheimer, Deborah. 2021. *Credible: Why We Doubt Accusers and Protect Abusers*. New York: Harper Collins.

Urwin, Rosamund, Charlotte Wace and Paul Morgan-Bentley. 2023. Accused: Russell Brand, the "sex predator" who hid in plain sight. *The Sunday Times*, 17 September.

Vincent, Alice. 2017. Did Kevin Spacey hint at his behaviour in his *American Beauty* Oscars speech? *Telegraph*, 31 October.

Weedle, D. 1995. *Straw Dogs*: They want to see brains flying out? *Sight and Sound* 5 (2): 20–25.

Weinstein, Harvey. 2009. Polanksi has served his time and must be freed. *Independent*, 28 September.
Weinstein, Harvey. 2017. Statement. *New York Times*, 5 October.
Williams, Jenessa. 2022. Music fandom in the age of #MeToo. Paper presented at *MeCCSA 2022: Silenced Voices*, Robert Gordon University, 7–9 September.
Zhong, Fan. 2018. What is Kevin Spacey thinking with this evil "Let Me Be Frank" YouTube video? *W.* 24 December. https://www.wmagazine.com/story/kevin-spacey-let-me-be-frank-youtube-video. Accessed 20 May 2019.
Zimmer, Ben. 2017. "Casting couch": The origins of a pernicious Hollywood cliché. *The Atlantic*, 16 October.
Ziv, Stav. 2017. At Oscars Harvey Weinstein thanked more than God, according to 2015 analysis. *Newsweek*, 10 October.

CHAPTER 7

Reconsidering Survivor Speech in the Media: Against Testimony

INTRODUCTION

Within weeks of #MeToo going viral, Tarana Burke commented that "amplification has happened" (Burke quoted in Serisier 2018: 115). In doing so, Burke suggested the success of #MeToo in the terms set out by Alyssa Milano's tweet. In this chapter, I consider—and question—the continued role of silence breaking more than six years on, when amplification *and* contestation have happened in ways detailed throughout this book.

In using the term testimony in the chapter title, I want to acknowledge the promise inherent in speaking out—namely that it will be *consequential*—and recognise that that promise is entangled with the law, and with justice for victim/survivors, in complicated ways (Serisier 2018: 71). Mediated victim/survivor testimony has become legally consequential for victim/survivors such that even to call oneself a victim or survivor is precarious, as the Depp v. Heard case starkly demonstrates (see Chapter 4). That both Bill Cosby's conviction and Harvey Weinstein's New York conviction could be overturned on technicalities about the conditions of testimony—regardless of the evidence within that testimony—is another example of the limitations of what testimonial speech can achieve. In this fraught context, to argue against testimony can seem to be doing the misogynists' work for them. However, if amplification has *already* happened what is to be gained by adding to the cacophony?

© The Author(s), under exclusive license to Springer Nature Switzerland AG 2024
K. Boyle, *#MeToo and Feminism*,
https://doi.org/10.1007/978-3-031-67314-6_7

Indeed, if we accept that justice for victim/survivors includes recognition and acknowledgement within their communities (e.g. McGlynn and Westmarland 2019; Herman 2023), for those same communities to demand that victim/survivors *keep* telling the same stories is arguably a form of injustice in itself. In this chapter I use Jilly Boyce Kay's (2020) notion of *communicative* in/justice to make sense of this, but here I want to acknowledge that communicative in/justice is inextricably linked to other forms of justice seeking in the experiences of victim/survivors.

This chapter begins with a consideration of "breaking the silence" as a commercial imperative before moving on to related narratives around "breaking the story" in the #MeToo era. As many of the cases discussed in this book have shown, investigative journalism has been key to the #MeToo moment. Here, I am particularly interested in how accounts of "breaking the story" have provided corroboration of the silencing of victim/survivors in ways that, simultaneously, decentre their voices. This sets up questions about representativeness, expertise and experience which are taken up more fully in the penultimate section. In considering the relationship between experience and expertise, my aim is not to present one as inherently better than the other, but rather to consider the different *representational* claims they can make and, importantly, the ways in which those claims can be interrogated. In the final section, I bring these concerns together in a discussion of the #MeToo documentary (Horeck 2024). This chapter thus recognises both the limitations and possibilities of mass media forms as tools for feminists working to end men's sexual harassment and assault of women, children and other men. But it also insists that that work is never solely personal and never solely discursive.

Breaking the Silence (Again)

In February 2023, a news story about actor Armie Hammer caught my eye. Two years earlier, Hammer had been publicly accused of sexual misconduct and abuse by multiple women. What was "new" in February 2023 was that Hammer had given his first interview on the topic:

> Armie Hammer Breaks His Silence: Two years after some of the most shocking allegations of the #MeToo era lit up the Internet and destroyed his career, the actor has finally decided to tell his side of the story.
>
> (Kirchick 2023)

This headline stayed with me whilst I was working on this book and this section is my attempt to think through what accounts of silence breaking like Hammer's have to do with the silence breakers whose collective speech has transformed our understanding of sexual harassment and assault, as discussed in Chapter 2. To investigate this, I used the Nexis database of news stories to identify uses of "breaks his silence" and "breaks her silence" in English-language news media in 2017 and 2023. These searches yielded some interesting results: first, in both periods, men are far more likely than women to be the silence breakers; and, second, the use of these phrases increases massively between the two periods.[1] However, in both years, a minority of these stories relate to sexual harassment and assault specifically.

In both the 2017 and 2023 corpus, breaking the silence is something of a clickbait cliche, regularly deployed in slightly salacious celebrity stories or in relation to potentially contentious political events or sports news. Notably, in these stories "breaking the silence" is used primarily to mean choosing to speak publicly about something. What is entirely absent is any sense of *being* silenced. Indeed, a number of the same celebrities crop up so regularly in silence breaking stories that one headline slightly wearily announces "Prince Harry breaks his silence (again)" (Whitworth 2023). That there is no silence to break is also illustrated in a *Mail Online* article which has singer Sam Ryder "breaking his silence" about being beaten to the Christmas number one spot by Wham! in a social media post *immediately following* the broadcast of the Official Chart Show (Philips 2023). Although not with the same satirical intent as the Prince Harry headline, this example also prompts the question as to when, exactly, Ryder was silent.

These examples are relevant to my concerns in this chapter because they suggest not only an imperative to speak publicly but also the demand for immediacy. Moreover, the demand for public speech is not sated by a single speech act and this has particular significance in stories about sexual harassment and assault. For both victim/survivors and those accused of harassment and assault, there is a constant need to *keep* breaking the silence by speaking on new platforms in response to developments in their stories. This means that silence often functions in the absence of silenc*ing*: both silence and speech are predominately constructed as

[1] The search for "breaks his silence" returned 766 articles for 2017 and 1492 for 2023. The equivalent numbers for "breaks her silence" were 535 and 1323.

personal choices; there is no sense of power or risk; and, particularly in celebrity stories, it is assumed that those speaking will be heard, even though the seriality of the silence breaking story paradoxically demonstrates the failure to listen (Kay 2020: 65–67). What these stories demand of readers, then, is the work of a *moment*—to believe or not believe—not the work of cultural change, or of achieving justice for victim/survivors.

In relation to victim/survivors, "breaking the silence" is akin to the positioning of Tarana Burke as always and only the founder of Me Too rather than its leader (see Chapter 2): it traps victim/survivors at the moment of their vulnerability, repackaged to fit the needs of a different medium or moment. Take, for example, this headline from *Daily Mail* (Australia):

> Madeleine West breaks her silence: *Neighbours* star films emotional *60 Minutes* with Tara Brown after the "monster" who abused her as a child was finally brought to justice.
> (Manly 2023).

In the article which follows, it becomes clear that the actor had previously shared some aspects of her story on Instagram. It is the medium and tenor of her speech—not what she actually said—which makes this a news story in November 2023. Indeed, the article has nothing to say about the content of West's interview (beyond its assumed emotional tenor) but rather is based on her "being seen filming segments with a crew along Tallow Beach in Byron Bay on Wednesday". The article also notes that, "Daily Mail Australia witnessed reporter Tara Brown arrive at West's multimillion-dollar Suffolk Park home, 5 km south of Byron, after midday". Finally, the article documents the breakdown of West's marriage and her legal battles with her ex-father-in-law. In other words, "breaking her silence" in *one* context legitimates intrusive surveillance of West in *all* contexts: where she goes, with whom and when.

There are parallels here with Kay's discussion of how Monica Lewinsky was repeatedly represented as "finally" breaking her silence about Bill Clinton every time she gave an interview or speech over a period of years. Kay argues:

> The "voice" that has been granted here is conditional on a *logic of communicative self- transformation* in which the speaking subject must

strategically perform silence as a legitimating precursor to every expression of voice. (2020: 67)

Whilst Kay sees this as an example of the "gendered patterning" of voices, this reading is complicated somewhat by the more frequent attribution of silence breaking to *male* speakers in my Nexis searches. However, whilst both men and women may be subject to the repetitive commercial logic of breaking the silence, when stories relating to victim/survivors are compared to those focused on accused men the "gendered patterning" Kay observes comes back into focus.

Although it caught my eye, the Hammer headline is not, in fact, that unusual in #MeToo stories. Indeed, this formula is already well-worn in the 2017 corpus. For instance, in December 2017, a number of outlets reported Weinstein "FINALLY break[ing] his silence" to offer a rebuttal of a statement made by actor Salma Hayek (e.g. Griffith and Spargo 2017; Gardner 2017). These articles are not supportive of Weinstein; indeed, they adopt a slightly bemused tone that it is *these* allegations (among the many) that he has chosen to respond to. But the assertion of silence ignores what Weinstein had *already* said in response to the sexual harassment and abuse story including, but by no means restricted to: his statement to the *New York Times* (Weinstein 2017); an interview with the *New York Post* published almost simultaneously with Kantor and Twohey's story (Smith 2017); on-camera statements to reporters[2] and a statement responding to Lupito Nyong'o (Loughrey 2017). In other words, Weinstein had never *not* had access to a public platform though, tellingly, the two women who prompted his direct statements—Hayek and Nyong'o—were the first women of colour to speak publicly against him. There are different ways of reading this racialised refusal: Weinstein's rebuttal can be seen as an attempt to re-assert his liberal credentials (whatever else he did, he didn't abuse women of colour) and/or as a safe bet given the racialised and sexualised doubt which women of colour must overcome to be believed. Either way, a question mark is placed next to the speech of women of colour whilst, at the same time, Weinstein's reconstruction as silence breaker reinforces the backlash narrative that it is

---

[2] Filmed getting into his car in Los Angeles Weinstein told reporters: "Guys, I'm not doing OK, but I'm trying, I've gotta get help guys. You know we all make mistakes, a second chance I hope". See https://www.youtube.com/watch?v=Lx5cGNQv20w&t=29s (Accessed 21 February 2024).

men who are being silenced in the #MeToo era. In this way, Weinstein and other accused men can, as Sarah Banet-Weiser (2021: 70) argues in her examination of men's statements in the wake of assault claims, *perform* the #MeToo genre, claiming the position of victimisation, silence and powerlessness as their own, at the same time as asserting that it is precisely their power that has rendered them so vulnerable.

Two examples from 2023, relating to comedian Russell Brand and football chief Luis Rubiales, show how this backlash narrative has persisted. The night before the story about him was due to air on Channel 4's *Dispatches* in September 2023, Brand outed himself as the-celebrity-who-was-about-to-be-outed, ensuring he got his rebuttal in before the details of the *Dispatches/Sunday Times* investigation were made public (Brand 2023). Like Weinstein's statement in 2017, Brand's rebuttal was widely picked up by the news media and was included in the *Dispatches* documentary itself. Yet, when Brand posted another video to social media one week later this was described by both the *Sun* (Johnson 2023) and *Mail on Sunday* (Hind 2023) as Brand "breaking his silence". In Rubiales' case, his refusal to resign amidst the international outcry following his forced kiss on World Cup Winner Jenni Hermoso culminated in an extraordinary press conference on 25 August where he shouted down his detractors to the applause of the primarily male audience. Nearly a week later, the *Mail Online* had him "breaking his silence" to claim he was "advancing feminism" in response to new calls from Spain's Acting Sports and Culture Minister for him to resign. Rubiales' "explosive" statement was, the article notes, released "within minutes" of the Minister's claims (Rudling 2023). In what has become another familiar rhetorical move, Rubiales also claimed to be the victim of a "lynching" (Rudling 2023).

The idea that either of these men had been silent is laughable: both were loud, forceful and immediate in their denials; and both had consistent access to media, enabling their speech to be heard. Yet, even in the face of largely unsympathetic media coverage of both these men, the silence breaking claims persist. These claims resonate with backlash narratives I have identified throughout this book, suggesting it is *feminists* who are the silencing agents. This interpretation is leant some weight when these examples are placed alongside other articles in the 2023 "breaks his silence" corpus which speak to what we might call—following the discussion of Damonsplaining in Chapter 3—the "Damon effect": the sense that men and boys are being punished for speaking "common sense" about gender. Two headlines, both from the *Mail Online* demonstrate this:

> Parents of boy, 12, are suing school that kicked out son for wearing "there are only two genders" shirt, as kid breaks his silence: 'They took away my ability to have a different opinion. (Sultan 2023).
> EXCLUSIVE: Married at First Sight star Dean Wells breaks his silence after being dropped by his management for criticising a drag queen story time event for kids as young as three. (Friedlander 2023)

Note that in both these examples, the boy or man is "breaking his silence" in relation to the consequences of his own, prior, statements. As with Brand and Rubiales, the articles themselves provide the evidence they had never been silent in the first place. What is at stake here is not their ability to speak, or indeed, to command an audience for that speech, but, rather, the sense that they are speaking out in a context where the *legitimacy* of what they have to say can no longer be taken for granted.

Returning to breaking the silence about sexual harassment and assault, it is not only perpetrators and victim/survivors who are compelled to speech. Whilst, as I've argued throughout this book, there are legitimate questions for witnesses and bystanders to answer, it is notable that women are routinely asked to account for men to whom they are, or have been, connected. For instance, the responses of Brand's ex-wife Katy Perry and his sister-in-law Kirsty Gallacher to the *Dispatches/Sunday Times* investigation were extensively anticipated. Tabloid news media widely reported on the two women's first social media posts following *Dispatches* (e.g. Ngimbi 2023; Roberts 2023), despite the fact that neither Perry nor Gallacher address the Brand story in their posts. Though some reports speak positively of their "stoic" (Chester 2023) and "dignified" silences (Dean 2023), the Brand story legitimates increased surveillance of these women's lives: whatever they do now is read through the lens of their association with Brand; whatever they said about him in the past is subject to scrutiny and criticism.

This is also true of reports about comedian Katherine Ryan attempting to "break the silence" about Brand in her comedy. There are some parallels here with Seth MacFarlane's "outing" of Harvey Weinstein—discussed in Chapter 6—or with Hannibal Buress naming Bill Cosby as a rapist in his stand-up. However, whilst these men were widely praised for their attempts to speak out, Ryan faced criticism for failing to name Brand as though in doing so she enabled his abuse to continue (Lewis 2023). Again, the powerful effects of silenc*ing* are not evident here. Indeed, one report went as far as to suggest that Ryan stood to profit materially and reputationally from her role in the Brand story:

> How Katherine Ryan could have the last laugh on Russell Brand! Comic who warned of "sexual predator" in the industry could earn MILLIONS as new face of reignited #MeToo movement. (Matthews and Cotterill 2023)

With its construction of Ryan as #MeToo's richly rewarded brand ambassador, there is no clearer example of my claim in Chapter 4 that feminism is popularly configured as a product not a process. Notably, all of the "experts" called on to review Ryan's impact in this story are public relations professionals. The story of women speaking out about men's sexual violence is thus reduced to the story of women speaking; the speech itself is emptied of meaning and, so, denied the possibility to effect meaningful cultural, structural change.

Many of the cases I have discussed in this book have spawned books, podcasts, documentaries and speaking tours and victim/survivors have at times profited materially from their participation. This has then been used by accused men to cast doubt on their motivations for speaking out whilst casting wealthy men as inherently vulnerable to exploitation. This is evident in the statement provided by R. Kelly's lawyer, seen repeatedly on screen in *Surviving R. Kelly: The Reckoning* (Lifetime 2020):

> R. Kelly has denied all claims relating to sexual assault, domestic violence/abuse and sexual misconduct with minors.
> Kelly's lawyer claims that Kelly has witness statements and evidence showing his innocence but cannot release them due to the active court cases against him.
> His lawyer also alleged that R. Kelly "is the subject of a smear campaign" and that "the accusers have not acted like victims at all" because "they have used their accusations to promote contemporaneous books, albums and speaking tours."

Here, again, we see the double standards which surround women's speech about sexual violence: for that speech to be believable it must always and only come *at a cost* to victim/survivors. Indeed, part of what renders these women incredible in this account is their failure to remain fixed in the moment of their victimisation: to act *like victims*. The material wealth

Kelly accrued in music and performances which glorified the abuse of Black women and girls does not dent *his* credibility, indeed it makes him vulnerable precisely because he now has so much to lose. Of course, we cannot know what the earning power and professional standing of these women would have been had their careers not been derailed by Kelly's abuse.

Part of the difficulty here—attested to by many of the victim/survivors who have spoken "on the record" for and in relation to the stories discussed in this book—is that becoming a public survivor means that the abuse they experienced comes to define them, their names become "synonymous" with the abuse (Hill 1997: 2). This is perhaps particularly true for women who did not previously have a public profile and have become "known" through their speech about sexual harassment and assault. Anything they do publicly is then read through the lens of their assault so that, perversely, any evidence of material or professional success can be constructed as evidence that they have benefitted from being assaulted, or at least from speaking publicly about it. This benefit is then weighed against the cost to the men who abused them.

Yet, being known as a victim/survivor can limit the range of roles and opportunities available because of the stigma associated with sexual assault. As Hannah, a victim/survivor I spoke with on a project about news coverage of rape, told me:

> I can know someone for five years and they maybe think good things about my life, but I could go on the news tomorrow and talk about it [the rape] and I swear I would bump into them and they would look at their feet. And that's because of how it's portrayed on the news. I might come across fine in a particular interview, but they associate me with the portrayal that we all have in our heads, a sort of stigmatised message. And I do want people to understand, yes, I've been through horrific things, I've had a difficult time, as we all do, but we also don't want to be looked at as, that you know, our lives are over.
>
> (Hannah, quoted in Boyle et al. 2023: 115–116)

As Hannah suggests here, the "ruined life" discourse means that as a public survivor her capacity and capability in other spheres of her life are thrown into question. Indeed, this is why many women choose *not* to speak publicly, or decide to stop doing so (Brison 2008; Serisier 2020).

To go back to Louise Armstrong's account of breaking the silence about incest, these examples are suggestive of the ways in which noise can serve the same function as silence:

> How did we get from enforced secrecy, the suppression of children's experiences, women's experiences, such that they were not ever heard – to a level of cacophony such that children's voices, women's voices, are once more not, in any purposeful sense, being heard? (1996: 8)

The word *purposeful* is key here. Communicative justice, to use Kay's (2020) helpful term, is not secured by breaking the silence if the listener still fails to translate what they hear into action—or if that action has a solely commercial imperative (Banet-Weiser 2018). Communicative justice is also, importantly, not achieved by an individual speech act. As Kay puts it, communicative *in*justice

> relates to the multiple ways in which women, as well as LGBTQ people, people of colour, working-class people, disabled people, and other "others" are denied a voice that is sufficiently *expansive, complex and meaningful* so as to allow them a position of full citizenship and personhood in contemporary culture. (2020: 8, emphasis mine)

"Breaking the silence" has not achieved communicative justice in the examples I have given here. Instead, it has become a tried-and-tested formula for selling a story, suggesting newness, exclusivity and revelation. Ironically, this in itself may be a silencing strategy as the work and risk involved in speaking out about sexual violence is subsumed by the commercial imperatives of clickbait whilst the surveillance of all aspects of the lives of women in the public eye is legitimated. As we have seen throughout this book, breaking the silence was never an entirely accurate descriptor for the explosion of testimony in the long #MeToo moment: it was not that women had been silent but that they had not been listened to. The conditions under which their speech could become consequential are best understood not in relation to breaking the silence but breaking the story.

Breaking the Story

The years leading up to Jodi Kantor, Megan Twohey and Ronan Farrow's Pulitzer-prize winning journalism about Harvey Weinstein had established the importance of investigative journalism in uncovering systemic sexual abuse in a range of contexts. In 2002, the investigative staff of the *Boston Globe* also won a Pulitzer, in that case for their reporting on abuse within the Catholic Church (Carroll et al. 2016). The investigative team at the *Indianapolis Star* first broke the story about sexual abuse in USA Gymnastics in 2016 (IndyStar, n.d.), the same year that Twohey and Michael Barbaro's investigations into Donald Trump's sexual misconduct were published in the *New York Times* (Barbaro and Twohey 2016). In the months leading up to the Weinstein story, the *New York Times* broke the story about *Fox News'* Bill O'Reilly (Steel and Schmidt 2017) and published an investigation into sexual harassment in Silicon Valley (Benner 2017). Less spectacularly, but no less significantly, in the UK, child sexual abuse had been the focus of a slew of investigative documentaries in the years prior to #MeToo, focusing on "sex gangs", football, politics and, of course, on the abusive career of Jimmy Savile.[3] What these stories all had in common was their focus on men who had abused multiple victim/survivors over decades, often with the knowledge of those around them.

In addition to the sheer volume of reporting, it is notable how often the difficulties in breaking the story *become* the story in this period. The Oscar-winning film *Spotlight* (dir. Tom McCarthy, 2015), for instance, focuses on the *Boston Globe* journalists breaking the story about abuse in the Catholic church. The Savile case is another obvious reference point here, not only in relation to Merion Jones' and Liz Keen's frustrated attempts to break the story at *Newsnight* but also in the reflections of documentarian Louis Theroux (*Louis Theroux: Savile*, BBC2, 2016) and biographer Dan Davies (2014) on their inability to break the story in Savile's lifetime. More recently, Julie K. Brown of the *Miami Herald* has published a book about breaking the Jeffrey Epstein story (Brown 2021) and Jim DeRogatis has written about his role in breaking the story about R. Kelly (DeRogatis 2019). To return to Weinstein specifically, both Kantor and Twohey (2019) and Farrow (2019) have published best-selling books about their reporting. Kantor and Twohey's *She Said*

---

[3] For a list of relevant programmes see Boyle (2018).

was made into a film (dir. Maria Schneider, 2022) whilst Farrow hosted a *Catch and Kill* podcast (Pineapple Street Studios, 2019–2020) to coincide with Weinstein's first criminal trial and an HBO series, *Catch and Kill: The Podcast Tapes,* followed (HBO 2021). One of the journalists featured in *The Podcast Tapes,* the *New Yorker's* media critic Ken Auletta, has himself published a post-#MeToo biography of Weinstein which recounts how he *almost* broke the Weinstein story (Auletta 2022). These examples are just the tip of the iceberg.

Here I want to consider the breaking-the-story-story as a space where a feminist analysis and understanding of men's violence against women can emerge, albeit in contested ways. A common thread running through these stories is abusers' attempts to thwart investigations and/or publication. For instance, Kantor and Twohey (2019) and Farrow (2019) identify the many resources Weinstein and his supporters were able to draw upon to silence victim/survivors, witnesses and critics. Securing the "on the record" testimony of associates, witnesses and—most centrally— victim/survivors provides much of the suspense in the book-length accounts of these investigations. The risk involved in speaking out is extensively and sympathetically detailed, with attention not only to the legal jeopardy posed by non-disclosure agreements, but also to the psychological toll, impact on family and friends, and potential professional consequences. It is abundantly clear in these stories that breaking the silence is not the work of a moment and that journalists were eventually able to get sources on the record precisely because of the weight of *other* evidence. For instance, Kantor and Twohey (2019: 149) describe the "25 years of allegations, a clear pattern, names and examples, human resources records, legal and financial information, and quotes from male and female employees characterizing the problem" which they shared with Ashley Judd before she went on the record. Both *She Said* and *Catch and Kill* also establish the work, time and resources required to investigate and fact-check these stories, alongside the editorial and legal wranglings involved in getting to print (see also Robinson and Yoshida 2023). As Tanya Horeck and Diane Negra (2022) argue in relation to the documentary series *Allen v. Farrow* (HBO 2021), these stories can explain and interrogate the communicative injustice (Kay 2020) victim/survivors have historically encountered in ways that make social (and sometimes criminal) justice demands. As such, the response these stories require is not simply in relation to the abuser himself, they also highlight the need for community responses as well as organisational and sometimes legal change.

In the broader context of the long #MeToo moment, however, the long lists of evidence deployed in investigative exposés give me pause as—in some contexts at least—they seem to have become another tool in the abuse apologist's arsenal. To be clear, my argument here is not about the standards of evidence that do or should apply in courtrooms or newsrooms, but rather that the centrality of investigative journalism and the criminal justice system to the long #MeToo moment may establish unrealistic standards of evidence for more everyday encounters with victim/survivor speech. As in Chapter 3 where I reflected on the sometimes-jarring experience of encountering very different forms of sexual harassment and abuse side by side through the shared use of hashtags, this is a concern about the flattening of context which can occur in the multi-platform era. What is the effect, for instance, of encountering unreportable testimonies under #MeToo in the same thread as Kantor and Twohey's or Farrow's reporting on Weinstein? Are individuals really more likely to be believed when they speak publicly about sexual harassment and assault six years after #MeToo; or have we simply established new standards for scrutinising their claims? It is notable, for instance, that the four-part documentary series *Allen v. Farrow*, and its accompanying podcast, provided the "semantic thickness" (Serisier 2018: 108)—in the form of three years' worth of research against the backdrop of the #MeToo moment—that allowed Dylan Farrow's story to be heard differently, at least in some quarters (Strauss 2021). Dylan's story—which had been widely reported since the early 1990s—had not, in itself, changed.

It is also relevant here to consider the role of journalistic objectivity and of feminism in telling the story of sexual violence. Feminism functions as a professional "stain" in some journalistic contexts and can open journalists up to virulent online misogyny attacking their credibility and potentially limiting the impact of their reporting (Gardiner 2018; Møller Hartley and Askanius 2021). This was the tactic *Fox News* adopted in relation to Megan Twohey as a means of attacking the legitimacy and accuracy of her reporting on Trump (Kantor and Twohey 2019: 17). Ronan Farrow also describes how his objectivity was questioned because of his public support for his sister (Farrow 2019: 188–189). Given what we know about the prevalence of sexual assault, to require that journalists investigating these stories have not been personally impacted by sexual assault would leave a very narrow reporting pool. Moreover, far from being a "sexual assault crusader", in a 2016 column for the *Hollywood Reporter* Ronan Farrow describes his own complicity as a reporter in *not* previously asking difficult questions about sexual assault in the entertainment industry. As such, he makes clear the lack of objectivity which has long characterised reporting on sexual assault, where the scales are weighted against victim/survivors by journalistic norms and the ways in which abusers can control access and content. Ronan notes, for instance, that when the *New York Times* published Dylan's 2014 open letter she had just over 900 words embedded in a blog "with careful caveats". In contrast, their father's response—published in a prime position in the print edition—was twice the length and published without caveat.

She Said and *Catch and Kill* expose objectivity as a myth, but— at the same time—they remain invested in it, taking care to distance the reporters from feminist activists and others who are emotionally or politically invested in the story. Although Kantor and Twohey (2019: 25) acknowledge that the idea for investigating Harvey Weinstein came from "Shaunna Thomas, a feminist activist" there is no further mention of Thomas in the book, nor of feminist advocacy organisations or researchers. Instead, there is an emphasis on the accumulation of evidence: legal documents, internal memos, company records as well as interviews on and off the record. Similarly, Ronan insists that he not only believes Dylan *as a brother*, but "more importantly, I've approached the case as an attorney and a reporter, and found her allegations to be credible" (Farrow 2016).

Whilst Kantor, Twohey and (Ronan) Farrow are understandably cautious that anything other than a strictly "objective" orientation to their reporting might limit its impact, it is relevant to set this concern against the context of communicative injustice which has long shaped what stories are told and how they are told (Kay 2020; Horeck and Negra 2022). It is a central tenet of active bystander interventions that it is not possible to be a detached observer in cases of sexual harassment and assault: to do nothing is to do something. There are numerous examples of how media organisations have acted to—tacitly or explicitly—support abusive men and their legacies, from the BBC's shelving of the *Newsnight* investigation into Savile (Pollard 2012), to the "catch and kill" practices which protect men like Weinstein (Farrow 2019) or Chinese state-censorship of stories relating to media men (Li 2024). The long #MeToo moment thus brings debates about bystander intervention, journalistic objectivity and editorial independence crashing into one another. This is tricky terrain for journalists to navigate as their own industries—and their involvement in them—have been part of the story (Møller Hartley and Askanius 2021; Sreedharan et al. 2020). Yet, the meta-commentary on the reporting of sexual harassment and assault has allowed for connections to be drawn to the wider context of gender inequalities in newsrooms (Møller Hartley and Askanius 2021; Sreedharan et al. 2020). In this way, reporting on #MeToo has created possibilities to reflect on the conditions of production, albeit in ways which have often been highly personalised. In the next section, the relationship between the personal and political, individual and representative, is taken up more fully in relation to the function of expertise and experience in the long #MeToo moment.

Experience and Expertise

I start this section with a personal experience of the conditional nature of women's expertise. In April 2022, I was invited on Nicky Campbell's phone-in on Radio 5 Live, alongside Dr Charlotte Proudman (a feminist barrister and academic) and Nicky Clark (founder of the Act Your Age campaign) to discuss the latest example of misogyny in the Westminster Parliament.[4] The ostensible focus was a *Mail on Sunday* story in which an anonymous Tory MP accused the Deputy Leader of the Opposition, Angela Rayner MP, of using her legs—like Sharon Stone in *Basic Instinct* (dir. Paul Verhoeven, 1992)—to distract then Prime Minister, Boris Johnson, during Prime Minister's Questions. As I was waiting to be brought into the discussion, Campbell asked Proudman: did she have any similar experiences to share? Listening in, I panicked. What would I say if he asked me? At the heart of this panic was an uncertainty about what—or who—I was there to represent. I worried that my examples might seem too trivial and therefore be used by detractors to further their arguments about women reading too much into things.

As it turned out, I wasn't asked that question. But as I documented in Chapter 2, since the earliest days of #MeToo it has been common practice for women in public life to be asked variations of the "has it happened to you?" question. When women who are ostensibly invited to comment

---

[4] This discussion of the Radio 5 Live phone-in draws on a blog I wrote at the time for *Gender Equal Media Scotland* (Boyle 2022).

because of our *professional* expertise are questioned in this way, what are our options and what does it mean for how our expertise is understood?

There are many reasons women may not want to disclose personal experiences of this nature. Experiences may be too recent, too raw, or too traumatic to speak of (especially without forewarning) on national radio. Indeed, both Proudman and some of the women ringing in chose to speak about experiences from some time ago. One of the difficulties, however, is that these stories can then be used as evidence of how bad things were, whilst callers congratulate themselves on now being considerably more enlightened. This version of the "different times" narrative is Angela McRobbie's (2009) "double entanglement" in action: the recognition of the truth of past experiences in the present is evidence that the problem is fixed and the speech is no longer needed. And so to counter the complacency of now we are required to offer more recent examples, keeping the cycle of disclosure going. That is *not* how Proudman presented her experience, but that I feel the need to add this qualification demonstrates one of the problems with the question: it focuses our attention on what individual women's experiences represent; not on men's behaviour.

The invitation to speak also, implicitly, lays the responsibility for silence at women's feet whilst failing to engage with the ways in which victim/survivors' silence is secured and their speech disbelieved. In the context of this particular phone-in, speaking publicly about workplaces may have posed a risk to women's continued employment or opportunities, for instance. For women who are already seen as not "fitting in"—because they work in a particularly male-dominated workplace, or because they are further marginalised by race or class, for example—speaking out is even more fraught. And it is not just in our workplaces that we might worry about "fitting in": our role as media commentators can also be precarious. Women still make up just 24% of experts in leading news stories globally, according to the 2020 Global Media Monitoring Project (GMMP), but 42% of those sharing personal experiences are women, and 38% of those giving popular opinion (Macharia 2021: 17). In the Scottish context in which I write, these gendered patterns are also sharply racialised. In a study of women of colour in Scottish news media, Melody House, Talat Yaqoob and I found that women of colour made up only 1.3% of experts (Boyle et al 2024: 31).

The "has it happened to you?" question also assumes that personal experience *is* evidence and that it is on a par with the other kinds of evidence academics and campaigners might be expected to offer such as their own research findings, evidence from professional practice, or overviews of available evidence in a particular field. To have no experience to offer in response to this question is therefore to compromise your position as expert. But to refuse the question is equally loaded: remember how Uma Thurman's restrained fury in response to that question *became* the story (see Chapter 2). In other words, "has it happened to you?" makes *our* responses (not men's behaviour) and the position from which we speak the focus. It is difficult to imagine Campbell asking a male barrister, academic or campaigner if it had happened to them or, for that matter, if they have ever made misogynist comments or sexually harassed their female colleagues. Women's presence in the public sphere should not be contingent on our willingness to share personal experiences.

This is not to deny that the evidentiary quality of experience has been central to feminist research and activism. In trying to unravel the kinds of evidence experience provides—without falling into the trap of interrogating the evidentiary claims of individual accounts—I have found it useful to return to debates about standpoint in feminist epistemology. Standpoint theory emerged as a powerful counterpoint to the traditional assumption that research should be objective and disinterested. Early iterations admittedly tended towards essentialism, as in Dorothy Smith's (1974) argument for women's standpoint as a radical critique of sociology. Even so, Smith's theorisation of women's standpoint is structural not strictly experiential: that is, it is about the position which women occupy in relation to power and, so, knowledge. The value of women's standpoint in this sense is that it offers a unique position from which to interrogate patriarchal privilege. As Sandra Harding (2012: 49) puts it, standpoint "studies up"; it uses the margins to better understand the mechanisms of power. This has been an important challenge to historical constructions of women as subjective and so particular, as well as to the unacknowledged androcentrism of traditional knowledge projects.

However, it is important to recognise that occupying the margins does not *necessarily* equate to occupying a position critical of the status quo and women as a group have very varied relationships to both the margins and centre of power (e.g. hooks 1992: 115–132; Simmonds 1997; Collins 2000; Tyler 2020: 211–240). Standpoint is not an identity claim. To return to Sandra Harding:

> All understanding is socially located or situated. Yet the success of standpoint research requires only a degree of freedom from the dominant understanding, not complete freedom from it. And it requires collective effort. Thus *a standpoint is an achievement, not an ascription*. Women do not automatically have access to a standpoint of women or a feminist standpoint. Such a standpoint must be struggled for against the apparent realities made to appear natural and obvious by dominant institutions, and against the ongoing political disempowerment of oppressed groups. (2012: 51, emphasis added)

These struggles, Harding notes, need to be understood as "systematically knowledge producing" (*ibid.*): it is the struggle—a struggle played out in modes of consciousness-raising and collective action, for example—which generates knowledge. At the heart of the debate about standpoint is my central concern in this section with the relationship between an "I" claim and a representative one; between *being* a victim/survivor and speaking *for* victim/survivors. These positions are, of course, not mutually exclusive, but they are also not mutually constitutive. To return to Harding,

> experience is not itself public, authenticated knowledge, for the latter requires kinds of critical reflection and collective legitimation that are not characteristic of women's or anyone else's experiences in themselves. (2012: 57)

Part of the problem with the mainstream media's role in contemporary narratives around sexual harassment and assault is that it makes experience a condition of knowledge in ways that require the endless "confession" of victim/survivor identity and experience. My argument here connects with the work of scholars who have pointed to the "traumatic paradox" (Walker 2005) or "credibility conundrum" (Jordan 2004) victim/survivors face when speaking of trauma, including that related to sexual violence; namely that for their trauma to be believable it must be unspeakable, yet the failure to speak of it renders it unbelievable.

In a UK context, there has been something of a fetishisation of "lived experience" as an unmediated source of truth in policy circles too. Whilst, in some ways, this is a positive move, there is also reason to be cynical. Listening to *this* survivor can minimise the need for the more challenging work of participative policy making whilst simultaneously negating the need for the more time-consuming and expensive work of research and advocacy. Moreover, the emphasis on "lived experience" asks individuals to subject themselves to endless scrutiny and disbelief not only in relation to their own experience but their suitability to represent a group for which they have been determined (often by others) to be an exemplary representative. Given the historical construction of women's *particularity* referenced above, doubt is baked into women's representational claims in a way it is not for the "default male" (Criado Perez 2019).

There is also a promise—potentially a false promise—in the solicitation of "lived experience": a promise that you will be listened to such that your speech is consequential. But what if your speech is solicited and *not* heard, *not* acted upon? This is an all-too-familiar experience for victim/survivors of sexual harassment and abuse who have seen their words used against their stated interests, most obviously—though hardly exclusively—in the criminal justice system. Privileging victim/survivor speech can also mean fixing the victim/survivor at a moment of vulnerability and fixing the meaning of that experience. It negates the possibility of transformation of understanding and assumes a kind of ontological security as to what that experience is and how it shapes their identity (cf Brison 2008). This is at odds with accounts of sexual violence developed through research with victim/survivors which points to the messiness, uncertainty and contingency of meaning (e.g. Gavey 2005, Alcoff 2018, McGlynn and Westmarland 2019). However, given the way that women's public speech—particularly, but not exclusively, when related to men's violence—is always already subject to doubt (Kay 2020), for a victim/survivor to admit that messiness in public is to cast further doubt on their ability to represent themselves, never mind to represent others. As Tanya Serisier (2020: 170–171) notes, this also privileges a particular kind of storytelling, one which centres trauma and harm and is constitutive of the victim/survivor as a particular kind of person, one whose life is altered by events which are *therefore* deemed harmful, wrong and deserving of censure. This can extend the scrutiny of victim/survivors (as well as those who have experienced sexual harassment and assault but do not recognise themselves in those terms) as once again it is the believability and legitimacy of their claims—in this case of trauma and harm—which are at stake. This can also play into accused men's deniability: in the absence of clear and immediate evidence of trauma or harm, how could they be expected to know that their behaviour was wrong?

The verdict in Weinstein's original New York trial was widely heralded as evidence of a new willingness to grapple with the messy contradictions of victim/survivors' experiences. Whilst there are reasons to be cautious of these claims (not least in light of the 2024 decision by the New York Court of Appeal), they are not entirely without merit. Victim/survivors' own use of media has also created possibilities for more complex narratives to emerge though every platform seems to have its own conventions of believability (e.g. Serisier 2018: 93–116; Kay 2020; Banet-Weiser and Higgins 2023; Harrington and Gerrard 2024). My argument here is not that these forms of storytelling are *not* forms of evidence, but rather that we need to resist the demand on victim/survivors to always be the "face of" the sexual harassment and assault story as this does not, fundamentally, shift the burden of believability. Indeed, the emphasis on experience as expertise sets the stage for highly personalised contests *between* women over the meaning and consequences of men's violence. For instance, in her work on rape and narrative politics, Serisier (2018: 23–42) identifies a number of high-profile rape survivors from the 1980s and 1990s whose public platform was, at least in part, based on the fundamentally conservative orientation of their speech which sought to distinguish between victims of "real" rape, like themselves, and other categories of victims. There have been numerous similar examples in social media discussions surrounding cases discussed in this book—including most vividly in relation to the Depp v. Heard trial (Bedera 2022)—with conservative users mobilising their own experiences as evidence that other women are not "real" victims. Part of what is at stake here is that when a woman speaks in public about rape or any form of sexual assault she is routinely constructed as speaking for—or judged as *failing* to speak for—a category of experience and personhood. The public survivor—typically an atypical figure, given everything we know about media logics and the disproportionate focus on particular types of assaults and people—is too often deployed in place of a collective understanding, to represent the category by representing herself.

One of the advantages of de-centring experience, then, is that it enables a critique of representational claims which does not invalidate individual experiences. Thus, it is possible—as Serisier does (2018)—to accept and believe an individual victim/survivor's account of her own experience whilst questioning the ways in which it is deployed in or against the collective interests of victim/survivors, or of a particularly situated group of victim/survivors. A feminist project of collective voice is based on understanding what women share, as well as where their experiences are structurally differentiated, for instance on the grounds of race, class or location. It is a project of critical listening, of analysis and, to use Tarana Burke's term, of work. It is *not* an identity claim and it is not reducible to experience. Of course, the results of that listening and analysis, whether led by survivors or not, may make claims to representativeness and these can and should be interrogated. However, the difference is that these claims can be interrogated in relation to process—how are they arrived at, who do they include and exclude, how contextually specific are they?—not personal believability.

There is a necessary caveat here. As Serisier (2018: 119–144) demonstrates, debates *within* feminism—and specifically within feminist academia—about "speaking for" victim/survivors can also be heard in very personalised terms. Serisier's example is a debate that ensued following the publication of a controversial article by a white Australian radical feminist anthropologist (Diane Bell), jointly authored with an Aboriginal community leader (Topsy Napurrula Nelson), about violence in indigenous communities. When the article was criticised for ventriloquising and appropriating the experiences of indigenous women, what could have been productively understood as a critique of *process* that could lead to new insight was instead the focus of an extended, acrimonious and very *personalised* debate. The significance of this for my purposes here is that rather than help interrogate representational claims on the grounds of process—and so develop, improve and revise methods of knowledge production—the wounded response returns to the realm of the personal. There are parallels here with my discussion of my awkward exchange with the feminist film academic about Woody Allen in the previous chapter. Whilst I read that exchange through the lens of affective engagement with Allen and his films, it is equally possible to read it through the lens of the personal stake in feminist knowledge production.

This is consistent with the personalisation of feminist expertise in the mainstream media story about #MeToo. When I refer to feminist experts here, I do not mean feminist opinion-writers (who are nonetheless important), but rather feminists who give voice to specifically situated evidence gathered through activism, advocacy and/or research but still find their knowledge reduced to personal, subjective experience. This also means that, in the interests of "balance", feminist expertise can be juxtaposed with the opinions of the individual misogynist in media stories (Mumford 2017): what critics have referred to as "both-sides-ism" (e.g. Horeck and Negra 2022). In this way, the norms of journalistic practice can perpetuate the mediated entanglement of feminism and misogyny without interrogating the very different evidence bases which *should* support their representational claims. The Radio 5 Live segment with which I opened this section did not aim to "balance" feminists and misogynists in this way (at least until they opened the phone lines), but the deployment of the "has it happened to you" question still limited the terms of feminist engagement. The question resituated the feminist expert as the object to be known, not the knower. In her response to the "Bell debate" discussed above, Sara Ahmed (2000) suggests that the question "who speaks" only gets us so far; a more pertinent question may be "who *knows*"? In the context of the radio segment I have discussed here, the "has it happened to you?" question worked to resituate expertise in personal terms that had implications for *all* the knowledge claims in the segment, establishing—from the outset—the importance of experience as a form of knowledge in a way that potentially undermines other sources of knowledge as less immediate, less authentic. Given the well-documented costs of speaking publicly about sexual harassment and assault in an era of instantaneous backlash and sustained, intensive online misogyny and misogynoir, this is concerning.

The relationship between experience and expertise is central to feminist knowledge projects, but it is far from straightforward. My intent in this section is not to suggest that one form of knowledge is superior to another, but rather to demonstrate the contingency of all forms of knowledge at the same time as asking what kinds of knowledge are valued in different media contexts. In the final section, I turn to the #MeToo documentary (Horeck 2024) as a site where different kinds of knowledge about sexual harassment and assault have, at times, been productively brought together.

Surviving Speech

In her article on the US #MeToo documentary, Horeck focuses on a range of documentaries released "in the wake of #MeToo" (2024: 232) that "prioritis[e] the experiences of victim/survivors" (233). In keeping with the argument of this book, I want to acknowledge that the victim/survivor-centred documentary does not magically appear from nowhere post-Milano (Boyle 2018). Even so, the proliferation of this content post-2017 has been undeniable and shows no sign of abating.

In many ways, I share Horeck's analysis that these series have prioritised the experiences of victim/survivors. Indeed, some documentaries—such as the BBC's programmes on DJ Tim Westwood (*Abuse of Power*, 2022; *Hip Hop's Open Secret*, 2022)—focus exclusively on victim/survivor testimony. Although that exclusive focus is unusual, as Horeck notes a characteristic of the #MeToo documentary is the layering of victim/survivor testimony to build a picture of how abusers—primarily serial abusers in positions of power and/or celebrity—operate. The intercutting between victim/survivors' testimonies allows their common character to emerge and serves as a form of corroboration. Notably, victim/survivor testimony is not typically in doubt in the #MeToo documentary itself, although speaking out does open these victim/survivors (who are predominately, but by no means exclusively, women) to wider scrutiny, doubt and attack (see, for example, *Surviving R. Kelly: The Reckoning*, Episode 2.1).

Another feature of the #MeToo documentary is establishing a context for the abuser which provides a means of answering the question at the heart of many of them: namely, how did he get away with it for so long? As such, many of these documentaries make extensive use of archival footage of the abuser in his prime. So, for instance, in *Athlete A* (Netflix 2020) we see Larry Nassar mat-side at gymnastics competitions alongside his self-produced videos for his "Gymnasticsdoctor.com" channel; and ITV's *Rolf Harris: In Plain Sight* (2023) includes footage of the entertainer on stage and on television across his more than five decades in the public eye. This attention to context is both welcome and significant. However, there is a difficult balance to be struck between situating the abuser in context and allowing that context—*his* context—to shape the terms of the conversation. This can mean that whilst the layering of victim/survivor testimony can allow a collective story to emerge, it is a story about him where victim/survivors are defined primarily through their relationship with the abuser. It is with this concern in mind that it is relevant to consider the range of "knowers" featured in these documentaries.

Here I want to turn to Ursula MacFarlane's Weinstein documentary *Untouchable: The Harvey Weinstein Story* (Hulu 2019). As the title suggests, *Untouchable* is *Weinstein's* story: it follows his life and career. The abuse is threaded through that story from the very beginning in powerful victim/survivor accounts: indeed, the film's tagline is "Hear the voices that power could not silence". These voices are situated alongside interviews with people Weinstein worked with at Miramax/Weinstein Company and journalists who covered different stages of his career. In its final minutes, the film brings in #MeToo as the broader context in which Weinstein's abuses need to be situated. Ironically, although *Untouchable* introduces #MeToo through news footage of a protest march led by Tarana Burke, Burke is not identified in the clip nor is she mentioned at any point in the film. It is actor Rosanna Arquette—also one of the women who speaks about her experiences of Weinstein in the film and is pictured at the Women's March—who speaks of (and with) the impact of women's collective rage:

> This is a revolution, so go fuck yourselves! You know, how dare you. We are not going to be silenced. We will not be silenced.

Arquette's rage and identification with the collective "we" is undoubtedly important. In the interview clips which follow Arquette, journalist Rebecca Traister and Weinstein's former personal assistant, Zelda Perkins, are clear that simply locking up this one man will not solve the problem. But what concerns me here is that the route to social and cultural change remains locked to speaking out in and of itself. Over a montage of images of the victim/survivors whose testimonies we have heard in the documentary, we hear Ronan Farrow's voice:

> So after this interview, I will go back to struggling with brave sources, to see if they are willing to take that risk of putting their name on tough stories. That challenge goes on every day for people facing abuse all over the world.

As I have argued, investigative journalism *has* been an important driver in the long #MeToo moment and Farrow's statement points to the considerable risk in telling, investigating and publishing these "tough stories". We *do* need men to take on the work of challenging other men, but the marginalisation of (primarily) women's long-standing activism and advocacy here is striking. The failure to look outside Weinstein's immediate world to understand his behaviour means that his power is constructed as *situational*, indexed to his celebrity and business interests and *not* to gender, race or class.

Untouchable is not unique in this respect: specifically feminist expertise is rare in the #MeToo documentary. Journalists and experts in the abuser's field—film, television or music critics, media executives—are those who most commonly offer commentary. In the first episode of *Allen v. Farrow* (HBO 2021), for instance, the interviewees not directly connected to the case are film critics, a culture reporter, writer and film programmer. Their role is to situate Allen and his movies. Notably, Mia Farrow's career—considered in most detail in Episode 2—is framed very differently. Admittedly, the filmmakers have access to original interviews with Mia which they don't have for Allen, but it is still notable that there is no expert assessment of *her* career which is, instead, discussed alongside her relationship with Allen. As with *Untouchable,* there is much to admire in this documentary series. Moreover, it is unusual among #MeToo documentaries in focusing on abuse within the family (albeit a celebrity family) and later episodes do offer a wider range of expert commentary—including a "forensic psychologist", "child abuse expert" and "child abuse psychologist". However, the emphasis on culture critics on the one hand, and medical professionals on the other, means that the need for an explicitly *gendered* analysis is, again, undercut. #MeToo is acknowledged as the context that finally offers the possibility that Dylan Farrow's words will be consequential, but—again—the relationship between the discursive #MeToo and the feminist *work* which precedes and surrounds it is obscured. Instead, the work Dylan's words necessitate is framed as cultural—what should we do about Allen's work—and personal (the working through of trauma).

Interestingly, it is primarily in documentaries focused on the abuse of women and girls by Black American men—R. Kelly, Russell Simmons, Bill Cosby—that this feminist work has been most visible. Horeck (2024: 237) describes how *On The Record* (HBO Max, 2020)—featuring interviews with, among others, Kimberlé Crenshaw and Tarana Burke—"centr[es] black feminist thought on intersectionality and [...] historicis[es] racialised experiences of sexual violence" and marks "an important shift away from a focus on individual victims and perpetrators". *Surviving R. Kelly* is even more marked in this respect. Although still centrally focused on victim/survivor testimony and including interviews with people in Kelly's orbit as well as with journalists and other artists commenting on his career, the series makes extensive use of Black feminist activists who are explicitly identified as such. Some of those included alongside Tarana Burke are: #MuteRKelly founders Oronike Odeleye and

Kenyette Tisha Barnes; Mikki Kendall, the cofounder of Hood Feminism; President and CEO of Girls for Gender Equity, Joanne Smith; Natasha R. Johnson, the Executive Director of North Brooklyn Coalition Against Domestic Violence; and Salamisllah Tillet, scholar and cofounder of A Long Walk Home (a national art organisation working with young people to end violence against girls and women). Alongside these activists are Black women working within the criminal justice system, as journalists and as academics in psychology, criminology and cultural history. These women are constructed as *knowers*, as experts who can situate R. Kelly's behaviour and the experiences of victim/survivors in a gendered and racialised context. Importantly, this is not to undermine the expertise of experience—indeed, the series establishes that many of the victim/survivors featured have become activists or advocates—but experience and expertise are not seen as being synonymous.

We Need To Talk About Cosby has a slightly different emphasis. Unlike *Surviving R. Kelly*—which was to play an important role in criminal charges being brought against the singer—the reckoning *We Need to Talk About Cosby* calls for is primarily cultural. The "we" of the title is the Black audience and, more specifically, Black men who, in different ways, owe their careers to Cosby's pathbreaking comedy and television work. Like *Allen v. Farrow* it offers interviews with cultural critics, journalists and academics (including Black feminists), who are able to situate Cosby's work and achievements whilst reckoning with Cosby's contemporaneous abuse of women. As in other #MeToo documentaries, the veracity of the women's reports is never in doubt. A number of victim/survivor testimonies are included but they are not the series' focal point. This is in contrast to the later two-part series *The Case Against Cosby* (CBC 2023) which is much more tightly oriented around victim/survivor testimony. *The Case Against Cosby* places the emphasis on trauma, albeit collective trauma, and the im/possibility of criminal justice, rather than on the gendered, racialised context which enables the abuse. *We Need to Talk About Cosby* treats victim/survivor speech very differently: the first testimony we hear is from Victoria Valentina who is introduced first as a "Former Playboy Bunny and Playmate" talking about the Playboy clubs of the 1960s. In other words, she is situated in time and place before we learn about her experience with Cosby and this is true of the other original interviews with victim/survivors too. The series also makes use of existing footage of victim/survivors speaking in the media: this has the effect of situating the victim/survivors in the same televisual space as Cosby himself. At the same time, it is a reminder that this speech *already* exists and—as filmmaker W. Kamau Bell suggests in an opening voiceover—the question is "What do we do about everything we *knew* about Bill Cosby, and what we know now?" The series is interested in what is now known and does not demand of victim/survivors that they package their experience anew to make the case that action is required. Indeed, we do not hear the first direct victim/survivor testimony until near the end of the first episode. Arguably, what *We Need to Talk About Cosby* offers, then, is an extended reckoning with the role of the audience—and the Black community in particular—in contributing to justice for victim/survivors. It begins from a position of belief and starts to work through the consequences of that belief.

Without in any way minimising the impact of victim/survivor speech in *The Case Against Cosby*, there the victim/survivors are victim/survivors first and foremost, trapped in reliving their victimisation. Across the two episodes, the meaning of the women's speech is also interrogated and interpreted by Dr Gabor Maté—introduced as a "Physician and Best-Selling Author"—at a "Trauma Retreat" attended by all the victim/survivors featured in the series. This renders the ongoing work of the victim/survivor as fundamentally psychological and personal. This is not to minimise the importance of healing—and, indeed, of healing as an aspect of justice (Herman 2023)—but rather to highlight that personal stories do not *automatically* become political through collective sharing. Interestingly, the series ends by offering brief captions situating each of the victim/survivors rather differently, giving a sense of their *continuing* lives and work beyond the Cosby case and identifying a number of them as advocates working to change law and institutions. But that activist orientation is confined to the "after" of the documentary; it is not its substance.

Thus, the pattern I am observing in relation to *On the Record, Surviving R. Kelly* and *We Need to Talk About Cosby* is not a linear, chronological development of the #MeToo documentary but, rather, speaks to some of the different configurations of storytelling, expertise and, indeed, communicative justice which persist in the long #MeToo moment. That these documentaries all focus on Black male abusers is not accidental (though it is also not determining, as *The Case Against Cosby* reminds us). This chimes with work on news reporting which identifies that Black men—and other groups who can be easily "Othered"—are more likely to be seen as anchored to, and potentially representative of, their communities. This allows for *structural* issues to come into play in a way that is rarely seen in reporting of white men's violence and it is these legacies that these documentaries grapple with. But they also engage, explicitly, with the intersectional erasures of the #MeToo moment, building on the work of Black feminist activists online to ensure that Tarana Burke's Me Too is acknowledged in the mainstream discussion around #MeToo. The constraints around that acknowledgement are suggested by my discussion of Burke's voiceless cameo in *Untouchable*, but Burke's expertise is extensively drawn upon in both *Surviving R. Kelly* and *On the Record*. What is even more striking, however, is that Burke is not a lone voice but is so clearly embedded in a wider Black feminist community of activists, organisers, critics and academics. #MeToo documentaries about white male celebrity abusers see them in much narrower contexts where their professional exceptionalism precludes a sustained consideration of race and gender.

The documentary featuring white abusers that I think comes closest to the socio-cultural analysis of the "intersectional #MeToo" (Horeck 2024) documentaries is Netflix's *You Are Not Alone: Fighting the Wolfpack* (2023) which, tellingly, does not focus on a celebrity case. The documentary focuses on a gang rape at the San Fermín festival in Pamplino, Spain in 2016—a case commonly referred to as La Manada (the wolfpack), a term the abusers used to refer to themselves. As news of the gang rape broke, the festival became a flashpoint for feminist protest and this intensified after the initial criminal verdict in the case in 2018. Footage of these protests is central to the documentary and some of the protestors are also interviewed. The documentary takes its lead from the protestors in situating its account of this one case in a wider rape culture, linking the gang rape to other misogynist attacks over a number of years. That the links do not hinge on individual repeat offenders allows for a wider critique to emerge and, therefore, makes it clear that achieving justice is not about achieving *criminal* justice in one isolated case.

Looked at collectively, the #MeToo documentaries complement and at times complicate the accounts of individual cases that have spanned the long #MeToo moment. They demonstrate the enduring importance of victim/survivor speech, particularly for sectors or communities who have not had their "#MeToo moment" in the mainstream. They also demonstrate a new presumption of belief: none of the documentaries here are investigations of sexual harassment and abuse claims and the credibility of victim/survivors is not in doubt. As such, these documentaries have a larger canvas to explore the meaning and function of men's sexual abuse of women which—in some instances at least—means looking to victim/survivors not simply to recount their experiences but to articulate their understanding of that experience in a wider context. Particularly in series which unfold over many hours, there is more opportunity to achieve the "expansive, complex and meaningful" use of voice that Kay (2020: 8) describes as essential to communicative justice. That accounts which do critically engage with power in relation to gender, race and wealth emerge is significant and demonstrates that there are some spaces where #MeToo and Me Too have become more closely aligned—though this is by no means assured. Indeed, Tarana Burke has become a prominent media commentator, increasingly (though by no means universally) recognised not only as the founder of Me Too but as its leader whose continuing work has become the focus of her contribution. That this has been achieved largely through the cultural work of Black activists and creators—the Black women online who made sure her work was not erased by #MeToo, as well as the work of media-makers like *Surviving R. Kelly* executive producer dream hampton—is a reminder that we cannot change the story without also considering who has access to the most effective, most recognised ways of telling it.

Conclusion

In this chapter, I have looked across a range of media representations to examine how they use the personal to tell stories about sexual harassment and abuse and to explore how those personal stories are—and are not—used to make knowledge claims. When I initially proposed this chapter, I envisaged the argument being "against testimony" for a number of reasons: because to *keep* telling people absolves listeners of the requirement to act; because the endless claims to newness and revelation inherent in "breaking the silence" allow us to forget what we already know; because the emphasis on the personal can be both ahistorical and exploitative. Noise in and of itself cannot achieve (communicative) justice for victim/survivors or map a path to the kind of change required in families, schools, communities, workplaces, representations and laws which might mean that future generations do not have to say #MeToo.

Yet, it is very difficult to imagine routes to systemic change which do *not* include engagement with the media. Those who are excluded from, marginalised or misrepresented within, mainstream media spaces struggle for recognition beyond them. Treva B. Lindsey makes this point powerfully in the introduction to *America, Goddam: Violence, Black Women, and the Struggle for Justice*. Reflecting on her own experiences, as well as on the violence against Black women and girls she has witnessed throughout her life, Lindsey writes, "[o]ur stories didn't get mass media coverage or even widespread outrage from people I thought should or would care". Lindsey goes on to describe "[t]he pain of screaming into a void while fighting alongside my fellow Black women and girls to merely be healthy, housed, fed, decriminalized, and valued" (Lindsey 2023: 25). For Lindsey, the lack of media coverage denies Black women and girls recognition and frustrates change: coverage, outrage and care are inextricably linked. And so my conclusion retains the ambivalence now so characteristic of feminist media studies. Yes, media can be part of the solution as well as part of the problem; but we need to pay attention to who speaks and for whom, and to the conditions in which that speech is solicited and allowed to be consequential.

References

Ahmed, Sara. 2000. Who knows? Knowing strangers and strangerness. *Australian Feminist Studies* 15 (3): 49–68.

Alcoff, Linda Martín. 2018. *Rape and Resistance: Understanding the Complexities of Sexual Violation*. Cambridge & Medford: Polity.

Armstrong, Louise. 1996. *Rocking the Cradle of Sexual Politics: What Happened When Women Said Incest*. London: Women's Press.

Auletta, Ken. 2022. *Hollywood Ending: Harvey Weinstein and the Culture of Silence*. New York: Penguin.

Banet-Weiser, Sarah. 2018. *Empowered: Popular Feminism and Popular Misogyny*. Durham: Duke.

Banet-Weiser, Sarah. 2021. 'Ruined' lives: Mediated white male victimhood. *European Journal of Cultural Studies* 24 (1): 60–80.

Banet-Weiser, Sarah, and Kathryn Claire Higgins. 2023. *Believability: Sexual Violence, Media and the Politics of Doubt*. Cambridge: Polity.

Barbaro, Michael and Megan Twohey. 2016. Crossing the line: How Donald Trump behaved with women in private. *New York Times*, 14 May.

Bedera, Nicole. 2022. Why are so many survivors supporting Johnny Depp? *Harper's Bazaar*, 26 May. https://www.harpersbazaar.com/culture/politics/a40116993/why-are-so-many-survivors-supporting-johnny-depp/. Accessed 23 March 2024.

Benner, Katie. 2017. Women in tech speak frankly on culture of harassment. *New York Times* 30 June.

Boyle, Karen. 2018. Television and/as testimony in the Jimmy Savile case. *Critical Studies in Television* 13 (4): 387–404.

Boyle, Karen. 2022. Has it happened to you? *Gender Equal Media Scotland* [blog], 17 May. https://emcc.engender.org.uk/news/blog/has-it-happened-to-you/. Accessed 23 February 2024.

Boyle, Karen, Brenna Jessie and Megan Strickland. 2023. Rape in the news: Contemporary challenges. In *Rape: Challenging Contemporary Thinking—10 Years On*. (Second edition) eds. Miranda A.H. Horvarth and Jennifer M. Brown, 113–127. London: Routledge.

Boyle, Karen, Melody House, and Talat Yaqoob. 2024. Time to Pass the Mic: Gender and race in Scotland's news. *Journalism* 25 (1): 22–40.

Brand, Russell. 2023. So this is happening. [Video] YouTube, 15 September. https://www.youtube.com/watch?v=ZGr_PVUHn2I&t=3s. Accessed 21 February 2024.

Brison, Susan. 2008. Everyday atrocities and ordinary miracles, or why I (still) bear witness to sexual violence (but not too often). *Women's Studies Quarterly* 36 (1/2): 188–198.

Brown, Julie K. 2021. *Perversion of Justice: The Jeffrey Epstein Story*. Harper Collins.

Carroll, Matt, Kevin Cullen, Thomas Farragher, Stephen Kurkjian, Michale Paulson, Sacha Pfeiffer, Michael Rezendes and Walter V. Robinson. 2016. *Betrayal: The Crisis in the Catholic Church. The Findings of the Investigation That Inspired Spotlight*. London: Profile.

Chester, Jason. 2023. Kirsty Gallacher breaks her silence as she posts on social media for the first time since brother-in-law Russell Brand was accused of rape, sexual assault and predatory behaviour. *Mail Online*, 20 September. https://www.dailymail.co.uk/tvshowbiz/article-12540149/Kirtsy-Gallacher-breaks-silence-posts-social-media-time-brother-law-Russell-Brand-accused-rape-sexual-assault-predatory-behaviour.html. Accessed 22 March 2024.

Collins, Patricia Hill. 2000. *Black Feminist Thought: Knowledge, Consciousness, and the Politics of Empowerment*. 10th Anniversary. New York: Routledge.

Criado Perez, Caroline. 2019. *Invisible Women: Exposing Data Bias in a World Designed for Men*. London: Chatto & Windus.

Davies, Dan. 2014. *In Plain Sight: The Life and Lies of Jimmy Savile*. London: Quercus.

Dean, Charlotte. 2023. Katy Perry breaks her silence as she posts on social media for the first time since her ex-husband Russell Brand was accused of rape and sexual assault. *Mail Online*, 19 September. https://www.dailymail.co.uk/tvshowbiz/article-12537833/Katy-Perry-breaks-silence-posts-social-media-time-ex-husband-Russell-Brand-accused-rape-sexual-assault.html. Accessed 22 March 2024.

DeRogatis, Jim. 2019. *Soulless: The Case Against R. Kelly.* New York: Abrams.

Farrow, Ronan. 2016. My Father, Woody Allen, and the danger of questions unasked. *Hollywood Reporter*, 11 May. https://www.hollywoodreporter.com/news/general-news/my-father-woody-allen-danger-892572/. Accessed 16 March 2024.

Farrow, Ronan. 2019. *Catch and Kill: Lies, Spies and a Conspiracy to Protect Predators.* London: Fleet.

Friedlander, Monique. 2023. EXCLUSIVE: Married at First Sight star Dean Wells breaks his silence after being dropped by his management for criticising a drag queen story time event for kids as young as three. *Daily Mail Australia*, 13 February.

Gardiner, Becky. 2018. "It's a terrible way to go to work": What 70 million readers' comments on the *Guardian* revealed about hostility to women and minorities online. *Feminist Media Studies* 18 (4): 592–608.

Gardner, David. 2017. Weinstein breaks his silence… to deny claim he threatened to kill Salma for refusing sex. *Evening Standard*, 14 December.

Gavey, Nicola. 2005. *Just Sex? The Cultural Scaffolding of Rape.* London: Routledge.

Griffith, Keith and Chris Spargo. 2017. "Gay sex scene was part of the story": Disgraced film mogul Harvey Weinstein FINALLY breaks his silence to respond to Salma Hayek claims that he stalked her and forced her to do a nude lesbian sex scene. *Mail Online*, 14 December. https://www.dailymail.co.uk/news/article-5177985/Weinstein-FINALLY-breaks-silence-respond-Salma-Hayek.html. Accessed 22 March 2024.

Harding, Sandra. 2012. Feminist standpoints. In *Handbook of Feminist Research: Theory and Praxis* (2nd Edition), ed. Sharlene Nagy Hesse-Biber, 46–64. Thousand Oaks: Sage.

Harrington, Carol and MacKenzie Gerrard. 2024. Telling an authentic, relatable #MeToo story on YouTube. In *The Routledge Companion to Gender, Media and Violence*, ed. Karen Boyle and Susan Berridge, 213–221. London: Routledge.

Herman, Judith L. 2023. *Truth and Repair: How Trauma Survivors Envision Justice.* London: Basic.

Hind, Katie. 2023. 'An extraordinary week': Brand breaks his silence on latest claims. *Mail on Sunday*, 23 September.

hooks, bell. 1992. *Black Looks: Race and Representation.* Boston, MA: South End Press.

Horeck, Tanya. 2024. Sexual violence and social justice: The celebrity #MeToo documentary in the US. In *The Routledge Companion to Gender, Media and Violence*, ed. Karen Boyle and Susan Berridge, 232–241. London: Routledge.
Horeck, Tanya, and Diane Negra. 2022. Reconsidering television true crime and gendered authority in *Allen v. Farrow*. *Feminist Media Studies* 22 (6): 1564–1569.
IndyStar. N.d. How IndyStar investigated USA Gymnastics. *IndyStar*. https://eu.indystar.com/story/news/investigations/2016/08/04/usa-gymnastics-sex-abuse-investigation/87907306/. Accessed 22 March 2024.
Johnson, Morgan. 2023. BRAND SPEAKS. Russell Brand breaks his silence in bizarre Instagram rant after being accused of rape and sexual assault. *Sun*, 22 September.
Jordan, Jan. 2004. *The Word of a Woman? Police, Rape and Belief*. Hampshire: Palgrave Macmillan.
Kantor, Jodi, and Megan Twohey. 2019. *She Said: Breaking the Sexual Harassment Story that Helped Ignite a Movement*. London: Bloomsbury.
Kay, Jilly Boyce. 2020. *Gender, Media and Voice: Communicative Injustice and Public Speech*. Cham: Palgrave Macmillan.
Kirchick, James. 2023. Armie Hammer breaks his silence. *AirMail*, 4 February.
Lewis, Isobel. 2023. Katherine Ryan explains why she made decision 'to call Russell Brand a predator'. *Independent*, 3 October. https://www.indepe ndent.co.uk/arts-entertainment/tv/news/katherine-ryan-russell-brand-des ert-island-discs-b2422832.html. Accessed 21 February 2024.
Li, Jun. 2024. Media, courts and "#RiceBunny" testimonies in China. In *The Routledge Companion to Gender, Media and Violence*, ed. Karen Boyle and Susan Berridge, 163–173. London: Routledge.
Lindsey, Trevi B. 2023. *America, Goddam: Violence, Black Women, and the Struggle for Justice*. Oakland: University of California Press.
Loughrey, Clarisse. 2017. Harvey Weinstein responds to Lupito Nyong'o harassment allegations. *Independent*, 21 October. https://www.independent.co.uk/arts-entertainment/films/news/harvey-weinstein-lupita-nyongo-harassment-allegations-response-statement-denial-oped-a8012706.html. Accessed 21 February 2024.
Macharia S (2021) *Who Makes the News? 6th Global Media Monitoring Project*. https://whomakesthenews.org/wp-content/uploads/2021/11/GMMP2020.ENG_.FINAL_.pdf. Accessed 23 February 2024.
Manly, Lucy. 2023. Madeleine West breaks her silence: Neighbours star films emotional 60 Minutes with Tara Brown after the "monster" who abused her as a child was finally brought to justice. *Daily Mail Australia*, 22 November.
Matthews, Chris and Tom Cotterill. 2023. How Katherine Ryan could have the last laugh on Russell Brand! Comic who warned of "sexual predator" in the industry could earn MILLIONS as new face of reignited #MeToo movement.

Mail Online, 22 September. https://www.dailymail.co.uk/news/article-125 49583/How-Katherine-Ryan-laugh-Russell-Brand-Comic-warned-sexual-pre dator-industry-earn-MILLIONS-new-face-reignited-MeToo-movement.html . Accessed 22 March 2024.

McGlynn, Clare and Nicole Westmarland. 2019. Kaleidoscopic justice: Sexual violence and victim-survivors' perceptions of justice. *Social and Legal Studies* 28 (2): 179–201.

McRobbie, Angela. 2009. *The Aftermath of Feminism*. London: Sage.

Møller Hartley, Jannie and Tina Askanius. 2021. Activist journalism and the norm of objectivity: Role performance in the reporting of the #MeToo movement in Denmark and Sweden. *Journalism Practice* 15(6): 860–877.

Mumford, Alys. 2017. Why there aren't always two sides to every story. *Engender Blog*, 24 October. https://www.engender.org.uk/news/blog/why-there-arent-always-two-sides-to-every-story/. Accessed 20 May 2019.

Ngimbi, Emmanuella. 2023. Katy Perry posts on social media after ex-husband Russell Brand's allegations. *Express Online*, 20 September. https://www.express.co.uk/celebrity-news/1814811/Katy-Perry-Instagram-return-Russell-Brand-allegations. Accessed 22 March 2024.

Philips, Ellie. 2023. Sam Ryder breaks his silence after Wham! beat him to the Christmas number one spot. *Mail Online*, 23 December. https://www.dailymail.co.uk/tvshowbiz/article-12896145/Sam-Ryder-Wham-beat-Christmas-number-one-George-Michael.html. Accessed 22 March 2024.

Pollard, Nick. 2012. *The Pollard Review: Report*. 18 December. https://downloads.bbc.co.uk/bbctrust/assets/files/pdf/our_work/pollard_review/pollard_review.pdf. Accessed 24 March 2024.

Roberts, Jamie. 2023. Katy Perry breaks silence after ex-husband Russell Brand accused of sex assaults. *Mirror*, 19 September.

Robinson, Jennifer and Keina Yoshida. 2023. *How Many More Women? The Silencing of Women by the Law and How to Stop It*. London: Endeavour.

Rudling, Michael. 2023. Shamed Spanish FA kiss-gate chief Luis Rubiales breaks his silence to claim he is "advancing feminism" and says he is the victim of a "lynching" as he fights Jenni Hermoso's World Cup final claims. *Mail Online*, 1 September. https://www.dailymail.co.uk/sport/football/article-12471877/Shamed-Spanish-FA-kiss-gate-chief-Luis-Rubiales-breaks-silence-claim-advancing-feminism-says-victim-lynching-fights-Jenni-Hermosos-World-Cup-final-claims.html. Accessed 22 March 2024.

Serisier, Tanya. 2018. *Speaking Out: Feminism, Rape and Narrative Politics*. Cham: Palgrave Macmillan.

Serisier, Tanya. 2020. Speaking out, public judgments, and narrative politics: Researching survivor stories and (not) telling my own. In *Me too, feminist theory, and surviving sexual violence in the academy*, ed. Laura A. Gray-Rosendale, 167–180. Lanham: Lexington Books.

Simmonds, Felly Nkweto. 1997. My body myself: How does a Black woman do sociology? In *Black British Feminism: A Reader* ed. Heidi Safia Mirza, 226–239. London: Routledge.
Smith, Dorothy. 1974. Women's perspective as a radical critique of sociology. *Sociological Inquiry* 44 (1): 7–13.
Smith, Emily. 2017. Harvey Weinstein gives first interview after shocking sex harassment claims. *Page Six (New York Post)*, 5 October. https://pagesix.com/2017/10/05/harvey-weinstein-gives-first-interview-after-shocking-sex-harassment-claims/. Accessed 21 February 2024.
Sreedharan, Chindu, Einar Thorsen and Ananya Gouthi. 2020. Time's up Or is it? Journalists' perceptions of sexual violence and newsroom changes after #MeTooIndia. *Journalism Practice* 14 (2): 132–149.
Steel, Emily and Michael S. Schmidt. 2017. Bill O'Reilly thrives at *Fox News*, even as harassment settlements add up. *New York Times*, 1 April.
Strauss, Jackie. 2021. "This is a story that people thought they knew": *THR Presents* Q&A with the *Allen v. Farrow* creators. *Hollywood Reporter*, 27 May. https://www.hollywoodreporter.com/tv/tv-features/allen-v-farrow-creators-hbo-dylan-mia-farrow-woody-allen-1234959401/#. Accessed 16 March 2024.
Sultan, Kamal. 2023. Parents of boy, 12, are suing school that kicked out son for wearing "there are only two genders" shirt, as kid breaks his silence: 'They took away my ability to have a different opinion. *Mail Online*, 18 May. https://www.dailymail.co.uk/news/article-12099671/Parents-boy-12-suing-school-kicked-son-wearing-two-genders-shirt.html. Accessed 22 March 2024.
Tyler, Imogen. 2020. *Stigma: The Machinery of Inequality*. London: Zed.
Walker, Janet. 2005. *Trauma Cinema: Documenting Incest and the Holocaust*. Berkeley: University of California Press.
Weinstein, Harvey. 2017. Statement. *New York Times*, 5 October.
Whitworth, Damian. 2023. Prince Harry breaks his silence (again). *The Times*, 2 January.

CHAPTER 8

Conclusion: #MeToo, Now What?

In Chapter 1, I suggested that the appeal of writing a second edition of this book was that it aligned with my argument that feminism is always in motion. That makes the task of concluding this book challenging and, indeed, deciding where to draw the line is arbitrary. New stories anchored by #MeToo continue to break: in the week I wrote this conclusion, a four-part documentary series on Discovery + laid bare "Nickelodeon's #MeToo story" (Kliegman 2024). What #MeToo has achieved is impossible to answer not only because its achievements are not uniform or fixed but also because it is by no means over.

But what version of #MeToo am I referring to here? In *#MeToo, Weinstein and Feminism* I asserted the importance of distinguishing between the activities and stories associated with the hashtag that went viral after Alyssa Milano's 2017 tweet, and the work of Tarana Burke's Me Too movement. Although this second edition has further complicated the origin stories associated with #MeToo and Me Too, I have—with an important qualification—sought to maintain this distinction. The qualification has been to situate #MeToo in a *long* moment, displacing the Milano-tweet as its origin point to think instead about the conditions which enable and/or limit #MeToo's virality in different contexts.

The long #MeToo moment does not have a fixed origin point but the popularity of feminist protest—and, in particular, feminist protest against men's violence—has shaped the forms that #MeToo has taken in different

© The Author(s), under exclusive license to Springer Nature   237
Switzerland AG 2024
K. Boyle, *#MeToo and Feminism*,
https://doi.org/10.1007/978-3-031-67314-6_8

contexts. Whilst situating #MeToo in *specific* contexts allows for a far sharper sense of the way in which the hashtag can be mobilised in, or in relation to, existing activism, there are also some points which appear to be shared across contexts. Central among these is that feminism's popularity is always already contested, most obviously through the concurrent rise of popular misogyny (Banet-Weiser 2018). #MeToo stories may have mainstreamed *belief* as the accepted response to (some) victim/survivor testimony, but that has often been accompanied by doubt in, and suspicion of, feminism and feminists. This recalls Angela McRobbie's (2009) account of the "double entanglement" in which feminism is taken into account in responses to individual victim/survivors whilst the feminist analysis that enabled those accounts to come to the fore at all is discarded as redundant. Thus we should #BelieveSurvivors but—as Johnny Depp supporters asserted—simultaneously believe that #AbuseHasNoGender.

In the long #MeToo moment, this is further complicated by the fact that #MeToo is no longer primarily a hashtag of disclosure, but rather is better understood as, in Anat Schwartz's terms (2023: 4), a citational hashtag referring, first and foremost, to other #MeToos (Cheema 2023). Citational chains keep #MeToo in circulation and allow for links to be made between different kinds of abuse and differently situated perpetrators and victim/survivors. In an interesting counterpoint to the ahistoricisation which I have argued can accompany hashtag activism in an Anglo-American context, Schwartz's work in South Korea suggests that citational hashtags can historicise activism, creating "a collective feminist memory" (2023: 5).

However, it is worth pausing to reflect on the extent to which the architecture of the platforms on which #MeToo circulates determines and foreshortens these citational chains. The increasing restrictions imposed by companies like Twitter/X and Facebook/Meta on research access to posts freely shared on their platforms will undoubtedly have a significant impact on the ways in which we can analyse future #MeToos. It is also worth considering who makes the citations and in whose interests. For instance, to return to the Nickelodeon documentary *Quiet on Set*, whilst #MeToo is an implicit presence in the documentary itself—the context against which the investigation of Nickelodeon becomes possible—its citation in reviews works primarily to construct a genre of programming: the #MeToo documentary. In other words, it is a form of consumer advice, a means of identifying a product not a process. There is nothing inherently wrong with this, but this kind of generic construction further distances #MeToo from Me Too. For future scholars, the challenge is therefore how to keep moments and movements in *ongoing* conversation whilst being alert to which—of the many—#MeToos are at stake in a specific context.

This points not only to the need to contextualise #MeToo in the specific places in which it circulates, but also to consider how the function of the hashtag changes over time. *#MeToo, Weinstein and Feminism* was written in response to #MeToo's moment of peak virality in an Anglo-American context when its testimonial usage was dominant. This second edition finds #MeToo proliferating and becoming a reference point for contemporary representations of sexual harassment and assault more broadly. This has implications for how we think of what is shared among communities of #MeToo users. For instance, including instances of femicide as part of #MeToo's citational chain sits uneasily with Milano's invitation to users to situate *themselves* using the hashtag (the me of #MeToo). However, foregrounding the ways in which the knowledge and threat of femicide shapes the way many of us experience non-fatal sexual violence demonstrates a commitment to continuum thinking. It also helps to keep in view the non-fatal sexual violence which is frequently identified in the histories of men who go on to murder women and girls.

The long #MeToo moment is also a period characterised by contradiction and complexity. In terms of representation, there is no doubt that we now have many more accessible representations of sexual harassment and assault that complicate stereotypical assumptions about what abuse is and who is impacted by it. The analyses presented in this book demonstrate that there is no one feminist formula for representing sexual harassment and assault. Different platforms and genres can do feminist work in different ways and with different constraints. One of the strengths of the hashtag and much subsequent #MeToo-related content has been the focus on forms of sexual harassment and assault which have not typically been deemed newsworthy in the past precisely because of their everyday nature. Yet, in many of the contexts in which #MeToo has achieved mainstream visibility, this has been possible because the story has been told through the lens of celebrity with an emphasis on serial offenders. Whilst these stories are inherently atypical, nevertheless they can implicate the audience in potentially challenging and uncomfortable ways as witnesses to abuse whose approval prolonged women's suffering.

Challenging the cultural value of abuse to make victim/survivors' experiences legible in their own terms can be part of a kaleidoscopic approach to justice (McGlynn and Westmarland 2019).

Thinking about the audience as part of a kaleidoscopic approach to justice is to recognise the importance of what Jilly Boyce Kay calls communicative justice (2020). Communicative justice depends not only on being able to speak, but more fundamentally on that speech being heard—in its messiness and complexity—such that it can become consequential. This extends the notion of consequences beyond a narrow focus on criminal punishment to envisage a more holistic approach to justice. In *Truth and Repair: How Survivors Envisage Justice*, Judith Herman (2023) suggests that an important element of healing and restitution for survivors is repairing their relationship with their communities. Here, I want to suggest that re-imagining relationships to and through popular culture can be part of that process of repair. A necessary first step is to recognise that there are victim/survivors (and perpetrators and bystanders) in the audience for *every* sexual harassment and abuse story. This then raises questions—both for audiences and for future research—about how those stories, and the way they are received by those around them, impact victim/survivors, their relationships to their communities, and to other victim/survivors.

Throughout this book I have also provided evidence of how media can be mobilised to anti-feminist ends. Media can be tools in the abuser's arsenal, a means of recording, circulating and extending abuse and control. Media representations can also extend the suffering of victim/survivors and compromise their believability in their own communities. Against that backdrop, the imperative to speech in the long #MeToo moment does not necessarily promise recognition, dignity or connectedness and, in providing opportunities for networked disbelief, may work against prevention. Knowing that we are under misogynist surveillance may shape what we say and how we connect with others through our speech about sexual harassment and assault (Megarry 2018). Speech about sexual harassment and assault is never free.

In that context, it is important to take stock of what speech about sexual harassment and assault is *already* available rather than endlessly requiring more. Of course, there are groups and contexts missing, and part of our job as researchers is to work out how we can bring those who are missing into the conversation in a meaningful way whilst minimising risk to those speaking out. But whilst our knowledge of sexual harassment and assault—and those who perpetrate and experience it—is by no means complete, we know enough to make that speech consequential. Making speech consequential *can* be about individual belief: remember, for instance, Dylan Farrow's statement that "every message of support has been a gift" (*Allen v. Farrow*, Episode 4). But much of the victim/survivor testimony recounted in this book requires more than belief on the part of the audience. It requires work. It requires work to understand, evaluate and determine a course of action. It requires work on policy and law. It requires work on attitudes and behaviours. It requires work on our curricula and playlists. It requires an assessment of the conditions of pleasure.

#MeToo—in the diverse contexts in which it has been taken up—has given us a wealth of evidence. The question now is, what are we going to do about it?

References

Banet-Weiser, Sarah. 2018. *Empowered: Popular Feminism and Popular Misogyny*. Durham: Duke.

Cheema, Iqra Shagufta. ed. 2023. *The Other #MeToos*. Oxford: Oxford University Press.

Herman, Judith L. 2023. *Truth and Repair: How Trauma Survivors Envision Justice*. London: Basic.

Kay, Jilly Boyce. 2020. *Gender, Media and Voice: Communicative Injustice and Public Speech*. Cham: Palgrave Macmillan.

Kliegman, Julie. 2024. Nickelodeon's #MeToo story was hiding in plain sight. *Slate* 18 March. https://slate.com/culture/2024/03/quiet-on-set-documentary-nickelodeon-dark-side-kids-tv-dan-schneider-drake-bell.html. Accessed 24 March 2024.

McGlynn, Clare and Nicole Westmarland. 2019. Kaleidoscopic justice: Sexual violence and victim-survivors' perceptions of justice. *Social and Legal Studies* 28 (2): 179–201.

McRobbie, Angela. 2009. *The Aftermath of Feminism*. London: Sage.

Megarry, Jessica. 2018. Under the watchful eyes of men: Theorising the implications of male surveillance practices for feminist activism on social media. *Feminist Media Studies* 18 (6): 1070–1085.

Schwartz, Anat. 2023. Acceptable activism: the history of the anti-sexual violence movement and the contemporary #MeToo protests in South Korea. In *The Other #MeToos*, ed. Iqra Shagufta Cheema, 1–21. Oxford: Oxford University Press.

Index

0–9
#AbuseHasNoGender, 238
#AskHerMore, 177
#BalanceTonPorc, 108
#BeersForBrett, 141, 142
#BelieveSurvivors, 141, 238
#BringBackOurGirls, 104
#FastTailedGirls, 183
#HimToo, 136, 137, 141–146, 148, 184
#MeToo, 1. *See also* Burke, Tarana; feminism, digital feminist activism; child sexual abuse, Me Too movement
  in Africa, 10, 108
  Alyssa Milano tweet, 1, 4, 35, 71, 89, 98, 201, 237
  backlash against, 22, 23, 33, 54, 69, 71, 98, 112, 114, 206, 238
  and celebrity, 10, 17, 25, 101, 172, 185, 239
  in China, 108, 112, 214
  and criminal justice, 69, 116, 119, 213
  and documentary, 25, 110, 202, 222, 223, 225, 227, 238
  end of, 23, 98, 115, 121, 141
  feminist critiques of, 1, 6, 7
  in France, 108
  in Iceland, 108
  in India, 104
  intersectionality, 1, 8, 54, 136, 228
  in Japan, 108
  the long #MeToo moment, 2, 3, 7, 13, 19, 23, 25, 97–103, 105, 109–111, 113, 115, 117, 119–121, 123, 125, 127, 129, 131, 189, 195, 201, 210, 213–215, 224, 227, 228, 237–240
  male victim/survivors, 24, 134, 136, 137
  Me Too Rising, 5
  as a moment, 1, 23, 100, 111, 115, 194, 213, 228
  participants in, 9, 12, 20, 35
  in Poland, 108
  in Russia, 108

and social media affordances, 5, 10, 46, 71, 73, 80, 213
in South Korea, 108, 112, 238
#MenToo, 136
#MuteRKelly, 116, 145, 183, 185, 189, 190
#MyHarveyWeinstein, 16, 21
#NiUnaMenos, 20, 74, 106
#PrimeiroAssédio, 106, 107
#SeAcabó, 114
#SheWasJustWalkingHome, 74
#YesAllWomen, 44, 106
30 Rock, 174, 176

A

Academy Awards, 52
  Kevin Spacey 2000 acceptance speech, 181
  Seth MacFarlane's Weinstein joke, 174
Ahmed, Sara, 100, 114, 186, 222
Ailes, Roger, 54, 110
Ajayi, Titilope F., 9
Alcoff, Linda Martín, 76–79, 81
Alianza Nacional de Campesinas, 55
Allen v. Farrow, 187, 212, 213, 225, 226, 241
Allen, Woody, 57, 185–188, 192, 214, 221, 225
Allred, Gloria, 50
Alves, Dani, 150
Andreasen, Maja Brandt, 181
Anitha, Sundari, 75
Ansari, Aziz, 51, 54, 80–82
Argento, Asia
  allegations against Harvey Weinstein, 140
  Jimmy Bennett allegations against, 137, 140
  response to Catherine Deneuve, 51
Armstrong, Louise, 39–41, 58, 210

Arquette, Rosanna, 224
Auletta, Ken, 152, 212
auteur apologism, 139, 167, 180, 188, 193
  in academia, 139

B

Banet-Weiser, Sarah, 5, 8, 44, 47, 53, 56, 58, 71, 103, 105, 111–113, 120, 143, 206, 210, 220, 238
  and Kathryn Claire Higgins, 133
Banks, Brian, 148
Barnes, Kenyette Tisha, 183, 226
Bates, Laura, 72
Bell, W. Kamau, 111, 227
Bennett, Jimmy, 140
Blasey Ford, Christine, 121, 141–146
Bloom, Lisa, 49, 50, 52
Boies, David, 50
Bombshell, 110
Boston Globe, 211
Brand, Jo, 78
Brand, Russell, 150, 182, 184, 192, 206–208
Brook, Vincent, 152
Brownmiller, Susan, 70, 73, 87, 88, 91
Burke, Tarana
  activism, 2, 6, 35, 38, 97, 125, 221, 225, 237
  media representation of, 45, 48, 111, 183, 204, 224, 225, 228, 229
  origins of Me Too movement, 6, 12, 35, 73, 89, 99
  responses to #MeToo, 17, 18, 45, 100, 125, 201
  Ted Talk, 6
  Unbound (memoir), 99, 101
Butler, Judith, 139
Buzzfeed, 105, 117

INDEX

C
Cain, Herman, 148
Cameron, Deborah, 17, 90
cancellation, 24, 168, 181, 185, 189, 191–194
Carlsson, Gretchen, 110
Case Against Cosby, The, 226, 227
casting couch, 171
Catch and Kill, 212, 214
Chatterjee, Tupur, 103
Cheema, Iqra Shagufta, 105, 238
Chemaly, Soraya, 40
child sexual abuse, 178, 190. *See also* Armstrong, Louise; continuum thinking; Kelly, R. (Robert); Savile, Jimmy; Spacey, Kevin
  EastEnders, 194
  media coverage of, 39, 41, 109, 154, 194, 204, 210, 211, 225
  Me Too movement, 35, 54, 73
  statutory rape, 54, 167
Chiu, Rowena, 11, 13
C.K., Louis, 83–85, 182, 184, 189, 192
Clark-Parsons, Rosemary, 20, 21, 35
Clifford, Max, 150
Clinton, Bill, 47, 204
Clinton, Hillary, 50
communicative justice, 187, 189, 202, 210, 212, 214, 227, 229, 240
Connell, R.W., 69, 91
consciousness raising, 22, 37–39, 41, 42, 58, 101, 119, 120, 218
continuum thinking, 22, 69, 71, 81, 82, 85–88, 92, 118, 166, 169, 239
Cosby, Bill, 50, 54, 110, 111, 120, 125, 182, 201, 207, 225–227
Crenshaw, Kimberlé, 225
Crews, Terry, 135, 136
Criado Perez, Caroline, 138, 219

criminal justice, 23, 38, 76, 77, 116, 117, 119, 120, 150, 155, 168, 189, 219, 226, 228

D
Daily Mail (Australia), 204
Daily Mail (UK), 80, 139, 203, 206, 207, 215
Damon, Matt, 70, 72, 80, 82–86, 89, 174
DARVO, 147, 153
De Benedicitis, Sara, 57
Dederer, Clare, 186–188
defamation, 108, 121–124, 201
Deneuve, Catherine, 51, 52, 80
Depp, Johnny, 142, 147, 238
  Depp v. Heard defamation trial, 14, 98, 121, 123, 124, 147, 220
  Dior *Sauvage* deal, 121, 193
  Fantastic Beasts franchise, 121
  Sun libel trial, 14, 98, 122, 147
DeRogatis, Jim, 173, 182, 190, 192, 211
DiBennardo, Rebecca, 135
domestic abuse, 14, 23, 38, 101, 123, 147, 148, 192
Driver, Minnie, 85, 86
Duggan, Lisa, 140

E
EastEnders, 194
Entourage, 174
Epstein, Jeffrey, 50, 211
Estrich, Susan, 88
Everard, Sarah (murder of), 74
Everyday Sexism, 72, 73

F
Facebook, 5, 52, 101, 238
Fallon, Sir Michael, 90, 91

Farrow, Dylan, 185, 186, 213, 214, 225, 241
Farrow, Ronan, 212, 214, 224. *See also* feminist killjoy; rape and sexual abuse; sexual harassmen
  Harvey Weinstein reporting, 1, 16, 34, 46, 211, 213
  support for Dylan Farrow, 187, 213, 214
femicide, 20, 74, 103, 106, 239
feminism, 3. *See also* feminist killjoy; rape and sexual abuse; sexual harassment
  backlash against, 97, 125, 137
  Black feminism, 6, 8, 42, 46, 111, 116, 121, 125, 182, 225, 226, 228
  and consciousness raising, 37–39, 58
  definition of, 3
  digital feminist activism, 6, 7, 23, 42, 106, 107
  and generational conflict, 4, 37, 42, 50, 51
  and intersectionality, 12, 225
  media representations of, 4, 22, 46, 97, 112
  as site of suspicion, 49–51, 122, 139, 238
film studies, 193
Flynn, Emma, 7, 25, 102, 108, 147
forced marriage, 75
Foster, Jodie, 177
Fotopolou, Aristea, 44
Fox News, 110, 211, 213
Franken, Al, 83–85
Fraser, Nancy, 120
Friedan, Betty, 47

G
Gallagher, Erin, 9
Gavey, Nicola, 76, 77

Gay, Roxanne, 14, 74, 77, 166
George, Susan, 172
Gill, Aisha, 75
Gilliam, Terry, 85, 86
Gill, Rosalind, 7–10
Glitter, Gary, 150
Global Media Monitoring Project (GMMP), 216
Golden Globes, 51, 55
Good Will Hunting, 84
Google Trends, 5
Grant, Melissa Gira, 90
Greer, Germaine, 51, 87, 88
Guardian, The, 8, 57, 153
Guha, Pallavi, 106

H
Hague, Gill, 101
Hall, Stuart, 150
Hammer, Armie, 202, 203, 205
Hanmer, Jalna, 38
Harding, Sandra, 217, 218
Harrington, Carol, 12
Harrison, Rebecca, 193
Harris, Rolf, 150
Hayek, Salma, 205
Heard, Amber, 147
  Depp v. Heard defamation trial, 14, 121, 220
  Sun libel trial, 122
  Washington Post Op-Ed, 123, 124
Hearn, Jeff, 154
Hemmings, Clare, 101
Herman, Judith, 227, 240
Hermoso, Jenni, 113, 114, 206
Hill, Anita, 141, 145, 148
himpathy, 24, 81, 91, 141, 143, 144, 149, 150, 154
Hoffman, Dustin, 172
Hollywood Life, 57
Hollywood Reporter, 214
hooks, bell, 3, 217

Horeck, Tanya, 109, 212, 221–223, 225, 228
House, Melody, 90, 147, 216
House of Cards, 179
Huff Post, 57

I
Imitation Game, The, 151
Indianapolis Star, 211
incest. *See* child sexual abuse
intersectionality, 210
  in feminist theory, 37
  in #MeToo, 6–8, 54
  in rape and sexual assault, 107, 137, 228
Ito, Shiori, 108

J
Jennifer Robinson, 34
Johansson, Scarlet, 177
Jordan, Jan, 101, 102, 114, 136, 138, 170, 177, 218
Judd, Ashley, 10, 33, 115, 212

K
kaleidoscopic justice, 18, 24, 98, 117, 157, 189, 192
Kantor, Jodi, 56, 192, 211, 212, 214. *See also She Said* (book); *She Said* (film)
  Weinstein story (with Megan Twohey), 1, 10, 11, 16, 17, 19, 34, 48–50, 56, 84, 151, 205, 211, 213
Kavanaugh, Brett, 24, 121, 137, 141–151
Kay, Jilly Boyce, 202, 204, 205, 210, 212, 214, 219, 229, 240
Keller, Jessalyn, 73

Kelly, Liz, 22, 23, 70–72, 74–82, 99, 124, 167
Kelly, R. (Robert), 116, 120, 137, 143, 173, 182–184, 189, 190, 192, 208, 211, 225, 226
Kendall, Mikki, 183, 226
King's Speech, The, 151
Kramer vs. Kramer, 172
Kunis, Mila, 118
Kutcher, Ashton, 118

L
Lazard, Lisa, 20
Leiter, Brian, 138, 139
Le Monde, 51
Lewinsky, Monica, 204
Lindsey, Treva B., 230
Lion, 151
Los Angeles Times, 81, 135
Loureiro, Gabriela, 106, 107
Love, Courtney, 175

M
MacFarlane, Seth, 174, 175, 177, 178, 207
MacKinnon, Catharine, 15, 80, 89
Mail Online. *See* Daily Mail [UK]
Malin, Brenton J., 184
Manne, Kate, 24, 79, 143, 144
Martinez, Lizzette, 183
masculinity, 70, 84, 107, 133, 136, 137, 143, 153, 155, 178, 184, 193
Masterton, Danny, 118
McDonnell, Andrea, 183
McGlynn, Clare, 18, 24, 98, 117, 157, 189, 192, 240
McGowan, Rose, 17, 50, 52, 53, 173
McRobbie, Angela, 48, 57, 86, 92, 113, 114, 216, 238
Megarry, Jessica, 39, 42, 58, 240

Mendes, Kaitlynn, 43, 73, 165
Merkin, Daphne, 51
Merrick, Jane, 90, 91
method acting, 173
Miami Herald, 211
Mikkelsen, Mads, 85, 86
Milano, Alyssa
  #MeToo tweet, 2, 4, 14, 35, 71–73, 89, 98, 201, 237
  response to Matt Damon, 85
Miller, Chanel, 12, 105, 116, 117
misogynoir, 11, 44, 116, 222
M, Kaye, 44, 45
Modrek, Sepideh and Bozhidar Chaklov, 9
Morrison, Toni, 145–148
Muller, Sandra, 108
Mumford, Alys, 53, 221

N
Nassar, Larry, 223
National Treasure, 154
New Musical Express, 57
Newsweek, 57, 153
New Yorker
  Ken Auletta story on Weinstein, 212
  Ronan Farrow Weinstein stories, 1, 16
New Yorker
  Ken Auletta story on Weinstein, 151, 152
New York Post, 51, 192, 205
New York Times, 182
  Donald Trump story, 211
  Dylan Farrow open letter, 185, 187, 214
  Harvey Weinstein statement, 1
  Jodi Kantor and Megan Twohey story, 11, 34, 46, 176
  reporting of Avital Ronell case, 139
  Uma Thurman interview, 180
Ng, Eve, 189, 191
Nirbhaya. *See* Pandey, Jyoti Singh (murder of)
Nyong'o, Lupito, 205

O
O'Connor, Lauren, 11
Odeleye, Oronike, 183, 225
online abuse, 10, 42–44, 124, 148, 222
On the Record, 225, 227, 228
O'Reilly, Bill, 211
Orgad, Shani, 7–10, 57

P
Paltrow, Gwyneth, 176, 192
Pandey, Jyoti Singh (murder of), 103, 104, 155, 165
Peckinpah, Sam, 172
Perkins, Zelda, 11, 13, 224
Pitt, Brad, 191, 192
Polanski, Roman, 53, 54, 167
pornography, 89, 171
Portman, Natalie, 52
Powell, Anastasia, 119
Powers, Ann, 182
Proudman, Charlotte, 215, 216

Q
Quiet on Set, 237, 238

R
rape and sexual abuse. *See also* child sexual abuse; criminal justice
  conducive context for, 167, 191, 193
  definitions of, 76, 105
  feminist theories of, 36

and intersectionality, 155, 220, 224
male victims of, 134, 169
media representations of, 2, 50, 86, 102, 135, 209, 220, 227, 239
and race, 11, 76, 102, 116, 119, 135, 142, 145, 146, 149, 155, 189, 205, 209, 225, 230
Rape, Abuse and Incest National Network, 43, 56
rape crisis movement, 41, 43, 56, 57
rape culture, 24, 54, 74, 105, 165, 166, 228
rape jokes, 182
rape within marriage, 38
speak outs against, 22, 37, 39, 47, 48, 58, 87
speak outs against, 35
statutory rape, 167
victim/survivor terminology, 19
Rapp, Anthony, 136, 178–181
Rathnayake, Chamil, 142, 143, 145, 147, 184
red carpet, 55, 175, 176
Reitman, Nimrod, 136, 139, 140
Ringrose, Jessica, 73
Robinson, Jennifer, 34
Rolf Harris, 223
Romito, Patrizia, 138, 155
Ronell, Avital, 136–140, 144
Rotten Apples, 191, 195
Rottenberg, Catherine, 57
Rotunno, Donna, 52, 53, 153, 154
Rowling, JK, 121, 122
Rubiales, Luis, 113, 114, 206, 207
Ryan, Katherine, 207, 208

S
Salmond, Alex, 90
Savile, Jimmy, 49, 109, 137, 149, 150, 154, 168–170, 172, 173, 187, 188, 192, 211, 214

Schwartz, Anat, 108, 112, 238
Scottish Women's Aid, 38
Segato, Rita, 56
Serisier, Tanya, 6, 20, 21, 36, 37, 39, 44, 114, 185, 213, 219–221
Sexton, David, 79, 80
sexual harassment, 2
 feminist theories of, 58
 speaking out about, 5, 7, 10, 33, 35, 37, 39, 41, 43, 45, 47, 49, 51, 53, 55, 57, 59, 61, 63, 65, 67, 100, 203, 207, 212, 241
 street harassment, 23, 77
 Time magazine Person of the Year, 33, 47
Shandilya, Krupa, 103, 104
She Said (book), 56, 211–214
She Said (film), 56, 191, 192, 212
Shrew, 4
Simmons, Russell, 225
SlutWalk, 7, 8, 105, 106
Smith, Dorothy, 217
Spacey, Kevin
 Academy Award, 181
 coming out, 178
 "Let Me Be Frank" video, 168, 178–180, 184, 193
 memes about, 181
 "Merry Christmas From Kevin Spacey" video, 180, 181
 sexual assault allegations, 84, 178, 179
Spotlight, 211
Stamp, Shelley, 172
standpoint theory, 217
Steubenville rape case, 165
Stone, Emma, 175
Stone, Sharon, 80, 81, 215
Strauss-Kahn, Dominique, 107, 109
Straw Dogs, 172
Streep, Meryl, 50, 172, 173
Sun, The, 98, 121, 122, 206

Surviving R. Kelly, 120, 145, 182, 183, 189, 190, 208, 223, 225–229
Swank, Hilary, 177

T

Tambe, Ashwini, 104, 109
Tarantino, Quentin, 180
Tesis, Las, 56
Theroux, Louis, 187, 211
Thomas, Clarence, 141, 142, 145–149, 151
Thurman, Uma, 40, 217
Till, Emmett, 149
Time magazine, 33, 47
  Person of the Year 2017, 47, 115, 135
TimesUp!, 46, 48, 55
Tranchese, Alessia, 102, 103, 107
Trump, Donald, 50, 106, 110, 142, 144, 149, 165, 211, 213
Tuerkheimer, Deborah, 143, 144, 183
Tufnell Park Women's Liberation Workshop, 5
Turner, Brock, 12, 105, 116–118, 149
Twitter (X), 5, 9, 10, 20, 21, 45, 50, 53, 74, 101, 144, 175, 179, 183, 238. *See also* individual hashtags listed above
Twohey, Megan, 1, 10, 11, 13, 16, 17, 19, 24, 34, 46, 48, 49, 50, 56, 84, 91, 119, 151, 174, 192, 205, 211–214. *See also She Said* (book); *She Said* (film)
  and feminism, 50, 56, 213
  Trump story (with Michael Barbaro), 211, 213
  Weinstein story (with Jodi Kantor), 1, 10, 11, 16, 17, 19, 34, 48–50, 56, 84, 151, 205, 211–214

U

Untouchable: The Harvey Weinstein Story, 223
Un Violador en tu Camino (A Rapist in your Path), 56

V

Vera-Gray, Fiona, 23, 41, 77–79
victim blaming, 52, 53, 74, 135, 139, 153, 184

W

Washington Post, The, 55, 122
Waterhouse-Watson, Deb, 15, 140
Way, Katie, 51, 80
Weinstein, Harvey, 205. *See also* Argento, Asia; Bloom, Lisa; Hayek, Salma; Kantor, Jodi; McGowan, Rose; Nyong'o, Lupito; *Untouchable: The Harvey Weinstein Story*
  and Academy Awards, 174–176
  appeal of criminal conviction, 14, 119, 121, 156, 201, 220
  bullying, 151, 174
  convictions, 14, 16, 119, 156, 201, 219
  criminal trials, 2, 22, 48, 50, 52, 55, 110, 153, 175, 212
  defence of Roman Polanksi, 167
  and feminism, 14, 46, 48–52, 54, 56, 57, 140
  Jewishness, 151, 152
  jokes about, 176
  memes about, 177
  Miramax, 174, 192, 224
  #MyHarveyWeinstein, 16
  New York Post interview, 51, 192
  non-disclosure agreements, 13, 34, 91, 212
  as outsider, 17, 19, 151, 152

physical appearance, 79, 152, 153, 176, 177
sexual assault, 11, 16, 18, 33, 46, 88, 151, 173, 211
statement to *New York Times*, 50, 52, 84, 88, 91, 115, 116, 141, 179, 205, 206
We Need to Talk About Cosby, 111, 182, 183, 226, 227
Westmarland, Nicole, 18, 24, 98, 117, 157, 189, 192, 240
Westwood, Tim, 223
Williams, Jenessa, 188
Women's Liberation Movement
 consciousness-raising, 101
 movement publications, 4
Women's Liberation Movement, 101
Women's March, 55, 105, 106, 224

Y

Yoshida, Keina, 34
You Are Not Alone: Fighting the Wolfpack, 228

Z

Zellweger, Renée, 176

SPRINGER NATURE

GPSR Compliance

The European Union's (EU) General Product Safety Regulation (GPSR) is a set of rules that requires consumer products to be safe and our obligations to ensure this.

If you have any concerns about our products, you can contact us on ProductSafety@springernature.com

In case Publisher is established outside the EU, the EU authorized representative is:

Springer Nature Customer Service Center GmbH
Europaplatz 3
69115 Heidelberg, Germany

The manufacturer's authorised representative in the EU is Springer Nature Customer Service Centre GmbH, Europaplatz 3, 69115 Heidelberg, Germany. If you have any concerns regarding our products, please contact ProductSafety@springernature.com

Printed and bound by CPI Group (UK) Ltd, Croydon, CR0 4YY

23/03/2026

02076398-0002